# The Walsingham Gambit

# The Walsingham Gambit

## Deception, Entrapment, and Execution of Mary Stuart, Queen of Scots

R. Kent Tiernan

Foreword by John J. Dziak

LEXINGTON BOOKS
*Lanham • Boulder • New York • London*

Published by Lexington Books
An imprint of The Rowman & Littlefield Publishing Group, Inc.
4501 Forbes Boulevard, Suite 200, Lanham, Maryland 20706
www.rowman.com

86-90 Paul Street, London EC2A 4NE, United Kingdom

British Library Cataloguing in Publication Information Available

**Library of Congress Cataloging-in-Publication Data**

Names: Tiernan, R. Kent, 1944- author. | Dziak, John J., writer of foreword.
Title: The Walsingham gambit : deception, entrapment, and execution of Mary Stuart, Queen of Scots / R. Kent Tiernan ; foreword by John J. Dziak.
Other titles: deception, entrapment, and execution of Mary Stuart, Queen of Scots
Description: Lanham ; Boulder ; New York ; London : Lexington Books, [2023] | Includes bibliographical references and index.
Identifiers: LCCN 2022026696 (print) | LCCN 2022026697 (ebook) | ISBN 9781793647023 (cloth) | ISBN 9781793647030 (epub)
Subjects: LCSH: Walsingham, Francis, Sir, 1532-1590. | Espionage, British—History—16th century. | Mary, Queen of Scots, 1542-1587. | Elizabeth I, Queen of England, 1533-1603. | Great Britain—Religion—16th century. | Great Britain—History—Elizabeth, 1558-1603. | Great Britain—Court and courtiers—Biography. | Great Britain—Foreign relations—1558-1603.
Classification: LCC DA358.W2 T54 2022  (print) | LCC DA358.W2  (ebook) | DDC 942.05/5—dc23/eng/20220616
LC record available at https://lccn.loc.gov/2022026696
LC ebook record available at https://lccn.loc.gov/2022026697

*To Carole Sue*

Deception is the capstone of successful conspiracies and counter conspiracies.

—R. Kent Tiernan

# Contents

# Foreword

The historical period that frames Kent Tiernan's work, and the controversies associated with Mary, Queen of Scots, Queen Elizabeth I, Walsingham, the Babington Plot, the Gallows' Letter, etc., are generally well known and well researched, albeit with significant differences of interpretation. But this author's approach does not re-plow that well-worked ground. Instead, he offers new and unique insights into the "hidden history" dimensions of the multiple controversies associated with the regicide of Mary, Queen of Scots.

Those "hidden history" insights engaged the professional experience of a contemporary intelligencer who applies the crafts of counterintelligence, intelligence, and their handmaidens—deception, provocation, diversion, disinformation, ruse, false flag operations, et al.—to the totality of plots and counterplots in the book's narrative. Mr. Tiernan presents a counterintelligence analytical approach with a primary focus on deception in domestic (England, Scotland) and international politics (e.g., France, Spain, the Vatican). In that sense, his work is unique, original, and judgmentally sound, indeed, highly professional. Too often, major historical periods receive a standard working over from the purely political, personal, special interest group perspectives without probing the hidden dimensions. Those dimensions comprise, among others, intrigue, guile, and manipulation by secret services in the interests of the reigning authorities. These seldom appear in the accepted, standard narratives or even in state documents.

The unique feature of this work is its counterintelligence/intelligence method. We seldom see such an approach taken in historical analyses, per se.

In short, this is a very yeomanlike piece of scholarship and historical investigation that will add to the body of serious work on the history of the Elizabethan era.

John J. Dziak, Ph.D.
Former Senior Intelligence Officer and Executive
Office of the Secretary of Defense and the Defense Intelligence Agency
Author of acclaimed book *Chekisty: A History of the KGB*;
Recognized as the best intelligence book for 1988.

# Preface

In 1966, while attending Stanford University, I joined approximately eighty other students at a newly opened campus at Harlaxton Manor, near Grantham, Lincolnshire, England. For six fascinating months, Stanford allowed me to immerse myself in England's beauty, and I quickly fell in love with its people, culture, and time-honored traditions. I soon discovered that the university's academic schedule allowed me to travel throughout the countryside as often as possible. Not surprisingly, I returned to California, captivated by England's historical heritage.

During my twenty years serving in the United States Air Force, including receiving a Master's degree in Western European Area Studies at the University of Notre Dame, I became enamored with Tudor history, especially events surrounding the Elizabethan period. Following retirement from the Air Force in 1987, I spent the next twenty-three years working in various capacities supporting the military and other national-level intelligence entities. During this period, I gained an entirely new perspective from which to evaluate many of the long-standing historical controversies associated with Queen Elizabeth I's reign—one being the famous, or as some would call it, infamous Babington Plot of 1586. However, before writing a book about this subject, I asked myself why anyone would be interested in reading about a historical event that led to a Scottish Queen's execution more than four hundred and thirty-five years ago?

First, it is a riveting story, especially for those who enjoy espionage, conspiracies, a life-or-death struggle between two very talented, strong-willed women, and royal court intrigue and deceit. It is all that amidst a backdrop of overt/covert religious activities between two implacable foes—Catholics and Protestants.

Second, for people interested in the scholarship and study of English history, especially the Elizabethan period, this book provides, from a deception perspective, a unique and comprehensive explanation of how English Intelligence entrapped Mary Stuart in treasonous activities against Elizabeth.

It may also encourage further academic research on how deception and influence tactics played a role in the Scottish Queen's demise. At the very least, it reinvigorates the process of reassessing commonly held assumptions associated with the Babington Plot, Elizabeth's role in influencing and manipulating the Catholic conspirators' activities, and the reasons behind Mary's behavior and actions that inevitably sealed her fate at Fotheringhay Castle.[1]

Third, to the practitioners of the art of deception in military planning, politics, and foreign policy, the Babington Plot provides invaluable insights into the requirements for conducting successful, strategic, large-scale deception operations.

Fourth, for intelligence officers committed to the search for truth, the Babington Plot offers valuable lessons for those applying analytical methods to determine if an event is real or purposely distorted to protect or promote an opponent's military, political, economic, or psycho-social agenda. Throughout my career in the Intelligence Community, I regularly encountered what appeared to be a pervasive "historical myopia," or a diminishing historical perspective, creeping into the ranks of the younger intelligence cadre. I advised them that using past lessons could significantly improve their analytical tradecraft and techniques today. Drawing on the cautionary adage by Edmund Burke, I reminded them that *"Those who don't know history are doomed to repeat it!"*

Fifth, for civilian and government education institutions teaching history, political science, national security policy, intelligence, and counterintelligence studies in pre- or post-baccalaureate programs, this book could support a comprehensive case study addressing both the anatomy and autopsy of a strategic deception operation. Surreptitious activities designed to influence, distort, and turn a target's actions against themselves is an issue that has considerable interest and relevance today.

Finally, the art of deception has been employed throughout history and continues to occur today with greater awareness due to the global twenty-four-hour news cycle. There are many examples of governments interfering with or deceiving each other, political deception, media deception, military deception, special interests deceiving the people and their elected representatives, or business-related deception. The list goes on and on. The results often vary, but the critical point to remember is that deception is real and can have significant history-altering consequences when applied efficiently.

Throughout this book, facts and compelling circumstantial evidence are intertwined with inferential-based explanations of the deception planning process and its impact on Queen Elizabeth's national security strategy. While direct evidence revealed that English Intelligence successfully executed a successful deception operation against Mary, Queen of Scots, and her

Babington conspirators in 1586, the discussion and treatment of the operation's evolution from concept development through the implementation and execution planning phases lack direct source confirmation (See Appendix E: Facts, Fiction, and Inferences). However, these specific activities represent deception tradecraft, application of time-phased planning windows, and supporting analysis methods employed by deception practitioners today.

To separate fact-based information from plausible speculation, numbered endnotes identify sources of information and quotes, comments, or opinions of people, issues, and situations relevant to events leading up to, during, and immediately following the capture of the Babington Plot conspirators. Also, in the tradition of historical fiction that employs creative license, seven vignettes, whose titles are in quotes (e.g., "Elizabeth Ascending"), were written to add a greater sense of intimacy between the reader and the principal characters, situations, and events.[2]

I now invite you to join me in returning to an exciting period in history when Protestant-ruled England struggled to preserve its existence against an increasingly threatening Catholic juggernaut. Going back to Queen Elizabeth I's reign, we will experience first-hand the tumultuous events that dominated the English and Western European stage for decades. Our journey will also provide a front-row seat to watch how an idea grew into a remarkably complex deception operation that destroyed a legitimate, Catholic royal claimant to the English throne.

## NOTES

1. A scientific/philosophical principle referred to as "Occam's Razor" states that the simplest or most obvious cause of an event is usually the correct explanation. However, recorders of history have also discovered that some events do not conform to the Occam's Razor principle, especially when evidence appears to be consistent with and support more than one hypothesis. When these situations arise, intellectual and analytical honesty demand that each alternative position be given equal consideration and closer examination. Occam's Razor is a problem-solving principle attributed to William of Ockham (c. 1287–1347), who was an English Franciscan friar and scholastic philosopher and theologian.

2. "These portrayals of the personal reflections of the characters are not flights of fancy. They are fully grounded in the factual record." Comments by Dr. James B. Bruce, 26 April 2020.

# Special Acknowledgments

To

Robert Hutchinson, *Elizabeth's Spymaster: Francis Walsingham and the Secret War That Saved England.* Reprinted by permission of Andrew Lownie Literary Agency Ltd., Copyright 2006.

Mary M. Luke, *Gloriana: The Years of Elizabeth I*, Reprinted by permission of Harold Ober Associates, Copyright 1973.

Charles Nicholl, *The Reckoning: The Murder of Christopher Marlowe*, Reprinted by fair use permission of University of Chicago Press, Copyright 1992.

# Prologue

## *Conspiracy, Deception, and "The Moor"*

Myriad historians and interdisciplinary scholars have written volumes about the Babington Plot. Most have concluded that Sir Francis Walsingham, using intelligence-designed "dirty tricks," was directly responsible for Mary Stuart's ultimate demise.[1] However, in-depth research has revealed that no one has adequately documented how he and his cadre of intelligencers developed and conducted such a successful manipulative operation employing deception as a cornerstone.

Adding context to the anatomy of an Elizabethan deception operation designed to hijack and control a Catholic conspiracy against Elizabeth, a novel, historical conceptualization based on modern deception theory was applied. Further research into extant scholarship on the Babington Plot revealed several misinterpretations in contemporary thinking about the strategic actions to deceive and entrap Mary Stuart. Based on direct and compelling circumstantial evidence and inferential-based conclusions, this book will explain in detail:

*Why* Elizabeth's chief advisors, Cecil and Walsingham, chose deception as an asymmetrical counter-Catholic conspiracy course of action

*When* this shift in policy direction began

*How* the actual deception was structured and evolved

*Who* played key roles before and during the deception operation

*What* deception tactics led to charges of treason against Mary Stuart

Figure P.1. (Left to right) William Cecil and Francis Walsingham. Artist: Ronda Penrod. Reproduced by permission of Ronda Penrod

Cecil and Walsingham drew on myriad examples from their past when deciding to use manipulation techniques against their Catholic adversaries. Thus, it should come as no surprise that deceptive activities employed during the reign of Elizabeth I proved as effective then as similar deception actions used today.

Humankind's instinct to manipulate to survive or improve its existence in a hostile and unforgiving environment can be traced back to pre-historic drawings etched on cave walls. In those drawings, human-like figures wore animal skins akin to a herd of four-legged creatures they had surrounded during a hunting foray. However, visual historical evidence also showed that deceptive acts were not only used to enhance a person's or group's survival. In ancient Egypt, deception was used to gain an advantage over others in much less aggressive situations. For example, Egyptian hieroglyphics and pictograms show two men playing one of history's oldest sleight-of-hand games. Originally called the "up from under" trick, con men today call it the shell game. Magicians refer to it as "cups and balls."[2]

As civilizations evolved, philosophers, theorists, military leaders, historians, and practitioners of manipulative activities have addressed issues associated with the art of deception. More than two thousand years ago, the Chinese master strategist Sun Tzu in *The Art of War* recorded time-tested examples of manipulation techniques that offered more indirect alternatives to aggressive military courses of action.[3] Homer's *Iliad* underscored the effectiveness of the famous Trojan horse ruse. The Bible extolled the virtues of deception when Joshua attacked Jericho's walls, and Gideon created a notional military force and capability much larger than that which existed. Treatises titled

*Strategemata by Polyanenus* c. AD 162 and *De Re Militaria* by Vegetius c. AD 390 identified 900 ruses of war and stressed the importance and inter-relationship between surprise and stratagem.[4]

In the twelfth and thirteenth centuries, "the Mongols possessed a vast repertoire of ruses that included feints, demonstration attacks, and uses of camouflage" to mask military movements and activities. These invaders from the East into Central Europe also "developed groundbreaking psychological warfare programs" that included the use of forgeries and rumors to cause disruption and chaos within its enemy's ranks.[5]

By the sixteenth century, Sir Thomas More, an English scholar, empha-sized using indirect approaches in combating an enemy. Niccolò Machiavelli, an Italian diplomat and philosopher, encouraged the use of deception to gain and hold power in politics, diplomacy, and war. He asserted that duplicity was a legitimate tool of statecraft.[6] There could be little doubt that learned men like William Cecil and Francis Walsingham were aware that such courses of action were available to them should the situation require it.

The universal instinct to "hide the real and show the fake" can take many forms and manifest in nature and the human condition. Then, as today, the motivation to apply trickery against an adversary may arise for various reasons (e.g., survival, gaining the advantage, hiding a military strength or weakness, attaining power, greed, lust, etc.). Myriad examples of deceptive activities can be found in all societal domains.

Bernie Madoff-like activities on Wall Street, costing unsuspecting clients billions of dollars, have become commonplace today. Prestigious auction houses regularly lend their reputations to the authenticity of *objects d'art* only later to find that they had sold forgeries to their highly valued custom-ers. Well-known and respected universities and medical centers have backed and financially supported experimental projects focused on curing cancer, only to be publicly embarrassed to discover they had based their support on totally flawed and "doctored" data.[7] Innocent and unsuspecting believers in their chosen religious faiths are daily becoming victims to a burgeoning trade of fake biblical artifacts claimed to have been uncovered in newly excavated digs in the Holy Land.[8] The United States Treasury Department and its secret service continue to struggle to keep one step ahead of the plethora of expert counterfeiters whose actions threaten the credibility and viability of our coun-try's legal tender.[9] These are but a few examples of the ubiquitous, insidious nature, scope, and impact that manipulation has today on a predominately unsuspecting world.

So, then why is this a story about deception when conventional historians of this period posit the events leading to Mary's execution as the sole result of a conspiracy? Of course, it was a conspiracy, but so much more was at play to achieve the desired outcome of duping Mary into committing treason. However, a conspiracy[10] requires an effective deception plan to succeed and deceiving the intended target(s) is the objective. In *The Walsingham Gambit*, the conspiracy to remove Mary, Queen of Scots, will define the goal, but strategic deception planning became the tool to achieve that goal.

As the story of Cecil and Walsingham's response to England's growing Catholic threat unfolds, both men will concede that England was incapable of directly confronting the vastly superior Catholic forces of France, Spain, and the Pope. However, by the mid-1570s, an alternative for engaging their implacable enemy with a more indirect, cost-effective, and resource-efficient approach will become an increasingly attractive option. When Cecil and Walsingham choose to activate that option, it should come as no surprise that many of their manipulative actions in the sixteenth century are strikingly similar to the conspiratorial deception activities used during the Bolshevik Trust and German rearmament operations of the twentieth century (See Postscript).

Deception as a course of action consists of false, incomplete, or misleading data passed on to groups or individuals in a manner intended to inspire the recipient's full confidence that the message or information is entirely credible. The intent is not merely to deceive or trick but rather to cause damage to the enemy. The recipient of the deceiver's message must be motivated to unwittingly inflict harm on himself, directly or indirectly, causing many self-defeating actions or inactions.[11]

Provocation as a course of action "at the strategic geopolitical level is designed to penetrate the enemy's camp to take over the direction of the enemy's activity, inspire the enemy with concrete views, or to incite him to undertake actions intended to lead to his defeat."[12]

In our contemporary world, deception planning guidelines are typically consolidated into checklist/building-block paradigms to ensure that all critical details in the planning process receive full consideration and attention. Of course, William Cecil and Francis Walsingham never had the benefit of such detailed planning models. Instead, they depended on their intuition, a deep understanding of human psychological vulnerabilities, and knowledge of historical activities and theoretical treatises to guide them through the complex planning task ahead of them. Arguably, the Lord Treasurer (Cecil) and First Secretary (Walsingham) often found themselves reacting to unanticipated

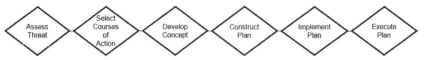

**Figure P.2. Deception Planning Phases.**
Source: R. Kent Tiernan

situations as their planning evolved. However, the mere fact that they achieved success in their endeavor, without a formal planning template at hand, speaks volumes about their intellectual, organizational, managerial skills, and brilliant statecraft.

However, as they embarked on their deception course of action in 1580, it is doubtful that Elizabeth's two top senior advisors fully understood the magnitude, complexity, and scope of the monumental task that lay ahead of them. Nevertheless, by 1585 and 1586, events proved that they were more than equal to the challenge.

Historians claim that Walsingham—called the "Moor" by Queen Elizabeth because of his swarthy complexion and propensity to wear dark clothing—was the man behind Mary, Queen of Scots' demise, but facts tell another story. He had significant help from others. A closer examination of the intricacies of strategic deception combined with the fact that he had many of Elizabeth's high priority duties to tend to, casts a long shadow on the contention that he should be credited as the sole architect of Mary Stuart's death.

Deception operations can be incredibly complicated.[13] A leader must continuously assess and direct his team to ensure the convergence of all interrelated, time-sensitive deception activities and seamlessly deconflict and coordinate resources. As events change and targets respond in ways outside of expected behavioral norms, a leader must immediately react and adjust. Deception planners at all levels must expend valuable time and resources to minimize the potentially negative impact of the unanticipated event on the deception operation. Such time-consuming challenges require detailed attention free of outside distractions.

Because of the burden of his other governmental duties, Walsingham was unable to effectively manage a complex deception operation by himself, especially during the deception plan's implementation. Fortunately, he had access to many talented people who would support his efforts to counter the growing influence of Mary and her loyal Catholic confederates.

History is replete with examples of great people leveraging the contributions of others. For instance, following Philip of Macedonia's footsteps, Alexander the Great applied his father's innovative military tactics in successfully conquering vast lands to the east of Greece. King Louis XIII of France could not have strengthened and consolidated the monarchy's power without his Chief Minister, Cardinal Richelieu, working diligently behind the throne. Abraham Lincoln would never have been recognized as the Great Emancipator and savior of the Union without the contributions of his tenacious military generals, Grant and Sherman. Erwin Rommel's reputation as Nazi Germany's most successful battlefield general was due to employing innovative military strategies and tactics based on Heinz Guderian and others' earlier works. Dwight

D. Eisenhower earned his reputation as a military genius. He organized, unified, and managed disparate allied coalition forces that brought victory to the
free world in 1945. However, he could not have achieved such monumental
success without the support of exceptionally talented men like George C.
Marshall at home and fighting "blood and guts" generals such as George
Patton on North Africa and Europe's battlefields.

At the time of young Queen Elizabeth's coronation in 1559, the thought
of using deceit to entrap Mary, Queen of Scots, in a plot to kill Elizabeth,
was not even a remote consideration in William Cecil's mind. But his and
Walsingham's ensuing, skillful use of deception is precisely what led to Mary
Stuart's execution.

Strategic deception—a new light on a famous historical event.

## NOTES

1. See Appendix I for historians' comments and conclusions about Walsingham's
methods to eliminate Mary.

2. J. Barton Bowyer, *Cheating: Deception in War and Magic, Games and Sports,
Sex and Religion, Business and Con Games, Politics and Espionage, Art and Science*
(St. Martin's Press, 1982), 10.

3. "Deception is the only weapon that a warrior can wield that, to the extent it suc-
ceeds, will impose uncertainty and the element of surprise on the opponent." Barton
Whaley, *Practice to Deceive,* Page 1.

4. Bowyer, 20–23.

5. Bowyer, 30.

6. Bowyer, 35.

7. CBS/60 Minutes, Video titled, *"Deception at Duke"* (March 2012).

8. Nina Burleigh, *Unholy Business: A True Tale of Faith, Greed and Forgery in the
Holy Land* (HarperCollins Publishers, 2008).

9. Jason Kersten, *The Art of Making Money: The Story of a Master Counterfeiter*
(Penguin Group, 2009).

10. *The Microsoft Encarta College Dictionary* (2001) defines a conspiracy as "a
plan or agreement between two or more people to commit an illegal or subversive
act." Page 306.

11. Dr. John Dziak, Unpublished manuscript on the subject, *"Counterintelligence."*

12. Dziak, Ibid.

13. Dr. John Dziak, *Disinformation*, Forward, Page xvii, writes "actual deception operations . . . are rarely found in published materials and even seldom in State
archives, if ever released at all. But that is the very nature of intelligence and counterintelligence—not everything is to be found in the accessible printed word. Human
sources were, and are still, the rare earth metals of the intelligence craft."

# PART ONE

# (1560–1579)

Deception Planning Phases.

## Chapter 1

# Exit the Old Order, Enter
# the New Chaos

### EARLY CHALLENGES TO THE CHURCH
### AND RISE OF PROTESTANTISM

While the Roman Catholic Church for hundreds of years had provided the spiritual guidance that saved people's souls and offered pathways to a divine afterlife, "the Church suffered political humiliation and moral decay through-out the fourteenth and early fifteenth centuries (1378–1417)."[1] As a result, the papacy's insatiable pursuit of wealth and increasing moral turpitude of its priests, secular clergy, and monks led to the eventual loss of papal independence and subjugation to the French monarchy (1378–1417). Nevertheless, despite the Church's fall from grace, and "amid all the complaints and revolts against its authority,[2] the popes continued to assert their absolute sovereignty over the kings of the earth."[3]

Such assertions in England did not go unnoticed. And, by the late fifteenth century, the English monarchy had already won the "support of a rising middle class," subdued the recalcitrant nobility, calmed the subjects in the countryside, and "felt strong enough to repudiate the claims of the Church's sovereignty over civil power." Seizing the opportunity presented by the deterioration of the Church's international and intellectual authority, secular rulers now dreamed of mastering every phase of life in their realms, including religion and the Church."[4]

### Rise of Humanism

As the shadow of Church excesses and concerns of papal overreach loomed over England, a new intellectual awakening[5] took root. Growing forces of industry, finance, and expansion of potential new markets, discovered in the New World, brought into being the realization that knowledge and the unrelenting search for truth were irreplaceable elements in seeking wealth, power, and societal improvement. As a result, calls for a "new learning" significantly expanded literacy rates and demands for more formally educated people to drive the engine of progress. Universities were also encouraged to develop new curriculums offering scholars subjects and methodologies that could further rationalize science, pedagogy, and philosophy disciplines. One significant offshoot of this renewed search for truth involved the Catholic Church revisiting its roots in Christianity's Greek and Roman origins.

At the outset of the sixteenth century, England became the focal point of humanistic studies and the home of the movement's most brilliant minds. During the reign of Henry VIII (1509–1547), men like Thomas More, Thomas Wolsey, John Colet, and Desiderius Erasmus, who on three different occasions visited from the continent, advised the English King on political, economic, and religious matters relevant to the impact of reform on the orthodoxy of the Catholic Church. Their general intent was to seek peaceful reform within the Church by reexamining Christianity's Greek and Roman origins. In their advisory capacity, they "stress[ed] the authority of original scriptures as opposed to current ecclesiastical traditions and rituals, denounce[ed] the worldliness of the clergy, simplify[ied] church liturgy and [supported] translating the New Testament into the vernacular of its worshippers.[6, 7]

## The Gathering Storm

The relationship between Church and State institutions was teetering on the razor's edge. On the continent, the monarchies of Spain and France, responding to the growing discontent leveled at the Catholic Church, sought to stem the tide of Protestant advances into the Low Countries, Germany, and Scandinavia by unleashing a whirlwind of terror, death, and destruction.[8]

In England, with Henry VIII's accession to the throne in 1509, hopes were high among those who believed that the Roman Catholic Church could be "peacefully and incrementally" reformed from within.[9] For the next decade, Henry did not disappoint. However, by the mid to late 1520s, the relationship with the Catholic Church soured as Henry, in retaliation for the constant papal rebuffs for permission to divorce his first wife, commenced a successful all-out attack on the independence and wealth of the English Catholic church. That dramatic political and religious change, of course, known as the Act of Supremacy 1534, would have a catastrophic impact on England and its subjects for years to come.[10]

As the storm of the Reformation roiled over the kingdom, Henry VIII, and his children for the next almost 50 years failed to steer the English "ship of

Figure 1.1. An Allegory of the Tudor Succession: The Family of Henry VIII. (Left to right) Mary's Husband King Philip II of Spain, Mary Tudor, Henry VIII, Edward VI, Elizabeth I. Yale Center for British Art, Paul Mellon Collection

state" into calmer waters. Henry VIII, Edward VI, son of Jane Seymour, and Mary I, daughter of Catherine of Aragon, sought very different paths to solving religious reform in their kingdom, but to no avail. In fact, their personal ambitions, disunity of purpose, conflicting governance strategies, and disparate approaches dealing with the growing Protestant challenge to Catholic orthodoxy further exacerbated the growing fears that England was falling into the abyss of disorder and destruction.[11]

The return to a relative sense of peace, religious tolerance, and domestic tranquility would prove too elusive for Elizabeth I's predecessors. It would now be up to the royal daughter of Anne Boleyn, and last of the Tudor line, to change the direction and recalibrate the trajectory of England's religious and political future.

## NOTES

1. Will Durant, *The Reformation* (Simon and Schuster, 1957), 6.

2. John Wyclif (1320–1384) Professor of Theology, Oxford, vociferously protested against the many Church excesses and abuses, and asserted that man's future was predestined by the will of God, and "good works [did] not win salvation . . . Hence, the relationship of man to God [was] direct and require[d] no intermediary." Will

Durant also observed that "Wyclif's strident call for reform of the Catholic church preceded Luther's ideas by nearly 155 years, reflected all the major elements of the Reformation and likely sowed the seeds of Luther's discontent." *The Reformation*: Pages 31, 35, 37, 152.

3. Durant, 7.

4. Durant, 253.

5. This "new learning" was called Humanism. "It was a secular, cultural and intellectual movement stimulated by the Renaissance's rediscovery of the arts and philosophy of the ancient Greeks and Romans." *Microsoft, Encarta College Dictionary,* Page 701.

6. By the end of Henry's reign, Thomas More had been executed. Colet, Wolsey, and Erasmus experienced better fates and were banished from court and declared *persona non grata.*

7. Durant, 123–125.

8. Durant estimates that in Germany, the Peasant War (1524–1526) alone cost an estimated 130,000 deaths in battle and hundreds of castles and monasteries destroyed. *The Reformation*, Page 392.

9. Durant, 428.

10. Peter Marshall opines that "The King of England and the Pope made use of each other for political ends . . . Henry's petulance in 1516–17, no less than his graciousness in 1521, suggests the contingent and quasi-contractual character of the attachment to the Holy See. To put it more simply, it reveals how Henry VIII was capable of reacting when he didn't get his own way." *Heretics and Believers*, Page 76,

11. Peter Marshall also writes, "Historians have often tussled over which side was 'winning' and which 'losing' the religious struggle of Mary's reign . . . divided and confused by the events of Henry's reign, and battered and demoralized by those of Edward's, there was emerging a more articulate, combative, and committed Roman Catholicism. On the other hand, the networks of reformers and evangelicals, who unexpectedly gained control of the kingdom in 1547, and unexpectedly lost it in 1553, were evolving into a more determined and doctrinaire Protestant movement . . . The intensification of religious persecution was a crucial development." *Heretics and Believers*, Page 415.

Twenty-four heretics were burned in the twenty-four years of Henry VII's reign; eighty-one during the thirty-eight years of Henry VIII; two in the six years of Edward VI; 280 in Mary's five-year reign; and four in Elizabeth's forty-four years of rule. *A Brief History of the Tudor Age*, Jasper Ridley, Page 77. Eamon Duffy, *Fires of Faith,* writes that the 280 heretics burned at the stake during Mary's rule took place during the last years of her reign from February 1555 to November 1558, Page 7. Duffy also claims that "Elizabeth I burned no Catholics, but she strangled, disemboweled and dismembered more than 200." Page 82.

## Chapter 2

# "Elizabeth Ascending"

*Westminster Abbey*
*Coronation Day*
*15 January 1559*

Sir William Cecil hugs his cloak tighter around him as an icy gust of wind blows across the yard that separates Westminster Hall from Westminster Abbey.[1] He is somewhat bemused that Dr. John Dee, the court astrologer, obviously misinterpreted his charts when he selected 15 January as the most propitious date for the official anointment of Elizabeth Tudor as Queen of England.

Just a day earlier, the traditional royal procession from the Tower of London to Westminster Palace took place under conditions of early morning snow and body-numbing temperatures. However, as the procession slowly

Figure 2.1. Pen-and-ink drawing of the procession for the entry of Queen Elizabeth I into London on 14 January 1559, the day before her Coronation. College of Arms MS M. 6, fol. 41v. Reproduced by permission of the Kings, Heralds and Pursuivants of Arms

wended its way through London's narrow and circuitous lanes, the soon-to-be anointed Queen's spirits were lifted by the growing crescendo of enthusiastic cheers from her subjects.

"She sat, now, in a chariot covered with gold brocade which accented the richness of her robe of cloth of gold, the exact color of a small crown which graced the abundance of coppery hair. A canopy was borne over the chariot, held by four knights. The chariot itself was drawn by two mules, gorgeously caparisoned in gold brocade."[2]

While some could interpret the inclement weather as a bad omen for Elizabeth's reign, Cecil hopes that yesterday's overwhelming public display of affection is a true harbinger of good times ahead.

Elizabeth's newly chosen Secretary of State and Chief Privy Council[3] advisor impatiently shifts his weight from one foot to the other as he waits for the opening anthem to start the coronation's procession. He understands the symbolic significance of officially legitimizing the return of Protestantism as the country's official religion through the holy anointment of Elizabeth. But he also knows there are many threats to her throne's stability that demand his immediate attention. The time to act is now! Consequently, he is anxious to have this ancient coronation ritual be over so he can proceed with the critical business of State.

To help overcome the growing fatigue that begins to creep through his body, Cecil reflects on the long, and at times, dangerous path that brought him to this point in time. He believes that despite his religious preference amid growing animosities between Catholics and Protestants, his measured, pragmatic approach to the rapid changes occurring with royal leadership's power places him in a favorable light. Yes, good fortune indeed smiles upon him today.

His father, Richard, had served both Elizabeth's father, Henry VIII, and grandfather, Henry VII, in a series of minor positions. At the age of eight, Cecil's father brought him to Henry VIII's court "to serve as one of the three Pages of the Robe." This experience impacted his future and helped him develop the skills necessary to deal with the significant religious differences between Edward VI and Mary Tudor's monarchies. He often recalled that even in the worst of times, "Queen Mary had called him an 'honest man.'"[4]

For as long as he could remember, he had sympathy for Elizabeth, whose status had degraded following Henry VIII's disposal of her hapless mother, Anne Boleyn. However, with the ascension of Elizabeth's half-brother, Edward VI, to the throne, her situation improved as Cecil provided counsel and managed matters that impacted her estate finances, health, and care. They had formed a great relationship, which helped Elizabeth immensely.

Figure 2.2. King Edward VI; mezzotint after unknown artist, eighteenth century. © National Portrait Gallery, London

*Fortiſsimi quique interfecti ſunt ab eâ.*

**Figure 2.3. Queen Mary I; line engraving after unknown artist, published 1630.** © National Portrait Gallery, London

Following Edward VI's early death and throughout Mary Tudor's reign, Cecil prided himself in remaining relatively unnoticed by the Marian Court as he successfully navigated the slippery slope of Catholic retribution. While performing minor tasks for the Catholic Queen, yet rarely appearing at court, he remained unswervingly dedicated to ensuring Elizabeth's safety and welfare while she was in the London Tower prison. The mere fact that it was from Cecil that Elizabeth received word that her sister, Mary, had died spoke volumes of the trust they shared with each other.[5]

Cecil is aware of the many challenges he will encounter following Elizabeth's ascension to the throne. He knows this young, twenty-five-year-old Queen is, indeed, a talented, impressive individual even though she represents the "weaker sex." Cecil learned it was against God's ordained will that women rule over men, a typical product of the patriarchal Tudor era.[6] The disruptive and tumultuous years of Queen Mary's failed rule certainly reinforced this gender-biased belief. It was a man's world. Nevertheless, contrary to the commonly accepted masculine view of women, Cecil remains fully committed to guiding his strong-willed, intelligent, yet unpredictable Queen Elizabeth to a long, successful reign. Service to God, Queen, and country will always be his top priority.

The sudden but long-awaited blare of royal trumpets shakes Cecil from his dreamlike reverie as the lengthy procession moves slowly toward the Abbey entrance. His thoughts return to the multi-faceted problems facing the new monarchy. As Secretary of State, he makes a mental note that he must make a concerted effort to find and recruit a new cadre of talented individuals to help him protect both England and Elizabeth from current and future threats. He is confident that in time, his concerns will prove to be well-founded.

As Cecil climbs the steps leading into the Abbey, he hopes the chair and footstool reserved for him to watch the royal coronation are fully cushioned. His feet and back ached him considerably.

## NOTES

1. Westminster Hall was the main public building where the most important official meetings were held by the reigning monarch (e.g., addresses to Parliament, sessions for the monarch's common law court, site for great State trials of traitors and traditional location for the coronation banquet). Before Henry VIII's abolition of the monasteries (1536–1539), Westminster Abbey was the most significant of the 513 monasteries in England. However, with its twenty-five monks, it was only the seventeenth in size, but it was the richest of all. *A Brief History of the Tudor Age,* Jasper Ridley, Page 30.

2. Mary M. Luke, *Gloriana: The Years of Elizabeth I* (Coward, McCann & Geoghegan, Inc., 1973), 40.

3. The Privy Council performed routine administrative functions concerning matters of religion, military, Queen's security, economics, and the welfare of the citizens. Members, or sometimes called advisors, were appointed by the Queen, and served at her pleasure.

4. Luke, 28.
5. Anne Somerset, *Elizabeth I* (Anchor Books, 1991), 62.
6. Alison Weir, *The Life of Elizabeth I* (Ballantine Books, 1998), 22.

*Chapter 3*

# The Worst of Times

Cecil's initial concerns for the future of England were not unfounded. Even before Elizabeth was anointed Queen of England, a contemporary of the soon-to-be new monarch succinctly described the deteriorating "State of the Realm."

> The Queen poor; the realm exhausted; the nobility poor and decayed; good captains and soldiers wanting; the people out of order; justice not executed; all things dear; excesses in meat, diet, and apparel; division among ourselves; war with France; the French King bestriding the realm, having one foot in Calais and the other in Scotland; steadfast enemies, but no steadfast friends.[1]

Compounding the future Queen's, and, by extension, William Cecil's problems was that of the approximately four million subjects living in England, an estimated 50% to 60% were adherents to the Catholic faith.[2] As a result of this demographic reality, the loyalty of Elizabeth's subjects became an issue of considerable import. Further complicating the situation, England was geographically isolated and surrounded by countries with substantially larger populations and superior military forces. Consequently, the English monarch faced what appeared to be several intractable challenges that threatened her throne, kingdom, and religious orientation. Yet, by the early 1560s, through the advice and leadership of Sir William Cecil, a reconstituted Privy Council sympathetic to the Protestant cause, the implementation of a frugal, fiscal plan, and a new tolerance toward the Catholic faithful, England had every reason to look to the future with a moderate degree of optimism.

However, beginning in 1568 and for the next two decades, England will experience a long series of unanticipated and unsettling events. Events that slowly, but inexorably, will create an ever-growing perception, especially among the Protestant-led government ministers and loyalists, that their country's survival was at risk from a vengeful and increasing Catholic resurgence.

Figure 3.1. Queen Elizabeth I; oil on panel by unknown continental artist, c. 1575.
© National Portrait Gallery, London

Now Elizabeth's chief advisor and First Secretary, William Cecil, is aware of the looming storm clouds on the horizon. As early as 1566, he informed Elizabeth that internal discord was growing among the English Catholics. Additionally, England lacked a formidable Protestant alliance to counter the growing Catholic threat from abroad. Sir Ralph Sadler, Minister of Parliament and Cecil's most trusted servant, diplomatic envoy to Scotland, and future custodian for Mary Stuart, also spoke in Parliament of rumors that a coalition of Catholic forces was forming on the European continent.

> We have heard, and we hear daily of secret conspiracies and great confederacies, between the Pope, the French King, and other Princes of the Popish confederacy against all Princes Protestant and professors of the gospel, of which the Queen's Majesty is the chief patroness and protectrix at this day.[3]

However, despite Cecil and others' earlier dire warnings, Elizabeth stubbornly continued to focus on what she considered a more immediate, pressing issue; the incessant turmoil centered in the north of England and its border with Scotland—a situation that would significantly worsen by 1568. From that year forward, it became irrefutably clear that the Counter-Reformation was indeed gaining momentum, much to the detriment of the country's national psyche.

## MARY STUART—UPRISING AND CONSPIRACY

On Sunday, 16 May 1568, many English subjects could not have predicted that Mary, Queen of Scots' escape from rebellious Scottish nobles, and her request for sanctuary in England, would have significant long-term implications that will plague the kingdom for decades to come. "The Queen of Scots was not seeking permanent political asylum. What she needed was a resting place to rally her forces, and she immediately called on her cousin Elizabeth for help."[4] However, much to Elizabeth's chagrin, Mary's expected short stay in England would, instead, last for nearly twenty years, giving Mary plenty of time to rally Catholics with the goal of re-establishing their faith in both England and Scotland.

In effect, the moment the Scottish Queen stepped foot on English soil, she brought with her political and religious "baggage" that would magnify, increasingly aggravate, and, finally, create irreconcilable differences between the two cousins. Mary herself soon realized that her choice of England as a temporary sanctuary was a poor decision.

In a 26 June 1568 letter sent from Carlyle Castle to King Charles IX of France, she opined "that the injustices of this queen [Elizabeth], or, at least

Figure 3.2. Mary, Queen of Scots; oil on panel after Nicholas Hilliard, inscribed 1578. © National Portrait Gallery, London

of her council, is preparing me for a much longer sojourn here . . . and that I fear to be more strictly guarded for the future . . . "[5]

For the English Catholic nobility residing along the Scottish-English border, the Scottish Queen's arrival became a *casus belli* for those committed to restoring the "old faith" to England. Poised to rally around Mary, a short-lived revolt led by the Earls of Northumberland and Westmorland against the Crown ensued.

Yet, even with the Northern Rebellion quickly and ruthlessly suppressed by an enraged Queen Elizabeth, it became abundantly clear that as long as Mary remained in England, her mere presence would encourage more aggressive, lethal, conspiratorial activities against the English Queen.[6] "The Northern rising [underscored the reality] that beneath the fragile crust of religious uniformity, divisive passions bubbled."[7]

Counter-Protestant activities continued to escalate for the next two decades as Mary Stuart became the nexus for an increasing number of plots designed to extirpate Protestantism in England. It is also during the post-Northern Rebellion time frame that Sir William Cecil and his new head of the English secret service, Sir Francis Walsingham, will seek alternative solutions to counter the growing and persistent enemy threat.

## PAPAL/SECULAR THREAT ACCELERANTS

### Excommunication of Elizabeth

In 1570, Pope Pius V further complicated matters for the Protestant Queen, her senior advisors, and especially Catholic-practicing English subjects when he delivered a papal bull excommunicating the heretic, Elizabeth, from the protective arms of Rome. As historian Alan Haynes explained:

> Late in February, "*Regnans in Excelsis*, a bull of excommunication and deposition . . . told distant English Catholics that rebellion was actually a duty and obeying Elizabeth was a sin. The pontiff took on the mantle of aggressor and, in Elizabeth's mind as well as Cecil's, the bull identified the religion of perhaps half her subjects with covert treachery."[8]

The Pope's proclamation immediately disrupted and destabilized a large segment of English society that had mostly complied with Elizabeth's religious tolerance and compromise policy for the previous twelve years. Before the Pope's interference, English subjects who still observed the "old faith" generally fell into two distinct groups.

One group reluctantly followed Elizabeth's religious compromise policy by paying nominal fines for not attending prescribed Protestant events but consciously resisted the idea that Protestantism was a permanent fixture in the kingdom. Now, with the Pope's permission to disobey and withdraw their allegiance to Elizabeth, Catholic agitators were provided further incentives to recruit a large, previously untapped pool of potential anti-Protestant supporters.

The second group willingly accepted the Elizabethan compromise, attended Protestant events, continued to celebrate Mass in the privacy of their homes, and gave their full allegiance to the Queen. But, to them, the Pope's proclamation created a dilemma. If the Pope condemned Elizabeth as a heretic and absolved from sin all Catholics who worked to destroy her, would those Catholics who continued to comply now be considered sinners?

**Figure 3.3. Pope Pius V. Artist: Ronda Penrod. Reproduced by permission of Ronda Penrod**

The Pope's interference in the Protestant Queen's affairs posed a clear and present danger to the kingdom's domestic and religious stability. It also provided Elizabeth's loyal Protestant subjects with conclusive proof that a unified front of Catholic secular and papal interests was allied against them. This inchoate perception would eventually turn into an unshakeable belief that England faced an international plot that threatened the very survival of Protestantism in England.

## The Question of Regicide

The question of the lengths Catholics would go to remove Protestantism from England ranged from guarded discussions of Elizabeth's removal by non-lethal means to the extreme act of assassination. However, by the Throckmorton and Parry Plots (early to mid-1580s), Spain, France, and even the Pope supported the more extreme measures.

The spiritual leader of the Catholic faith and successor to Pius V, Pope Gregory XIII, faced a dilemma. On the one hand, as vicar of Christ, he could not explicitly approve of assassination. But, on the other hand, many devoted followers inclined to support such an act looked to him for his assurance that such an extreme measure—the murder of a King or Queen—was morally justifiable.[9]

"From the outset [of his ascending to the papal throne in 1572], he made it clear that the principal objective of his pontificate would be the fight against Protestantism, together with the steadfast promotion of the decrees of the Council of Trent. . . . One could wish, for example, that he had not reacted to the news of the St. Bartholomew's Day Massacre of the Huguenots by ordering a special Te Deum to be sung . . . or he had not tried to persuade King Philip of Spain to launch an invasion of England from Ireland or the Netherlands, or when these dreams collapsed, that he had not given active encouragement to a plot to assassinate Queen Elizabeth of England—'the Jezebel of the North.' Such an act, he had declared, would be hailed as the work of God."[10]

In 1578, King Philip II of Spain, having a series of discussions with his chief representative in the Netherlands, also encouraged the idea of assassination as a legitimate tool of State. Accordingly, on 25 August 1580, Philip officially offered a reward for Prince William of Orange's death, the leader of the Protestant movement in the Low Countries of Holland and Belgium.[11] Less than four years later, on 30 June 1584, William of Orange fell victim to a Catholic assassin's bullet.

There can be little doubt that Philip's public support of William's assassination sent a clear message to England's Protestant leaders, including Elizabeth, that she was no longer immune from future attempts on her life. By the 1580s, regicide was openly discussed in England's exile communities in Europe and even the Vatican in Rome.

## Threat Perceptions Etched in Stone

Atrocities committed by Catholics against Protestants in Paris on St. Bartholomew's Day, 24 August 1572, undoubtedly left a vivid[12] impression in Elizabeth's Protestant loyalists' minds. What began as a failed attempt to disrupt the wedding of the Catholic French King's sister to the Protestant King of Navarre soon devolved into the murder of the Huguenot (French Protestant) leadership who also attended the marriage celebration. Attacks on the Huguenot leaders quickly spun out of control and rapidly engulfed all Protestants living in the city. For days, Protestant citizens, including those residing in the English embassy, became targets of unspeakable violence and bloodlust. The frenzy and human slaughter quickly migrated to the French provinces, where the carnage lasted even longer. The Paris massacre took three to four thousand lives. Deaths outside of Paris ranged from ten thousand to as many as seventy thousand.

The long-term impact the St. Bartholomew Day Massacre will have on the English Protestant psyche is indeed profound. This event alone would remain a constant reminder that the return of Catholicism to their kingdom could unleash the same fury and slaughter that had occurred under the reign of Elizabeth's sister, Mary Tudor. The hatred spilling onto the streets of Paris in late summer 1572 was recorded by England's resident ambassador in Paris, Francis Walsingham, who alerted his peers—many on the Privy Council—to the danger that awaited England should the avid supporters of the Counter-Reformation return.[13]

## "Bringing It"—Fifth Column Infiltration

"Missionaries from [Catholic] seminaries [in Europe] were trained with one object in mind; to provide a religious counter offensive to the heretics in England, Ireland and Scotland. Pope Gregory XIII gave papal support and blessing to all and singled out the Jesuit order as the main source of recruits. Beginning in 1574, the influx of Catholic priests into England to replace those who had grown old, retired, or died increased."[14]

During the first decade of Elizabeth's reign and in response to the perceived diminution of Catholic vigor and allegiance to the "old faith," Dr. William Allen, a leading intellectual within the Catholic-English exile community, established a missionary school in Douai, Spanish Netherlands. Later, similar English Catholic colleges opened in Rheims, France, Rome, Valladolid, and Seville, Spain. Their goal was to revitalize the spiritual energy of English Catholic subjects, roll back the deleterious gains of the Elizabethan compromise, and re-establish the Roman Catholic Church in England.[15]

The first wave of this new breed of proselytizing missionaries returned to England in 1574. Their mission was to revitalize the old faith by building resistance against increasing Protestant influence within the English Catholic community.[16]

That same year, the Bishop of London's warning to Francis Walsingham of the rising Catholic missionary threat proved to be a prescient prediction

Figure 3.4. Cardinal William Allen; stipple engraving by Joseph John Jenkins, possibly early to mid-nineteenth century. © National Portrait Gallery, London

of what was to come three years later. Based on numerous reports from peers across England, the Bishop reported: "that the Papists marvelously increase[d] both in numbers and in obstinate withdrawing of themselves from Church (Protestant supported) and service of God. He [was] adamant that the only way of countering this disturbing trend [was] to formulate legislation that [would] make the Catholics' lot more unpleasant."[17] Responding to the Bishop's concerns, the English Privy Council imposed more stringent laws heavily penalizing subjects who supported and protected Catholic missionaries from Europe.

However, despite increasing attempts to track down and severely punish recusants accused of aiding and abetting the influx of new arrivals dedicated to spreading the work of the old faith, a second wave of approximately one hundred radical Jesuit "Soldiers of God" infiltrated England in 1580.[18] Father Robert Campion and Father Robert Persons spearheaded this group of spiritually driven, fifth columnists. Even though Campion was eventually executed on 1 December 1581, he and Persons successfully advanced the Catholic cause embarrassing Elizabeth's advisors responsible for countering Campion and Persons's subversive activities. Shortly after Campion's arrest, Persons safely returned to Europe in August 1581. However, before he departed from England, he urged recusant conspirators to action, which would lead to the 1582 Throckmorton Plot designed to remove Queen Elizabeth and her senior advisors.[19]

From 1580 to 1583, political and religious polarization in England rapidly reached a breaking point. Perceiving that the forces of Catholic resistance were growing in intensity, Sir Francis Walsingham and his mentor, Sir William Cecil, were determined to find a way to stop their Catholic opponent's momentum. In concert, they boldly set forth to develop an innovative, high-risk/high-reward offensively focused course of action that would assist them in taking the fight to the enemy.

## NOTES

1. Mary M. Luke, *Gloriana: The Years of Elizabeth I* (Coward, McCann & Geoghegan, 1973), 32.

2. Luke, 473.

3. Anne Somerset, *Elizabeth I* (Anchor Books, 1991), 191.

4. John Cooper, *The Queen's Agent* (Pegasus Books, 2012), 51.

5. *Letters of Mary, Queen of Scots. Volume I* (Henry Colburn, Publisher, MDCCCXLIV, 1864), 85.

6. Five thousand men rose under the leadership of Earls Northumberland and Westmorland. However, the rising was suppressed before King Philip II of Spain had time to send aid. More than six hundred rebels were executed.

7. Somerset, 241.

8. Alan Haynes, *The Elizabethan Secret Service* (Sutton Publishing, 1992), xxi.

9. Stephen Alford, *The Watchers: A Secret History of the Reign of Elizabeth I*, Page 76, writes that "Gregory was minded to deprive Elizabeth of her princely dignities by either conspiring her death or supporting open rebellion and an invasion."

10. John Julius Norwich, *Absolute Monarch: A History of the Papacy* (Random House, 2011), 321.

11. John Hungerford Pollen, *Mary, Queen of Scots and the Babington Plot*. Edited from the original documents in the Public Record Office (T. and A. Constable for the Scottish History Society, 1922), Introduction, "Loyalty to Queen Mary," xix–xx.

12. Vividness—A term in psychology that describes the impact of an extremely traumatic or catastrophic situation on the psyche of the person or persons who experience the event. The vividly horrendous event is irrevocably embedded in the person's memory and can often be recalled in detail. The experience will also reinforce and strengthen psychological biases that existed before the event.

13. Neville Williams, *The Life and Times of Elizabeth I,* Page 117, writes that "the St. Bartholomew Massacre was a grim moment for Protestantism in Europe, for the news from France was interpreted as an evil conspiracy by the powers of the Counter-Reformation and yet, before long, it provoked greater solidarity among Protestants of different persuasions and countries than any other single event." G. J. Meyer, *The Tudors: The Complete Story of England's Most Notorious Dynasty*, Page 498, writes that "What matters here is that the massacre of 1572 horrified the Protestants of England, [and] seemed to provide rich justification for their insistence that Catholicism had to be extinguished . . . "

14. Luke, 434.

15. Eamon Duffy writes that "all of his [Cardinal Allen's] politics were tuned to the reconversion of England . . . Allen believed he knew how to convert England: between 1553 and 1558, he had seen it done and had taken part in the process. He never doubted that what was needed for the success of this great work of God was, in essence, the repetition of the Marian restoration . . . He did not believe that Catholics and Protestants could live in peace together." *Reformation Divided*, Page 153.

16. John Cooper, *The Queen's Agent: Sir Francis Walsingham and the Rise of Espionage in Elizabethan England*, Page 137, estimates that three missionaries who had received their education and training at Douai returned to England in 1574, followed by sixteen more shortly after that. Despite the execution of Cuthbert Mayne in 1577, the first of the "new breed" to be executed by Protestant authorities, the numbers of priests surreptitiously returning to England continued to increase exponentially. Eamon Duffy asserts that "four priests returned to England in 1574, and by 1580, about a hundred in all had been sent on the mission." *Reformation Divided*, Page 147.

17. Somerset, 385.

18. Stephen Alford, *The Watchers: A Secret History of the Reign of Elizabeth I*, Page 125, estimates that by the end of Elizabeth's reign, approximately four hundred seventy missionaries had infiltrated England. Of that number, one hundred sixteen were executed, two hundred ninety-four were sent to prison where seventeen died while incarcerated, and ninety-one were banished from the kingdom. John Cooper, *The Queen's Agent: Sir Francis Walsingham and the Rise of Espionage in Elizabethan England,* Pages 143–145, estimates that by 1586 there were approximately three hundred missionaries in England. Of that number, thirty-three had been executed, fifty were in prison, and sixty were banished from the kingdom.

19. On 23 June, two days after Campion's arrest, Robert Person, who was still in England, wrote to his superior in France that the persecutions of Catholics in England were on the increase and estimated that there were twenty thousand more Catholics

in England than a year before. However, the numbers might have been greatly exaggerated to impress his superior or mislead the English government should his letter be intercepted. *Calendar of State Papers—Domestic Series, 1581, 23 June,* Page 21, #51.

# Chapter 4

# Becoming the Fox

At the beginning of her reign, "She [Elizabeth] and her First Secretary [Cecil] . . . wanted beyond anything, to make a success of running the country and on three major points they were agreed as to how this was to be done. They saw the nation's future as bound up with the Reformation, and they abhorred the ruinous waste of war . . . they [also] agreed that a re-establishment of the national credit was a step without which nothing else could be done and that this itself could not be achieved without a vigilant economy."[1] However, Cecil soon discovered that the best intentions do not always achieve the best results.

Cecil, and later Walsingham, quickly realized that implementing and executing Elizabeth's single-minded commitment to her national security priorities was both incredibly frustrating and counterproductive when dealing with the looming Catholic threat. Early in her reign and despite her successful foray against the French along the English/Scottish border, her reaction to various aspects of the operation provided Cecil an unsettling preview of what lay ahead.

"Elizabeth's successful excursion into Scotland had given her no taste for war . . . There was also less risk of a Treasury enlarged by chronic frugality being depleted in very short order."[2] The extent of her parsimony even dictated how Cecil would conduct government business with his foreign counterparts.

"Mr. Secretary returned to court on 28 July (1560) . . . he had been away sixty-three days, incurring expenditures of 252 pounds [from his own pocket] . . . when he recommended that Elizabeth send some small present to the Scottish nobles who had done him good service during the negotiations, she would not listen, sarcastically referring to his Scottish friends as his 'brother saints.'"[3]

In 1562, Elizabeth's inflexibility, penny-pinching proclivities, and war avoidance posture were again on display in her half-hearted support of the French Protestants when her negotiators agreed to have " . . . English troops

**Figure 4.1. (Left to right) Sir William Cecil, 1st Baron Burleigh; Queen Elizabeth I; and Sir Francis Walsingham; line engraving by William Faithorne, 1655. © National Portrait Gallery, London**

occupy Le Havre and Dieppe in exchange for the return of Calais when the Protestants won the war. However, when the towns proved difficult to hold, the Huguenots made peace with their Catholic countrymen. The expedition collapsed amid a savage bout of the plague. English honor had been hazarded and forfeited, while the Queen's aversion to war had been vindicated [and likely reinforced]. Persuading her to pursue a hawkish foreign policy would henceforth be more difficult than ever."[4]

By the early 1570s, uncomfortably aware of their sovereign's idiosyncratic and frustrating behaviors, Cecil and Walsingham concurred that they had to find a way to shake England out of its defensive and somewhat inward-looking posture. The kingdom's national security policy required a more innovative and unorthodox approach.

## SELECTING THE DECEPTION ALTERNATIVE

"The Machiavellian mode had been exported to England, and so flourished hot and cold, that foreign rulers could not escape the shivery conclusion that they knew and understood far less about foggy English policy than the English divined about them." Alan Haynes, *Elizabethan Secret Services*, Page 193.

Despite Elizabeth's consistent, stubborn reluctance to accommodate her advisors' concerns, William Cecil and Francis Walsingham eventually find a solution to their dilemma. In seeking other creative, asymmetric approaches to protect and promote the benefits and gains of the Reformation and the Protestant cause, they revisit the writings of Sir Thomas More and Niccolò Machiavelli.

Knowing Elizabeth would not approve new initiatives that could further drain her royal coffers, Cecil and his recruit, Walsingham, *in camera,* looked for anti-Catholic strategies by studying More's *Utopia* and Machiavelli's *The Prince* and *Discourses of Titus Livius*. Their studies led to an innovative, foundational strategy that would not only satisfy Elizabeth's priorities but still permit them the flexibility to develop more dynamic counter Catholic initiatives.

In *Utopia,* Sir Thomas More wrote that a righteous and perfect, God-fearing country should never opt for a direct, force-on-force confrontation, especially against a stronger enemy. Instead, he theorized that the use of indirect physical and psychological, non-kinetic means, coupled with a heavy emphasis on wit, cunning, and deceit, would ultimately undermine and eventually preempt an aggressor's ability and intent to wage physical war. Sir Thomas also proposed that adopting such an approach ultimately resulted in an efficient, less internally disruptive, and more cost-effective path to victory. In so doing, cunning, wit, and deceit would always prevail over an enemy's warlike intentions.

They be not only sorry, but also ashamed to achieve the victory with bloodshed, counting it great folly to buy precious wares too dear. They rejoice and avaunt themselves, if they vanquish and oppress their enemies by craft and deceit. And for that act they make a general triumph . . . by the might and puissance of wit.

For with bodily strength (say they) bears, lions, boars, wolves, dogs, and other wild beasts do fight. And as the most part of them do pass us in strength and fierce courage, so in wit and reason we be much stronger than they all.[5]

More also extolled the virtues of offering incentives to kill those in leadership positions and urged the use of various psychological actions to promote confusion and suspicion within the enemy camp. Such actions, he professed, would destabilize leadership and weaken the enemy's resolve to go to war.

Immediately after that war is once solemnly denounced, they procure many proclamations signed with their own common seal to be set up privily at one time in their enemy's land in places most frequented . . . they promise great rewards to him that will kill their enemy's prince . . . Whatsoever is prescribed unto him that killeth any of the proclaimed persons, that is doubled to him that bringeth any of the same to them alive . . .[6]

For his part, Niccolò Machiavelli emphasized deception and manipulative techniques as keys to success and victory.

Since a prince must know well how to use the nature of the beast, he must choose the fox and the lion from among them, for the lion cannot defend himself from traps, and the fox cannot defend himself from wolves. It is, therefore, necessary to be a fox to recognize traps and a lion to frighten wolves. Those who live simply by the lion do not understand this.[7]

His [Machiavelli's] argument that "the ends justified the means" likely resonated with both Cecil and Walsingham as they wrestled with Elizabeth's restrictive domestic and foreign policies. Ironically, their familiarity with Machiavelli's chapter on "Conspiracies" in *Discourses of Titus Livius* may have planted the early seeds for an idea that Cecil and Walsingham will later grow into an audacious, high-risk/high-reward intelligence operation. Machiavelli stated that "I maintain that one finds in history that all conspiracies have been made by men of standing or else by men in immediate attendance on a prince, for other people, unless they be sheer lunatics, cannot form a conspiracy; since men without power and those who are not in touch with a prince are devoid alike of any opportunity of carrying out a conspiracy successfully."[8]

## CHANGE OF COURSE

Using the guidance espoused by More and Machiavelli, Cecil and Walsingham will refocus their attention from the adversary's military command and control structures and warfighting capabilities (hard targets) to more vulnerable supporting institutions and infrastructures (soft targets). This new strategy of "Indirect Preemption" will buy England valuable time to strengthen its military forces. It will also delay Catholic military action against England by diverting Spain and France's attention through tactics that will disperse Catholic naval and ground forces worldwide and drain their overextended warfighting resources.

"Walsingham's mind encompassed a remarkable grand strategic vision focused on containing the Spanish, [French] and papal threats and recognizing that his front-line defenses lay not along the English coast but on the continent of Europe. He fully understood the necessity of using naval power to exert political and diplomatic pressure; he utilized economic warfare to hinder Armada preparations; he employed black propaganda to lower morale amongst the forces of England's enemies."[9]

Embarking on this new journey, Cecil, ably assisted by Walsingham after 1568, developed and employed an array of assertive, preemptive-focused initiatives that, in time, would become unrelenting and costly irritants and distractions to their Catholic adversaries.

## Use of Proxies

Even before England's foreign policy reorientation a decade later, Cecil, with Elizabeth's reluctant concurrence, experimented with an idea to rid Scotland of French military support. "The plan was simplicity itself—England would subsidize the Protestant-based Scottish Lords of the Congregation to fight secretly what England could not fight in the open; primarily the eviction of French and Catholic influence from Scotland."[10] However, the scheme failed due to the lack of Protestant Scottish noble resolve.

Using that early example as a springboard for future actions, "In October 1578, [even though the Queen balked] at sending her bond for 100,000 pounds, which she had earlier promised the rebels . . . she was hoping to achieve the same end at less cost and with less chance of directly antagonizing Spain by entertaining the recently renewed marriage suit of Francis, the former Duke of Alençon, who was proposing to lead his own expedition to the Low Countries."[11]

In 1580, "Walsingham plan[ned] to boldly kidnap the Papal Legate to France . . . Huguenot pirates from La Rochelle were paid to seize the Legate so that he could be questioned about the Vatican's scheme for a possible military expedition against Ireland involving Spanish troops."[12]

## Use of Black Propaganda

In September 1579, pamphlets appeared in London and abroad, criticizing the possible marriage of Queen Elizabeth to the French Duke of Alençon.[13] "The text was a masterpiece, combining intimate knowledge of the very arguments that had been advanced by opponents of the marriage." Although never proved, Elizabeth suspected that some Council members were behind the pamphlet. The rumor in Paris was that Walsingham was linked to it.[14]

In 1585–1586, Walsingham developed a disinformation plan to isolate London's French ambassador, preventing him from interfering in Mary Stuart's trial for treason.[15] Walsingham also directed his agents to write an anti-Jesuit pamphlet to exploit and leverage an already acrimonious divide between two English exile factions.

## Penetrating Communication Networks

Cecil and Walsingham penetrated the Catholic communications system in the French embassy in London in 1582. The action disrupted plans to liberate Mary, Queen of Scots, and laid the groundwork for a unique communication intercept operation at Chartley Hall to successfully co-opt renewed attempts to free the Scottish Queen in 1586.

## Use of Diplomacy

Diplomatic envoys attempted to induce the Ottoman Turks to start a war with Spain. If successful, "Philip II would be forced to deploy ships which could otherwise be used against England. In 1585, Walsingham instructs [the English representative] to explain to the vizier how the rise of Spain threatens the dignity of the sultan. The remedy that Walsingham prescribe[d] [was] a [Turkish] military strike, either on Spain itself from the coast of Ottoman-controlled Africa, or an assault of naval galleys on Habsburg territories in Italy. [The English representative] dutifully spen[t] the next three years petitioning the sultan to commit some portion of his forces against Spain . . . "[16]

## Specific Seaborne Tactics

Walsingham "advanced for stealthy raids by English privateers and small naval squadrons upon Spanish interests across the breadth of its vast empires . . . proposed sending three warships to snap up the Spanish fishing fleet on the Newfoundland Banks. . . . backed and promoted other voyages of discovery that promised to combine private profit, scientific discovery,

English interests, and Spanish discomfiture . . . Mr. Secretary's spies in Italy reported that the news had shaken Philip's credit with the Genoese bankers: they had just refused him a loan of a half-million crowns."[17]

## Mary's Frequent Relocations

From 1568 to December 1585, the frequent relocations of Mary Stuart's incarceration, coupled with an increasing emphasis on security measures, kept those seeking to free her in a constant state of planning uncertainty. Beginning with Mary's initial incarceration in 1568, the growing breakdown of trust between her and Elizabeth became tense and fractious. As the years progressed, Mary's presence in England continued to encourage Catholic resistance to Elizabeth, thus posing an increasing threat to the country's stability and the English Queen's physical well-being.

However, Walsingham will blunt the incessant Catholic attempts to spread discord throughout the land by controlling Mary's location of imprisonment, which limited contact with her supporters. Whether through Cecil's intervention with Elizabeth or her direct consent, he virtually had *carte blanche* to move the Scottish Queen to increasingly restrictive environments making it difficult for the Catholic conspirators to find and free her. Mary Stuart was moved to different locations approximately twenty-one times before her execution in 1587.

## Momentum Shift

By the late 1570s, a significant change in English focus based on More and Machiavelli's writings would provide a new, dynamic, and more effective national security policy that would significantly misdirect and ultimately drain Catholic resources and manpower.

During this critical transition period from 1570–1580, the most tangible benefit derived from Cecil and Walsingham's Indirect Preemption strategy was the restructuring, centralization, and expansion of the English intelligence secret service. In addition, the service's vastly improved collection and analysis functions significantly increased England's ability to accurately understand its Catholic adversary's intentions, plans, and capabilities.

## NOTES

1. Elizabeth Jenkins, *Elizabeth the Great* (G.P. Putnam's Sons, 1958), 63.

2. Mary M. Luke, *Gloriana: The Years of Elizabeth I* (Coward, McCann & Geoghegan, Inc., 1973), 181.

3. Luke, 104–105.

4. Cooper, 61–62.

5. Sir Thomas More, Ralph Robinson (trans.), *Utopia* (Barnes and Noble Classics, 2005), 118.

6. More, 119.

7. Niccolò Machiavelli, Wayne A. Rebhorn (trans), *The Prince* (Barnes and Noble Classics, 2003), 75.

8. Miles J. Unger, *Machiavelli: A Biography* (Simon and Schuster, 2011), 204.

9. Robert Hutchinson, *Elizabeth's Spymaster* (Thomas Dunne Books, St. Martin's Press), 264.

10. Luke, 92.

11. Stephen Budiansky, *Her Majesty's Spymaster: Elizabeth I, Sir Francis Walsingham, and the Birth of Modern Espionage* (Penguin Books, 2005), 110–111.

12. Hutchinson, 89–90.

13. Ensuring a legitimate heir to succeed Elizabeth was an immediate priority once she ascended the throne in 1559. This priority became more urgent when Elizabeth nearly succumbed to smallpox in late 1562. Among the many suitors asking for Elizabeth's hand were two younger brothers of the French King—Henri, Duke of Anjou, and Francis, Duke of Alençon. Francis found himself involved in an approximately three-year courtship as a political pawn being manipulated by both England and France as they vied for an advantage in countering Spain's growing influence in the Netherlands. Given his strident Puritanical, anti-Catholic leanings, Walsingham was certainly not a supporter of Francis's marriage proposal. Although the First Secretary was never explicitly identified as the force behind John Stubbs's anti-Alençon pamphlet, Walsingham without question possessed the motive, opportunity, and means to undermine and resist the Alençon-Elizabeth relationship.

14. Budiansky, 111.

15. The idea for this contingency plan occurred c. 1584–c. 1585. It was probably based on three assumptions: 1) that Elizabeth would resist condemning Mary to death, 2) the French ambassador in London would attempt to influence Elizabeth's decision, and 3) the already antipathetic relationship between the First Secretary and Sir Edward Stafford would worsen over time. All these assumptions proved valid. Elizabeth was extremely hesitant to carry out Mary's death warrant. The French ambassador attempted to intercede in clearing the charges of treason against Mary, and the scheme involving Stafford's brother, William, would forever tarnish the reputation of Sir Edward Stafford. (For more details on The Stafford Plot, see Appendix B, Lingering Questions and their Implications, Section V.)

16. Cooper, 177.

17. Budiansky, 179–180.

# Chapter 5

# Elizabeth's Eyes and Ears

In the "Rainbow portrait," her cloak is scattered with eyes and ears—as if her extravagant claims made to a French ambassador to know everything that happened in her kingdom were possible through secret surveillance." Alan Haynes, *Elizabethan Secret Service*, Page xii

"Given the urgency of England's situation in Europe, the Queen's secretary [Walsingham], who ran her government, needed eyes and ears throughout the kingdom and beyond. The secret trade [intelligence] grew to meet the political need."[1] When Elizabeth claimed in 1586 that her intelligence organization was a formidable force to be reckoned with, she was without question "spot on." However, her boast of England's intelligence apparatus's exceptional skill was undoubtedly not the case when she first ascended the throne.

When William Cecil became Elizabeth's chief advisor in 1559, he immediately took control of her intelligence arm. Like many other pressing issues that required immediate attention, he encountered a hodge-podge of competing information gathering groups that at times served high-ranking court officials' interests as much, if not more, than those of the royal monarch.[2]

However, by the early 1570s, William Cecil and Francis Walsingham would steer the Queen's intelligence service in a new direction. After the Northern Rebellion in 1569, the Anglo-Netherlands trade rupture, the Pope's excommunication of Elizabeth in 1570, and the short-lived Ridolfi Plot, both men realized the growing threat to the survival of their Queen, kingdom, and Protestant religion demanded drastic innovative changes.

Fortunately for the English Crown, the first significant counter-spy operation abroad under Cecil's direction, the Ridolfi Plot, was so successful "that it set the standard for excellence throughout Elizabeth's reign . . . In addition, as the benchmark for clandestine operations, it prepared the way for the future successes of Walsingham when he became Principal Secretary of State

**Figure 5.1. Queen Elizabeth I, the "Rainbow Portrait" / Oliver, Isaac (c. 1565–1617). Hatfield House, Hertfordshire, UK / Bridgeman Images**

[20 December 1573], and on the following day gained a seat in the Privy Council."[3, 4]

Walsingham and Cecil would gradually assume control of the fragmented intelligence fiefdoms, delineate intelligencer responsibilities, and consolidate the intelligence service into a more cohesive and mission-focused group dedicated to countering existential threats to Elizabeth's reign. These actions would result in a more efficient and effective government national security apparatus. Thus, by the early 1580s, Walsingham, again with Cecil's support, significantly shifted the momentum of English intelligence activities from a defensive posture to a more aggressive stance.[5]

## THE SHIELD AND THE SWORD—
## "BIRDS OF A FEATHER"

It is virtually impossible to overlook Cecil and Walsingham's vital roles in this story as they navigated the English ship of State around the dangerous shoals of anti-Protestantism. Being two of the three most influential men on Queen Elizabeth's Privy Council (the third being Robert Dudley, Earl of Leicester, and the Queen's close friend and rumored paramour),[6] their ability to work with and often around Elizabeth would keep the government afloat while gaining valuable time to reorient England's foreign policy focus.

Early in Elizabeth's reign, Cecil recruited the younger Walsingham following Walsingham's return from exile in Italy, Switzerland, France, and Germany.[7] Reviewing his background, Cecil immediately recognized that adding this talented young man to his intelligence portfolio promised to be of inestimable value to countering the increasing Catholic threat. Cecil considered Walsingham ideally steeped in the spirit and ideals of the Renaissance and Reformation and verbally agile in three foreign languages: all qualities required to advance the national interest of Protestant England.[8]

From the beginning, Francis Walsingham proved to be the perfect choice to fill Cecil's position as First Secretary later. To no one's surprise, when Elizabeth selected Sir William Cecil to be her new Lord Treasurer in December 1573, Cecil chose his protégé to be his replacement. Earlier under Cecil's mentorship, Walsingham had gained invaluable intelligence tradecraft experience by assisting in defeating the Northern Rebellion, providing collection and analysis support during the Ridolfi Plot, and overseeing England's agent network while in Paris. Few past occupants of this critical position would bring to the job such extremely impressive credentials backed by an intuitive sense of the changes needed to revamp and improve the overall effectiveness of English intelligence.[9]

What initially began as a mentor/apprentice relationship would later turn into a strong partnership of professional equals working together to deflect a resolute adversary's attacks. Over time, their efforts will result in a unique blending of shared values and objectives that will naturally focus on serving their Queen.

However, in matters of style, there were discernible differences between them. While they initially, but somewhat hesitantly, supported Elizabeth's national security policy priorities, Walsingham differed from Cecil in policy emphasis and the courses of action he considered best for England. Cecil tended to be more pragmatic in carrying out his duties and readily sought a compromise to avoid confrontation with opposing Privy Council members. On the other hand, Walsingham was more ideologically driven, strident, and dogmatic. He believed that directly confronting threats to his Puritan-oriented Protestantism was always preferable to subtle, indirect courses of action.[10]

Early in his career, when ambassador to France, "Walsingham . . . forbidding in aspect, hard-working and outspoken . . . was the most militant of Protestants, and his religious outlook accounted for his contentious views on the conduct of foreign policy . . . Because he was sure that war with the forces of the popish Antichrist was inevitable, he took the view that the English must strike the first blow, and he had no patience with those who pleaded that the country could not afford to squander its resources on military adventures overseas."[11]

However, Walsingham eventually moderated his aggressive stance and adopted an Indirect Preemption strategy against England's Catholic enemies. This radical about-face for the new First Secretary occurred when it became clear to him that England could not compete against its enemies on a confrontational force-on-force basis. At that point, Walsingham grudgingly concluded that, even with Cecil's support, he could not overcome Elizabeth's near-pathological tendency to procrastinate.[12]

The working relationship between the two men did turn tense at times, but flare-ups between them were rare. Interestingly, their two most significant points of contention involved the question of intelligence source control and who should be the first recipient of a specific source's sensitive information. However, in the end, they resolved both incidents successfully.[13] In general, their differences were minor compared to the significant contributions they provided to their Queen, country, and religion.

When selected First Secretary in 1573, Sir Francis Walsingham, with Sir William Cecil's assistance, injected into Elizabeth's "body politic" and England's Secret Service a sense of revitalization. He also brought a distinctive leadership and managerial style with a new, asymmetric approach to countering and mitigating the growing Catholic threat. For Walsingham to achieve even a modicum of success in reaching that objective, he would have to:

- Remain unswervingly committed to protecting Elizabeth, England, and the Protestant faith[14]
- Believe that Protestant England was in a fight for its very survival[15]
- Support Elizabeth's National Security priorities while seeking other asymmetric alternatives that would obtain those same priorities

- Be knowledgeable about evolving historical and contemporary political statecraft and warfighting theories and philosophies
- Believe reform of the Secret Service and expansion of intelligence capabilities were key to Protestant England's survival[16]
- Focus on identifying and attacking the Catholic opposition's most vulnerable target(s)[17]
- Be capable of identifying and exploiting the Catholic leadership's psychological vulnerabilities and biases[18]
- Think strategically and demand, for himself and others, close attention to details[19]
- Consistently select the right people for the right jobs[20]
- Prove adept at multi-tasking and managing disparate governmental activities[21]
- Be able to work effectively in an unpredictable, frustrating, and emotionally-filled work environment[22]
- Always avoid public visibility, especially when conducting sensitive activities and consistently "holding one's own counsel"[23]
- Be adept at taking advantage of unanticipated opportunities[24]
- Possess the ability to judge and evaluate situations from a historical perspective[25]
- Be recognized by the Catholic opposition as an excellent intelligencer who is a formidable Protestant opponent[26]
- Be kept constantly informed of current events, trends, and innovative ideas, etc.; people who are avid readers and bibliophiles meet this requirement[27]

As their careers progressed and matured over the years, Cecil and Walsingham resembled a "Yin and Yang" relationship—one person using his strengths to cover the other person's weaknesses. For example, should Walsingham find himself in a difficult situation (e.g., personality conflicts with Elizabeth), Cecil would immediately intercede to protect him from Elizabeth's fury and recriminations. Likewise, should Walsingham fall ill, Cecil would take on his duties until the First Secretary was well enough to return to court. If, on the other hand, Cecil wished to distance himself from activities that might put him in an uncomfortable political position with Elizabeth, Walsingham would step in to protect Cecil from situations that could compromise or implicate his involvement in sensitive, potentially embarrassing, intelligence-related situations.

In concert, both men worked to provide Elizabeth with the most accurate, timely information possible. In pursuit of that objective, the First Secretary and Lord Treasurer developed an energetic, systematic program of initiatives that by 1580 significantly expanded, consolidated, and rationally organized

English intelligence collection and analysis capabilities. Together, they created the vital means and force multipliers to permit them to take the battle to the hated Catholic enemy. Both men, no doubt, subscribed to the adage: "Knowledge is never too dear."

## ELIZABETHAN COLLECTION AND
## ANALYSIS ENVIRONMENT

Elizabethan intelligence was confined to just two forms of transmission: the written word and the spoken word. Intelligence, like all forms of news, moved physically. Whether written down in letters, or coded dispatches, or committed to memory, it had to be carried from place to place [from the source to the customer]. The fastest that intelligence could travel was the speed of a horse.[28]

Elizabethan England and the countries of Western Europe were extremely limited in their point-to-point communication capabilities. Walsingham, his adversaries, and allies all had the option of moving information by means other than horseback—on foot, by ship, using flags, semaphores, bonfires, *etcetera*. However, the speed and accuracy of the transmitted information via those alternatives were affected by the variables of long distances, inclement weather, and road or sea conditions. Intangibles such as loyalty, commitment to the mission, physical health, and courier personnel's safety were also contributing factors to the problem. The multiplicity of these impediments to the smooth and rapid flow of information invariably affected the time lag between the collection point and the information collection center.[29]

### Keys to Success

Throughout the 1570s, the First Secretary and Lord Treasurer implemented the following initiatives that significantly broadened the scope and improved the accuracy and timeliness of England's intelligence collection and analysis capabilities. As a result of their efforts, they:

- *Expanded and exploited information supplied by domestic and international commercial trading sources. The First Secretary gained access to a new pool of valuable information by significantly increasing the use of English commercial and trading associations that were widely dispersed and located in major commercial centers and international markets. The significant impact of this economically based information provided greater insight into other countries' political and military events as well as rumors and leadership intentions that were previously unattainable.*

*Tapping into this new supply of information further strengthened England's national security through greater access to previously unexploited collection sources. Expansion into these sources provided new communication conduits supporting future disinformation, propaganda, or psychological operations.*[30] *Impact:* Acquired improved collection, analysis, and deception capabilities.

- *Increased the consultative services of intelligence and intelligence-related Subject Matter Experts (SMEs).* Walsingham and Cecil elevated the quality and scope of the English intelligence service's intellectual, scientific, linguistic, technical, human behavior, cryptologic, and foreign specialist expertise. In so doing, they aggressively sought out SMEs in a diverse number of intelligence-related and associated fields and integrated that expertise into existing intelligence collection and analysis tradecraft. This integration process transformed a reactive force of minimally qualified, less educated intelligencers into a more proactive, knowledgeable, and educated group of agents.[31] *Impact:* Changed the direction, focus, and character of English intelligence; improved operational, collection, and analysis capabilities.

- *Established an intelligence-sharing relationship with foreign Protestant allies.* England and Protestants abroad faced the same enemy. This mutual concern led to the increasing exchange of knowledge, technical expertise, and strategies to redress Protestant military force-on-force imbalances.[32] *Impact:* Improved analysis, collection, technical, and operational security capabilities; expanded knowledge and provided more timely and accurate information on Catholic activities on the continent.

- *Increased the number of intelligence collection, analysis, surveillance, and agent/provocateur assets.* The expansion of these collection and analysis capabilities between 1573 and 1580 significantly extended the English intelligence service's reach and enhanced its overall offensive and defensive readiness posture.[33] *Impact:* Widened the scope and improved the understanding of Catholic activities, plans, and intentions in England and abroad; increased the frequency and number of reports; improved source and information credibility and assessment processes; created a perception in Catholic ranks that English intelligence was a ubiquitous, formidable foe.

- *Utilized English artistic, literary, academic, scientific, topographical, and medical community members for collection, propaganda, provocation, disinformation, and consultative tasks.* Cecil and Walsingham took advantage of the many non-government elements of English society that are typically outside the boundaries and interests of intelligence matters.

By extending into non-government segments of the kingdom, the two men exploited new resources to expand English intelligence effectiveness into future targets of opportunity.[34] *Impact:* Broadened the scope of the intelligence support base and intelligence collection, propaganda, and disinformation capabilities.

- *Created an Intelligence Headquarters framework.* Walsingham established a precedent-setting reorganization that differentiated subject matter roles and responsibilities within the English intelligence service. He consolidated and dispatched most of his intelligence work from Seething Lane. He established a leadership style emphasizing the principle of centralized control and decentralized implementation and execution of intelligence activities: an approach that facilitated offensive-oriented intelligence operations. *Impact:* Provided a more effective means to coordinate and control several simultaneously run intelligence operations, streamlined command and control communications, and enabled delegation and multi-tasking while fulfilling other pressing government duties.

- *Expanded the number of domestic security and surveillance agents and capabilities.* Mirroring the expansion of agents working outside England's boundaries, the same expansion of security forces also occurred within England's borders to protect the government from internal seditious actions. Walsingham and Cecil now have a competent organization to counter both foreign and domestic enemies.[35] *Impact:* Improved the defensive and offensive capabilities of English intelligence; enhanced protection around the Queen; increased intelligence flow for further analysis; improved and expanded threat warning capabilities.

- *Developed considerable intelligence capabilities for their offensive-focused deception and influence/provocation operations.* Between 1574 and 1580 saw a significant improvement in the English intelligence service's ability to transact its business more efficiently and effectively. Walsingham successfully developed courses of action to counter England's adversary's attacks and improved his secret service's ability to take the battle to the enemy.[36] *Impact:* Provided the means and capabilities to conduct more effective manipulative tactics, techniques, and procedures against Catholic, anti-Protestant initiatives, in general, and conspiratorial actions, in particular.

- *Emphasized the importance of recognizing certain aspects of human behavior and attendant psychological vulnerabilities.* Walsingham increased his emphasis on understanding how an opponent's psychological vulnerabilities could be fully exploited. The First Secretary's knowledge of human behavior was legend. He integrated human factors considerations into his organization's operational thinking. *Impact:* Provided an invaluable focal point, knowledge base, and reference point for future analysis, source and information credibility assessments, and offensive-oriented intelligence operations.[37]

- *Established permanent locations for intelligence activities away from the royal court.* Walsingham consolidated his organization's critical components under one roof, creating the perception that English intelligence was an independent, exclusive group of government professionals dedicated to promoting Elizabeth and England's common good. Seething Lane, close to the Tower, and two outlying annexes at Mortlake and Barn Elms, became focal points for Walsingham's intelligence secretariat, communications network, research, archival storage, analysis, planning, and interrogations. All three locations also served as safe houses for other sensitive matters.[38] *Impact:* Consolidated essential intelligence functions and support activities primarily at one central location, promoted unity-of-command and line-of-sight tasking, and significantly improved the means of transmitting information to and from Seething Lane, Barns Elm, and Mortlake to collection points abroad. Created a sense of professional exclusivity and *esprit de corps*; improved the ability to de-conflict, synchronize, and coordinate ongoing and future intelligence operations.

- *Set higher "quality of analysis" and intelligence "best practices" standards.* The First Secretary took action to ensure the information his intelligence service analyzed was credible and accurate. Perhaps the fact that early in his career, he passed manipulated and deceptive data to Cecil sensitized him to the fact that accepting information at face value could result in harmful, catastrophic consequences. Once Walsingham replaced Cecil as head of the English secret service, Walsingham encouraged his intelligencers to view all collected information's reliability through a filter of healthy skepticism. He established this approach for all of his analysts to follow. His analysts now possessed the independent, verifiable means to confirm or refute information acquired from many of the new collection sources in place. In effect, Walsingham created an environment within his intelligence construct that significantly improved its ability to determine truth from falsity. *Impact:* Improved accuracy of analysis and search for truth. Sensitized analysts to the possibility that information they received from their collectors may have been manipulated and not credible. Introduced and integrated the concept and use of "independent verifiable means" as a more reliable source and information vetting approach.[39]

- *Developed stricter employment guidelines and established a government budget to support secret service activities.* Government funding for
  Walsingham's activities significantly increased as the threat of Catholic
  anti-Protestant movements gained momentum in the late 1570s and early
  1580s. Cecil, as Lord Treasurer, convinced Queen Elizabeth that increasing expenditures were essential to countering the growing threat.[40]
  Elizabeth's additional financial support provided Walsingham with the
  funds to expand the intelligence service's agent cadre. A much-improved
  merit and reward system was developed and put into effect.[41] *Impact:*
  Infused new energy into the intelligence service, expanded access to
  previously unattainable critical resources, and reinforced a sense of
  exclusivity and importance of mission. It further changed the nature,
  character, focus, and momentum of the pre-Cecil and Walsingham
  intelligence groups, developed financial "reimbursement" cut-outs to
  obfuscate the intelligence service's money trail, and increased the sense
  of permanency, job security, and stability among full-time employees.

The accumulative effect of Cecil and Walsingham's efforts to implement
their Indirect Preemption strategy in the early 1580s resulted in a significantly
improved and restructured intelligence arm, an arm strengthened with new
capabilities that permitted English intelligence to go on the offensive. With
the new intelligence construct now in place, Walsingham and Cecil begin
developing a conceptual planning framework upon which they will build their
deception operation.

## MOTIVE AND MEANS IN PLACE—
## AWAITING THE OPPORTUNITY

The *motive* behind Cecil and Walsingham's initiative to develop a bold course
of action against the Catholics grew out of the unsettling, anti-Protestant
events during the late 1560s and the 1570s. By the early 1580s, new English
intelligence capabilities will provide England with the necessary *means* to
plan and execute a strategic deception operation. Now, all that was required
was the *opportunity*—or *raison d'être*—that would put the plan's development into full motion. That opportunity would present itself with the uncovering of the Throckmorton Plot in 1582.

While waiting for that opportunity to arrive, Elizabeth's two most influential advisors commenced a comprehensive series of retrospective pattern
analysis studies to better understand how their Catholic adversaries organized, developed, and conducted their past clandestine activities. At this point

in the deception planning process, Cecil and Walsingham believe that once they integrate and operationalize that data, knowledge, and insight into their deception planning process, they will possess a distinct advantage in defeating future Catholic intrigues.

# NOTES

1. Stephen Alford, *The Watchers: A Secret History of the Reign of Elizabeth I* (Bloomsbury Press, 2012), 15.

2. This balkanization of intelligence collection groups in England was a direct result of a dynamic found in all royal courts of Western Europe. For example, a noble's status and position at court was dependent on perceived or real power and wealth. Maintaining or advancing that same noble's status and position was a direct function of how much that noble knew about his monarch, peers, and other activities within the court, country, and outside the realm. Thus, access to and control of information increased a nobleman's knowledge of what forces threatened him or could be used to advance his interests. At the risk of mirror-imaging, most environments surrounding power centers today have similar dynamics at play regardless of the organizational level.

3. Upon becoming Lord Treasurer, Cecil divided the responsibilities of the First Secretary between Francis Walsingham and Thomas Smith designating Walsingham as the Principal Secretary. Three years later, "Smith is afflicted with throat cancer and leaves government service. Upon Smith's departure, Walsingham takes control of the Privy seal and assumes the title of First Secretary." Hsuan-Ying Tu, *The Pursuit of God's Glory*, Pages 67 and 71; *Queen Elizabeth and Her Times*, a series of letters, Volume II, Pages 32–33.

This somewhat unorthodox move may have been due to 1) Cecil's concern that Walsingham's governmental inexperience required extra support to cover the anticipated increasing responsibilities created by the growing Catholic threat and expanding counter-espionage activities, 2) A power move designed to ensure that Cecil was aware of all information emanating from the First Secretary's office, 3) Cecil's acknowledgment that Elizabeth and Walsingham had difficulty working together, and would alternatively use Thomas Smith as the go-between to minimize contact between Walsingham and Elizabeth, or 4) Cecil's belief that Smith would help revitalize England's struggling economy. Smith, like Cecil, was dedicated to the idea that the practice of alchemy could potentially solve Elizabeth's economic problems. Refer to Campbell, *The Alchemical Patronage of Sir William Cecil, Lord Burghley*, Pages 25–27; Harkness's *The Jewel House*, Pages 173–174; and Sherman's *John Dee: The Politics of Reading and Writing in the English Renaissance*, Pages 75–76.

4. Alan Haynes, *The Elizabethan Secret Services* (Sutton Publishing, 1992), 1; Hsuan-Ying Tu, *The Pursuit of God's Glory: Francis Walsingham's Espionage in Elizabethan Politics, 1568–1588* (University of York, September 2012), 67.

5. John Cooper is quick to point out that this new approach should not be construed as the early organizational forerunner of intelligence bureaucracies that exist today. He also underscores the fact that "the Elizabethan secret service was [still] less a formal structure than a web of relationships. Walsingham turned his household into a seat of government." *The Queen's Agent,* Page 163.

Walsingham's significance in creating this "new scale of surveillance" may indeed have been more evolutionary than revolutionary. However, the fact remains that he and Cecil's early contributions in expanding the depth, scope, and specialization of English intelligence capabilities did provide a viable template, or roadmap, for future intelligencer generations to follow. Consequently, the precedents set by Cecil and Walsingham would years later significantly influence how modern-day intelligence organizations are structured. Also, Walsingham's successful initiatives in countering anti-Protestant challenges might not have succeeded without Cecil's encouragement, support, and timely personal intercession and influence with Elizabeth. Therefore, giving Francis Walsingham top billing as the Father of MI5/MI6 may be somewhat overstated. Instead, suggesting that Cecil and Walsingham were the co-fathers or forerunners of modern British intelligence may be closer to the truth.

6. Stephen Budiansky, *Her Majesty's Spymaster: Elizabeth I, Sir Francis Walsingham, and the Birth of Modern Espionage* (Penguin Books, 2005), 88–89.

7. Eamon Duffy states that with the accession of Mary Tudor more than eight hundred protestants escaped to the continent "including most of the best brains in the evangelical camp." Francis Walsingham was one of them. *Fires of Faith,* Page 11.

8. John Cooper, *The Queen's Agent: Sir Francis Walsingham and the Rise of Espionage in Elizabethan England* (Pegasus Books, 2012), 29–30; Robert Hutchinson, *Elizabeth's Spymaster* (St. Martin's Press, 2006), 30.

9. Haynes, 26–27.

10. Cooper, 32–33.

11. Anne Somerset, *Elizabeth I* (Anchor Books, 1991), 267–268.

12. Somerset, 280.

13. Haynes, 35; Cooper, 172–174.

14. Hutchinson, 262–263; Cooper, 194; Alford, 261.

15. Hutchinson, 262–263; Charles Nicholl, *The Reckoning: The Murder of Christopher Marlowe* (The University of Chicago Press, 1992), 103.

16. Alison Weir, *The Life of Elizabeth I* (Ballantine Books, 1998), 214; Alford, 15, 268; Somerset, 406; Nicholl, 103–105.

17. Somerset, 203; Cooper, 72–73; Mary M. Luke, *Gloriana: The Years of Elizabeth I* (Coward, McCann & Geoghegan, Inc., 1973), 519.

18. Hutchinson, 42; Alford, 88; Cooper, 161.

19. Hutchinson, 264; Antonia Fraser, *Mary Queen of Scots* (Delacorte Press, 1969), 530.

20. Nicholl, 106–108; Haynes 69–70; Alan Haynes, *Walsingham: Elizabethan Spymaster & Stateman* (Sutton Publishing, 2004), 152–154; Cooper, 163, 183, 185.

21. Haynes, 28; Hutchinson, 265; Cooper, 91–92.

22. Cooper, 93, 103–104, 108–109; Somerset, 69; Alan Haynes, *Walsingham: Elizabethan Spymaster & Statesman* (Sutton Publishing, 2004), 240–241.

23. Neville Williams, *The Life and Times of Elizabeth I* (Doubleday and Company, 1972), 170; Budiansky, 92.

24. Cooper, 237.

25. Cooper, 29–30.

26. Nicholl, 102; Haynes, *The Elizabethan Secret Services*, 192; Elizabeth Jenkins, *Elizabeth the Great* (G.P. Putnam's Sons, 1958), 170; Cooper, 92, 161–163.

27. Haynes, *Walsingham: Elizabethan Spymaster & Statesman,* 77–78.

28. Nicholl, 105.

29. A royal postal service had been established in 1509 to facilitate official diplomatic and ambassadorial communications. However, the system proved restrictive and slow in its transfer of information to and from the English royal court. Consequently, recipients of the royal postal service abroad began to develop their own means of receiving and transmitting information. Hsuan-Ying Tu, *The Pursuit of God's Glory*, Pages 84–85. Benjamin Wooley in *The Queen's Conjurer* writes that "As every sixteenth-century prince and general knew, distance was the first enemy. Roads were often impassable, 'noisome sloughs,' 'so gulled with the fall of water that passengers cannot pass.'" Page 67.

30. Cooper, 175–176; Haynes, *The Elizabethan Secret Services*, 13–14.

31. Cooper, 172, 205–206; Haynes, 13–14; Budiansky, 93.

32. Budiansky, 143–144; Cooper, 201–203.

33. Cooper, 175; Alford, 263; Hutchinson, 84, 89; Haynes, 15–16.

34. Cooper, 270–271, 291, 325; Haynes, *Walsingham: Elizabethan Spymaster & Statesman,* 74–76, 80.

35. Williams, 162–163; Stefan Zweig, *Mary Queen of Scots and the Isles,* 285; Luke, 474–475; Hutchinson, 17, 94.

36. Nicholl, 112–113; Somerset, 63–64.

37. Hutchinson, 223–224; Budiansky, 34–35.

38. Nicholl, 116; Cooper, 47, 95, 167–168, 272, 302; Hutchinson, 97–98; Tu, 84–87.

39. Alford, 253, 268, 313; Hutchinson, 35–36; Cooper, 169; Haynes, *The Elizabethan Secret Services,* 14–15.

40. There are also indications that Cecil and Walsingham may have independently developed an untraceable funding line hidden from the Exchequer's records.

41. Nicholl, 104, 109–110; Cooper, 178, 182; Budiansky, 99; Haynes, 54–56.

# PART TWO

# (1580–1582)

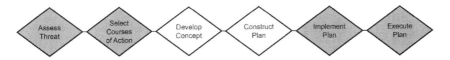

Deception Planning Phases.

# Chapter 6

# Looking Back

Before 1580, Cecil and Walsingham possessed only a rudimentary understanding of Catholic conspiracy planning and operational patterns. But now, with a revitalized and restructured intelligence arm having a new, comprehensive research and analysis effort focused on past Catholic conspiratorial practices, they hope to acquire a clearer understanding of the dynamics that will drive future anti-Protestant activities.

Both men conclude that if their use of deception to counter future Catholic activities is to succeed, they must: 1) discover how Mary's background experiences may drive her current actions and behaviors, 2) acquire a more comprehensive understanding of the tenuous relationship that exists between the English and Scottish queens, 3) develop and prioritize a future Catholic conspirator target list, 4) compare and contrast past Catholic conspiracy planning and operational patterns, 5) identify Mary Stuart's behavioral patterns and psychological inclinations, and 6) determine to what extent Elizabeth's well-known unpredictable and disruptive behavior could enhance or degrade the success of their future deception initiatives.

## TORTUOUS ROAD TO ENGLAND

In studying Mary's past, they found that the Scottish Queen was all too familiar with personal tragedy and proved to be highly resilient when faced with adversity. Six days after her birth, Mary became Queen of Scotland following her father's death, James V. At the age of five, her mother sent her to France to marry Francis II, the son and heir of King Henry II. She married in 1558, but tragedy struck her twice in short succession. First, Mary's loving mother, Margaret of Guise,[1] died in June 1560, and six months later, Mary's young husband, Francis II, succumbed to an ear infection. Left without allies to maneuver within the oppressive, byzantine-like environment of her scheming

mother-in-law, Catherine de Medici, Mary, encouraged by supporters still living in Scotland, chose to return to her country's birthplace.

For the first several years after she arrived in Scotland, except for her
frequent confrontations with Calvinist firebrand John Knox and his followers, Mary's hope of bringing unity to her country appeared possible. Then,
however, a series of tragic and disappointing setbacks once again stalked her
with a vengeance.

She struggled to maintain power over her recalcitrant, clan-based nobility that repeatedly broke their pledges of allegiance to her legitimacy as the
Queen of Scotland. Moreover, her unsuccessful attempts to quell a growing
number of uprisings, inflamed by rebel claims that her religious faith and
moral turpitude was anathema to the commonwealth of a free and independent
Scotland, left her even more vulnerable to the persistently defiant nobility.

Adding to her problems, she endured two marriages in Scotland with men
of dubious motives and character. Both turbulent relationships ended in scan-
dals that would haunt her for the rest of her life. Finally, overwhelmed by an
intractable opposition, the Scottish Queen found herself in a remote prison
and was forced to abdicate the throne to her only child, James VI. However,
when all seemed lost, the besieged Mary managed to escape her captors and
seek sanctuary in England.

## WHAT TO DO ABOUT MARY?

From the first day of Mary's unexpected arrival in England, Cecil knew that
dealing with the Scottish Queen would be a delicate matter, especially when
more severe measures against her would undoubtedly become necessary.
Mary's royal status made it difficult to take any action that would be considered denigrating or disrespectful. Further complicating the situation, Mary
was unwilling to be controlled by her new English "protectors." Before being
moved deeper into the country's interior, she explicitly threatened repercus-
sions if her treatment did not improve.[2] Mary, at the same time, implicitly
encouraged Catholic sympathizers to rescue her from her Protestant captors.

## COMMENCING BASELINE TARGET/
## PATTERN ASSESSMENTS

While the two royal cousins never meet face-to-face, their complicated relationship often changes in tone and tenor when seen in public or restricted
to private communications. Both are public-image conscious and create the
impression that they are reasonable and caring cousins. Elizabeth is especially

sensitive to her subjects' opinions and always tries to project a public image of tolerance toward her Scottish royal cousin's religion.

Both women are also acutely aware of the reality that they live and rule in a predominantly man's world. Therefore, it is incumbent upon them to prove their worthiness, "manly attributes," and strengths daily. Thus, to dispel any attacks on their capabilities, they purposely present themselves as mature, decisive, resolute, and single in purpose when seen by their subjects. Emotional outbursts or anything construed by their loyal followers as stereotypical female behavior is to be strictly avoided; emotions both Elizabeth and Mary, at times, find difficult to control. During the first few years of Mary's presence in England, public displays of mutual respect mask the underlying conflict between the two queens.[3] However, behind the curtain of private communications, a different reality exists where irreconcilable differences lurk just below the surface.

## Mirror, Mirror on the Wall

Like her mother, Anne Boleyn, Elizabeth's main appeal is her personality and not her physical appearance. To compensate, she takes advantage of her lovely skin, piercing black eyes, stunning red hair, and graceful, delicate, long-fingered hands by wearing elaborate dresses accented with precious gemstones sewn into her gowns or worn in her hair. Breathtaking jewelry would always adorn her hands, wrists, and arms. Elizabeth is considered "tall and very slender, with a tiny waist and small bosom . . . She possesses a swarthy, 'olive' complexion like that of her mother although she makes a habit of whitening it with a lotion made up of egg whites, powdered eggshell, poppy seeds, borax and alum which makes her face appear white and luminous . . . Always dignified and stately in her bearing, she can also be vain, willful, dictatorial, temperamental, and imperious. Her sense of humor sometimes has a malicious edge to it and is capable of making sharp, cutting remarks, yet she can be warm and compassionate when occasion demanded."[4]

On the other hand, while Mary's two disastrous marriages show she is not a particularly good judge of men when romance is concerned, she is well-liked by people who meet her, regardless of their religious orientation. Mary possesses an alluring grace, charm, and charisma that wins over even the most ardent anti-Catholic stalwarts. "Wherever she went she won friends, even among her foes. As the bride and a widow, on every throne and in every prison, she radiated an aura which aroused sympathy and made the environing atmosphere warm and friendly"[5]

"Mary, like her mother, Margaret of Guise, is very tall (probably close to 6 feet), gracefully slender, and her erect stature only emphasize[s] her well-endowed figure. Her face [is] a delicate and piquant oval, with clear skin and abundant chestnut hair. The almond-shaped eyes, alert and intelligent beneath a smooth, clear brow, offset the too-thin mouth and sharp nose. Normally her manner [is] soft and gracious. It [is] difficult not to be swayed by such loveliness . . . It [is] ever Mary's gift—in whatever state she [is] in—to induce in men a compassion for her distress. She invites[s] a desire to protect and help."[6]

Over time, Elizabeth becomes increasingly irritated by the frequent, glowing reports about her royal cousin's exceptional beauty, comportment, wit, and charm. Elizabeth seethes with a full-blown sense of jealousy and envy.[7] Elizabeth's puerile pettiness will continue to fester beneath the façade of seemingly civil communication between them for as long as Mary remains in England.

Soon after Mary's return to Scotland following her first husband's death in 1560, Elizabeth's curiosity revealed itself during several extended discussions with the Scottish ambassador, Lord Melville. Elizabeth asked "to discern what color of hair was reputed best, and whether [Mary's] hair or hers was the best, and which of them was fairest . . . Then out came another question, she enquired which of them was of highest stature . . . then asked what kind of exercises she used . . . she asked if she played well and who played better . . . she enquired whether she or Mary danced best."[8] Apart from their competing egos, Mary and Elizabeth's governance styles and attitudes toward their subjects also differed considerably.

## Governance Styles and Attitudes

"The difference between Mary and Elizabeth was summed up in their attitude to their own kingdoms. Mary never troubled to conceal the fact that her ambition was to gain the throne of England . . . She was ready to submit Scotland to invasion . . . to destroy the Scottish Reformation . . . Had [Elizabeth] been Queen of Scotland, the Scots would have known that they had a Queen who was as proud of them as they were proud of themselves." Elizabeth Jenkins, *Elizabeth the Great*, Page 92.

Mary was raised to be a Queen. Her birthright provided access to all the luxuries and comforts of the French and, later, Scottish royal elites. Still, her isolation from the commoners created an aloofness and inability to identify with those of fewer means and social status. Before coming to England, she had been a Queen in both France and Scotland.

Mary always attempted to play the gracious sovereign . . . she had little real interest in her people's (Scotland) customs, their history or their future . . . The depth of Elizabeth's devotion to the welfare of her people and England would have puzzled Mary Stuart . . . Mary Stuart never possessed the genius that was Elizabeth Tudor's: a capacity to relate to her subjects, to know their thoughts and feelings and anticipate their reactions.[9]

Elizabeth's tension-filled experiences as a young woman created an entirely different person who was better prepared to empathize and deal with those of lesser economic and social status. "One goal superseded all. Her subjects came first. She appeared to draw strength and sustenance from such encounters, and always these meetings with her subjects acted as a stimulant from which Elizabeth appeared to gather a radiant strength. Their love, acclaim, and trust were all she needed. The Spanish Ambassador to England wrote his King, Philip II, that Elizabeth was without question very fond of her subjects, and they, in turn, felt the same way about her."[10]

Being a strategic thinker and tactician, Elizabeth was superior in that respect to Mary. The English Queen was familiar with the writings of Machiavelli and viewed the world as a giant chessboard. She responded deliberately (some argue today that this was a designed strategy and not a behavioral flaw or characteristic), taking into consideration both short- and long-term impacts as well as the possible unintended consequences that could result from her decisions. Such a decision-making approach required detailed research and information collection prior to choosing the most effective course of action. When making decisions of national import, Elizabeth was calculating, cautious, and excruciatingly deliberate. In a passing reference to Elizabeth's statesmanship and diplomatic acumen, Pope Sixtus V allegedly said, "if she were not a heretic, she would be worth the whole world."[11]

On the other hand, Mary was impulsive and prone to react to situations with little thought to her action's unintended consequences. Elizabeth always considered the impact her decisions could have on the kingdom. In vivid contrast, Mary only seemed to care about how her decisions affected her personally.

When considering personal goals, there was absolutely no room for compromise and reconciliation between the two sovereigns. Mary's claim to the English throne was legitimate, and her commitment to succeed Elizabeth as the rightful heir was unswerving and unassailable. Her refusal to recognize the Treaty of Edinburgh[12] made clear her intentions to claim the English throne once Elizabeth died. Her dedication to returning the Catholic faith to England and Scotland was unshakeable and became a rallying cry for her supporters to remove Elizabeth and her advisors from power.

Elizabeth, on the other hand, found herself in an untenable situation. Faced with the delicate balancing act of protecting the sanctity of Mary's royal, divine rights of governance, Elizabeth, at the same time, defended her throne from Mary's incessant internecine intrigues that demanded the removal of Elizabeth and Protestantism from England.

After the Ridolfi Plot of 1571–1572, civility and the friendly exchange of messages between the two queens quickly soured. Whatever rapport had previously existed steadily deteriorated as English security around Mary tightened. As a result, the public façade of cordiality quickly faded as survival became the overriding objective for both royal monarchs.

Not surprisingly, the balancing act increased in difficulty as the years passed. By the early 1580s, Cecil and Walsingham will begin in earnest to seek a final solution to this seemingly intractable situation.

## THOMAS, CHARLES, AND JOHN

Ironically, three men identified by English intelligence agents in the 1570s as sympathetic supporters of Mary, Queen of Scots, will later become influential players in the 1586 Babington Plot. Having been shadowed and monitored by Walsingham's agents early in England's intelligence revitalization program, Thomas Morgan, Charles Paget, and John Ballard will unknowingly contribute vital information and provide an unprecedented window into the status of all Catholic clandestine activities designed to liberate Mary.

Thomas Morgan served in the Earl of Shrewsbury's household in 1568 when Elizabeth commanded Shrewsbury to act as custodian and "watcher" of Mary's activities. Like many men who encountered Mary, Morgan was smitten by her well-known charm and quickly sympathized with her cause. Subsequently caught informing Mary about English agents spying on her, Morgan spent most of 1572 in the Tower of London prison. Upon his release, he became Mary's courier delivering messages between her place of incarceration and her supporters in England and abroad. In 1575, Morgan was implicated in a scheme using a bookseller's shop in London as a distribution point for Mary's letters. Warned of Walsingham's warrant for his arrest, Morgan escaped to Paris, where he was offered, at the behest of Mary, a cipher clerk position working for Archbishop Beaton, Scotland's ambassador in France.

An English aristocratic family member, Charles Paget, supported the Northern Rebellion against the Crown but found himself on the losing side. He escaped to France while many of his compatriots were left to experience the dire consequences of Elizabeth's wrath. While in Paris, he became a close friend of Thomas Morgan, who, like Paget, was committed to advancing the cause of Mary Stuart. With his flight from England and self-imposed exile, Paget forfeited his right to collect desperately needed tax revenues on his properties confiscated by the English Crown.[13]

The third of the future Babington conspirators, John Ballard, was educated at Cambridge University and fled England in 1579. In Rheims, he studied at the English exile university, was ordained a secular priest in March 1581, and left the college in December 1581. Ballard returned to England to spread the word of the old faith. Arrested and incarcerated in the Gateway prison, he is befriended by Anthony Tyrell, who, unbeknownst to Ballard, works for Francis Walsingham. Both men "remarkably" escape finding their way back to France.[14, 15]

Walsingham's knowledge of and ability to "watch" the activities of these three Catholic conspirators will later provide him with considerable access and insight into the inner workings of his fiercely loyal opposition. Possessing this invaluable gift of clarity, Cecil and Walsingham will incorporate this newly acquired knowledge into developing their ambitious but still incipient deception plan.

## UNDERSTANDING CATHOLIC CONSPIRACIES

By the end of the 1570s, the First Secretary and Lord Treasurer, based on operational pattern analysis, had a much clearer understanding of how the Catholic opposition planned and developed their conspiratorial courses of action. With this invaluable insight, they were now prepared to predict with a moderate degree of confidence how future conspiratorial planning would evolve and result in the following actions:

1. English Catholic exiles would direct and coordinate their conspiracies from their intelligence center in Paris. (When Sir Amyas Paulet was an ambassador in Paris, he informed Walsingham that Thomas Morgan and Charles Paget were key representatives for Mary, with Morgan acting as her *de facto* secretary of state and chief intelligencer in exile.)[16]
2. Agitators from outside the country would infiltrate, coordinate, and assist Catholic supporters, especially English nobles sympathetic to Mary Stuart's cause.
3. Military forces from Spain, France, and Rome/Italy would spearhead the invasion.
4. English Catholic nobles, primarily residing in the northern counties, would provide the in-country military support to free Mary and overthrow the Protestant government.
5. Spanish and French embassies in London would act as clearinghouses for communications between the Catholic intelligence center of gravity in Paris and Mary's incarceration location.

6. One or several individuals would be specifically selected to remove Elizabeth from her throne by whatever means necessary.
7. Not more than two trusted agents would act as couriers between Mary and her key contacts via a foreign embassy in London.[17]

Walsingham and Cecil's ability to counter future Catholic operations was further enhanced by their new intelligence capabilities to penetrate and observe the covert activities of Paget, Morgan, Ballard, and others. The First Secretary and Lord Treasurer were now significantly better positioned to design tailored courses of action to exploit Catholic vulnerabilities.[18]

## DEVELOPING ESSENTIAL ELEMENTS OF INTELLIGENCE

### Questions Requiring Further Investigation

In the process of gathering baseline information to gain more in-depth knowledge of the opposition's strengths and vulnerabilities, Walsingham and Cecil discover intelligence gaps that will require additional collection and analysis. Once these baseline assessments are complete, they will determine if this newly gathered information can more effectively leverage, manipulate, or influence their adversaries' behaviors and actions. Both men know that if their future deception plan is to have any chance of success, they must find answers to the following questions:

*Could Mary's Behavioral Tendencies Be Used Against Her?*

Analyzing her bold escape from Lochleven Castle[19] in 1568, Walsingham and Cecil find that Mary used her seductive charm to influence several men to assist her. In addition, they learn she employed deception tactics combined with a willingness to take perilous risks. Also, examining the Scottish Queen's past behaviors revealed that her sense of royal entitlement and privilege, vanity, and love of intrigue are behavioral patterns that might be subject to future exploitation.

*How Does the Scottish Queen React to Stressful Situations?*

Again, using Mary's incarceration at Lochleven Castle as a predictor of future behaviors, Walsingham and Cecil find that Mary is also a person who, when faced with extended periods of isolation, will become stressed to the point of mental and physical instability. In addition, other factors, such as being held in spartan or unhealthy conditions and without communication with the outside world, will further impact her psychological stability. Therefore, replicating similar stressful situations could force her to take risks that she would typically not consider.[20]

## How Unified is the English Catholic Resistance Community?

After a cursory investigation, Elizabeth's two chief advisors also discover that Catholics living in England and the English Catholic exile community residing abroad is not a monolithic body of recalcitrant dissidents sharing a unified strategy in opposition to Elizabeth and the Protestant faith. Instead, they find that recusants living in England are either inclined to tacitly accept the restrictions placed on the practice of their religion or stubbornly resist any attempts by Elizabeth to strike any compromise that would mollify her Catholic subjects' concerns.

As for the English Catholic exile community in Europe, they learn two leading groups differ on how best to reintroduce Catholicism into England. The Welsh or secular faction seeks more tolerance and reconciliation with Elizabeth. In contrast, the opposing Jesuit faction wants to reestablish the old faith as the kingdom's official religion using all means possible. Walsingham and Cecil will find this factional split a lucrative target for future manipulation-designed courses of action.

## Is There a Single Point of Failure Between Mary's Location of Imprisonment and Her Supporters in England and France?

As a result of the Throckmorton Plot, discovered in 1582, the Lord Treasurer and First Secretary find that Mary's vital communication lifeline with the outside world is channeled through the French and Spanish embassies in London. Knowledge of that communication link could be exploited by English intelligence should another Catholic conspiracy be discovered in the future.

## What Role Should Queen Elizabeth Play in the Deception Planning Process?

By 1580, Cecil and Walsingham know their sovereign's unpredictable, unsettling behavior will negatively affect their plan's success if they cannot find a way to control her emotions. Therefore, they conclude the root cause of Elizabeth's behavior is likely due to her experiences before becoming Queen of England.

"During her younger years, she had suffered abandonment by a father who had ordered her mother's head cut off. She had subsequently been shunted about to a series of dreary royal manors, reminiscent of a royal orphan with whom no one wished to be bothered. Twice she had been bastardized by a compliant Parliament and twice had been imprisoned for suspected treason against the very woman who, so conveniently, had just died . . . Those four years had been dangerous and uncomfortable ones for Elizabeth Tudor . . . She remembered the terror of those days"[21, 22]

Examples in 1572 and 1575 also underscore Elizabeth's inclination to procrastinate and delay decisions on issues of State believed by Walsingham and Cecil to require resolute and immediate actions.

Such behavior was on public display in the aftermath of the Ridolfi Plot in 1572. Charged with high treason for his involvement in a scheme to marry the Queen of Scots and participation in a plot to have Mary replace Elizabeth as Queen of England, the Duke of Norfolk was sentenced to be executed in January 1572. However, Elizabeth, on four different occasions, found reasons to revoke the Duke's death warrant, delaying the execution by four months.[23]

In 1575, Walsingham discovered a clandestine network of people in Elizabeth's court carrying messages to Mary, Queen of Scots. This discovery that some of the top Catholic recusants were involved prompted the First Secretary to advise Cecil. Elizabeth's subsequent refusal to take direct action against them reinforced the First Secretary and Lord Treasurer's belief that Elizabeth's indecisiveness could eventually be her undoing.[24]

Whether this indecisiveness was a consciously applied technique to manipulate her political opponents, a pathological character defect caused by emotional traumas experienced during her childhood or something randomly inherited from her parents was irrelevant to Cecil and Walsingham. Whatever the cause of her indecision, they found it incredibly frustrating and often counterproductive to satisfying Elizabeth's policies and the kingdom's best interests. Therefore, they believed it imperative to find ways to work around Elizabeth's dilatory decision-making inclinations, or their risky operation would never get off the ground.

## DELICATE BALANCING ACT

Early in their tenures, Sir William Cecil and Sir Francis Walsingham had faithfully but, at times hesitantly, carried out Elizabeth's orders. However, they also learned that creative, counter-intuitive courses of action enabled them to reconcile her policies with their plans to thwart the growing Catholic threat.

### An Uneasy Relationship

Walsingham's frequent encounters with Elizabeth were often tense and emotional. As a result, many at court believed that Elizabeth and Sir Francis disliked each other. For Elizabeth's part, she grudgingly relied on Walsingham's skills to manage government programs with effectiveness that far surpassed his peers. She also looked to Walsingham for invaluable worst-case counsel to her national security decisions. However, because of their divergent views, they were never genuinely comfortable working together. Because of personality conflicts between them, Cecil attempted to minimize contact between the two whenever possible. However, for her part, Elizabeth permitted Walsingham to act independently as long as she believed Cecil controlled his leash.

From Elizabeth's perspective, Sir Francis was the most hawkish of her advisors. At court and in private, she outwardly disliked his radical, ideological stance on dealing with Catholics in England and Europe. Elizabeth considered him an alarmist with doctrinaire views that diametrically opposed her own. She found it incredibly difficult to tolerate his deportment at court. Adding to the tension between them, Walsingham's manner in her presence was always frank and, at times, rebuking and patronizing in tone. His mode of communication never played to Elizabeth's vanity, and his opinions were devoid of court protocol and etiquette. Particularly grating to her sensibilities was his incessant claim that she refused to face up to the realities of the world. Walsingham often criticized Elizabeth's assumption that England's enemies were rational actors who believed compromise was the solution to England and Europe's religious and political problems. Such sessions between them in private or publicly at court not only tried her patience but regularly drove her to mental and emotional distraction and public displays of temperamental outbursts.[25]

For his part, Walsingham believed that there was less danger in "fearing too much than too little," thus, viewing the world and conducting his actions accordingly. However, over time, Elizabeth's constant rebuff and refutation of his opinions and recommendations left him in a permanent state of frustration that eventually created a paranoiac-like suspicion that Elizabeth was no longer confident in his work. Given the preponderance of responsibilities and multitude of tasks, coupled with the constant frustration of dealing with a very demanding and difficult Queen, Sir Francis was willing to resort to desperate means even if it resulted in taking actions without Elizabeth's consent.

Walsingham eventually learned how far he could push before she refused his counsel. Unfortunately for him, his fervent convictions and desperation for action frequently exceeded those boundaries and led to heated confrontations with her. Much like Elizabeth's feelings toward him, he often lost his patience with her inability to act aggressively against perceived enemies, especially concerning her safety and plotters conspiring to return the old faith to England. By 1580, Walsingham resented Elizabeth's lack of appreciation toward his services. Experiencing the brunt of Elizabeth's many physical and verbal tirades further aggravated his sense of being underappreciated and undervalued.

Unlike Walsingham's stormy relationship with Elizabeth, Cecil developed a unique partnership with her that endured for over forty years. She rarely made an important decision without first seeking his opinion. His "man of moderation" persona drew Elizabeth to him and treated him with great respect valuing his judgments and counsel. Even when she did not follow his advice, he always attempted to avoid confrontations with her and sought other subtle ways to bring affirmation and support to his opinions. Affable, self-controlled with unflappable nerve and, like Walsingham, limitless capacity for work, Cecil became a master at influencing and cajoling Elizabeth. He was influential in virtually all areas of government.[26]

## STILL MORE TO DO

Personality conflicts and erratic royal behavior aside, both men concurred it was still not the right time to rush into a bold, intelligence-focused deception operation. Instead, they opted to wait until a better opportunity presented itself to strike the enemy. In the interim—between the period of developing a conceptual framework and actual execution of an operational plan—Cecil and Walsingham will devote most of their time brainstorming best courses of action, evaluating probable enemy reactions, and considering the unintended consequences of putting those deception actions into play. Both men were acutely aware that details mattered if their future intelligence-oriented deception operation was to be successful. They also agreed that success depended on how well they prepared their battlespace or "field of play." Thus, their next step was to create a basic deception planning framework.

---

### **Recap of Pre-Phase 1: Concept of Operations Development**

By 1580, Cecil and Walsingham began a systematic and comprehensive data collection and analysis process that will provide them with a greater understanding of their adversary's leadership and infrastructure strengths, weaknesses, and vulnerabilities. During this period, they conducted the following:

1.) Assessed both the domestic and foreign Catholic threats

2.) Expanded data collection on key Catholic conspirators

3.) Assessed potential Catholic vulnerabilities to English manipulation

4.) Identified potential English vulnerabilities that could be exploited by the Catholic opposition

5.) Discovered how Catholic conspiracies were constructed

6.) Restructured and expanded English intelligence collection and analysis capabilities

7.) Developed a new collection driven EEI list (Essential Elements of Information) to monitor Catholic activities at home and abroad

---

**Figure 6.1.**
Source: R. Kent Tiernan

## NOTES

1. The House of Guise was a noble Roman Catholic family who played a significant role in French politics during the Reformation and Counter-Reformation. In support of defeating the growing threat of Protestantism in England, Scotland, Ireland, and the continent, the family and its avid supporters became influential power brokers at the French court. Mary's mother was Margaret de Guise, thus giving the House of Guise a great incentive to support Mary's claims to the English throne.

2. "She [Mary] knew that she was a potential threat to the English queen, and she flaunted the fact with wild indiscretion. When told that, against her wish, she was being removed from Carlisle to Bolton Castle, she exclaimed: I have made great wars in Scotland—I pray God I make no trouble in other realms also." Elizabeth Jenkins, *Elizabeth the Great,* Page 136. Mary Luke, *Gloriana: The Years of Elizabeth I*, Page 322, writes that Mary's letters sent abroad had promised that "she would be Queen of England in three months if an armed force were sent to her assistance."

3. A.N. Wilson, *The Elizabethans* (Farrar, Straus, and Giroux, 2011), 37–38, 40.

4. Alison Weir, *The Life of Elizabeth I* (Ballantine Books, 1998), 16–17; Mary Luke, *Gloriana: The Years of Elizabeth I* (Coward, McCann & Geoghegan, Inc., 1973), 304; Will and Ariel Durant, *The Age of Reason Begins, Vol. VII* (Simon and Schuster, 1961), 5, 7, 11.

5. Stefan Zweig, *Mary Queen of Scotland and the Isles* (Lancer Books, 1933), 249; Luke, 378.

6. Luke, 168.

7. Rosalind K. Marshall, *Elizabeth I* (HMSO, 1991), 76.

8. Marshall, 85–86.

9. Luke, 195, 272.

10. Luke, 36, 211; Durant, 8.

11. Durant, 8–9.

12. Sections of the Treaty of Edinburgh stipulated that 1) the French would remove its troops from Scotland, 2) governance of Scotland would remain under the Protestant Scottish council, and 3) Mary would renounce all claims to Elizabeth's throne.

13. Stephen Budiansky, *Her Majesty's Spymaster: Elizabeth I, Sir Francis Walsingham, and the Birth of Modern Espionage* (Penguin Books, 2005), 95–96.

14. Being that Tyrell was already Walsingham's "man," it is likely the First Secretary "looked the other way" to facilitate Ballard's escape.

15. Robert Hutchinson, *Elizabeth's Spymaster* (St. Martin's Press, 2006), 125; Alan Haynes, *The Elizabethan Secret Services* (Sutton Publishing, 1992), 69–70; Alan Haynes, *Elizabethan Spymaster & Statesman* (Sutton Publishing, 2004), 153.

16. Haynes, *The Elizabethan Secret Services*, 17.

17. The ability to anticipate how the opposition would probably conduct future conspiratorial activities, reinforced with their newly acquired English intelligence capabilities, now allows Walsingham and Cecil the opportunity to design specific counter-conspiracy courses of action against the Catholics. By 1580 at the latest, Mary Stuart, Thomas Morgan, Charles Paget, and John Ballard represent the foundational core of future Walsingham deception targets.

18. Stephen Alford identifies four principal threads for a conspiracy: 1) financial support from the Pope, 2) invasion led by a Spanish general, 3) liberation of Mary, and 4) support of a powerful English nobility. *The Watchers,* Page 127.

19. Mary Jenkins, *Elizabeth the Great,* Page 135, describes Lochleven, "as one of four islands in the middle of the lake. The castle was dour and lacked furniture suitable to her rank. Antonia Fraser, *Mary Queen of Scots,* Page 336, writes that "the castle was suited to be a prison rather than a pleasure haunt. It was a bleak and desolate place."

20. Cecil was advised of Mary's status at Lochleven by reports sent from Thomas Throckmorton, Elizabeth's emissary to Scotland, and other sources.

21. "When she came to the throne, her subjects knew relatively little about her. Nurtured in a hard school, having suffered adversity and uncertainty from her infancy, and having gone in danger of her life on at least two occasions, she had learned to keep her own counsel, hide her feelings, and live by her wits. Already, she was a mistress of the arts of deception, dissimulation, prevarication, and circumvention, all

admired attributes of a true Renaissance ruler." Alison Weir, *The Life of Elizabeth I*, Pages 9–10.

22. Luke, 21–22.

23. Luke, 378–380; G.J. Meyer, *The Tudors: The Complete Story of England's Most Notorious Dynasty* (Delacorte Press, 2010), 500.

24. Hutchinson, 88–89.

25. Anne Somerset, *Elizabeth I* (Anchor Books, 1991), 276–277.

26. Somerset, 63–64; Budiansky, 45; Stephen Alford, *The Watchers: A Secret History of the Reign of Elizabeth I* (Bloomsbury Press, 2012), 264.

# Chapter 7

# Deception Roadmap

"Oh, what a tangled web we weave, when first we practice to deceive."

—Sir Walter Scott, *Marmion,* Canto VI-The Battle (XVII).

Between 1580 and the discovery of the Throckmorton Plot in 1582, Cecil and Walsingham devoted much of their time to discussing various deception approaches. They intuitively understood that regardless of their chosen options, their plan had to be clear in purpose, believable by the targeted opponents, and achievable using resources available to their deception planners. Most importantly, their deception gambit had to be consistent and adhere to their overall Indirect Preemption strategy.[1]

To successfully develop, implement, and execute their intelligence operation, they acknowledged that they must strictly adhere to the following fundamental planning criteria: First, operational security measures had to hide the operation's existence from domestic and foreign scrutiny. Second, their operation's details had to be limited to a select few individuals. Third, individuals knowledgeable of the plan had to have the freedom to control their specific part in the operation without interference from other unwitting government entities. Fourth, the First Secretary and Lord Treasurer would require unlimited access to manpower, financial, and material resources supporting the operation. Fifth, and most importantly, the operation's evolution from concept development to termination would involve multi-year planning cycles. They also concluded that unity of command and continuity of leadership would be critical to the operation's success.

## DETERMINING THE DECEPTION OBJECTIVES

Before 1581, both men realized that their Queen and the kingdom's survival depended solely on their ingenuity in developing asymmetric overt and covert actions that would effectively thwart the growing Catholic threat. To achieve this objective, Cecil and Walsingham had to concentrate their efforts on developing deceptive initiatives that would cause Mary to implicate herself in treasonous activities against the English Crown. Moreover, they needed compelling evidence that the Scottish Queen was personally and directly involved in such activities for this gambit to succeed.

In developing a fundamental concept of how to rid their country of Mary's presence, Cecil and Walsingham, at the very least, addressed three fundamental questions. First, what actions or inactions did they want their deception targets to take (*the "do"*)? Second, what did they want their adversarial targets to believe (*the "think"*) to cause the desired actions or inactions? Most importantly, the First Secretary and Lord Treasurer had to decide what they wanted their targets to observe or experience (*the "see"*) to cause the desired actions or inactions that would lead to the Scottish Queen's eventual demise.[2]

## PHASE 1—CONCEPT OF OPERATIONS

Unlike today, Cecil and Walsingham worked in an environment where rapid communication and the smooth flow of logistic support were virtually impossible. To overcome these impediments to their complex deception operation, they divided their plan into a series of discrete, sequential, interrelated segments. Once laid out, they applied the insight gained from their initial baseline assessments and identified and prioritized key Catholic individuals and centers of gravity within and outside England's borders.

Once they determined these critical focal points, Cecil and Walsingham commenced a second tightly controlled internal baseline target assessment process that gathered more detailed information on the adversary's intelligence and counterintelligence capabilities and potential systemic and individual vulnerabilities. In this process, Elizabeth's two chief advisors also developed new collection strategies to close information gaps when discovered. These iterative procedures progressively added more significant substance and context to their earlier planning activities.

## Key Target List

With additional intelligence resources and assets brought into this iterative process, Walsingham improved his ability to determine how to effectively deploy his agents to infiltrate, penetrate, and exploit the enemy's command and control infrastructure.

## A Pair of Queens

The most immediate problem facing the First Secretary and Lord Treasurer involved both queens. Walsingham and Cecil had to develop workable solutions to rid them of Mary's presence and minimize the negative impact that Elizabeth's unpredictable behavior could have on their future deception planning activities. Without question, both issues carried potential liabilities that would require final resolutions before planning could move forward.

At this time, a solution to remove Mary from their kingdom lacked the *raison d'être* to begin direct action against her. However, as the Scottish Queen's presence in England became an accepted fact, they found that having her activities under their constant control and surveillance had paradoxically turned her unwelcome presence from a liability into a critically important

Figure 7.1. Pair of Queens—Cartoon that underscores the threat to Elizabeth's Protestant-ruled England—Mary Stuart's claim to the throne. Reproduced by permission of Carlyn Beccia, *The Raucous Royals* (Boston: Clarion Press, 2008), cover image. © 2008 by Carlyn Beccia

intelligence collection asset. Walsingham will use this advantage to build a case that eventually implicates Mary in treasonous acts against Elizabeth.

As for their concern about Elizabeth, they soon must determine to what extent she should be aware of their deception planning initiative. Regardless of their final decision, they recognized that the "Elizabeth factor," at some point, had to be integrated into their future planning considerations.

## Thomas Morgan (Mary's Chief Intelligencer)

Walsingham and Cecil select Thomas Morgan, Mary's chief intelligencer and influential member of the more moderate English-in-exile faction, as a critical intelligence collection priority because of his prominent role in Mary's communication network. His value to the Scottish Queen in moving her funds and coordinating plans to liberate her from Elizabeth's clutches also promises a wealth of information and insight into the activities of a large segment of the English Catholic exile community.

## John Ballard (Firebrand Ideologue)

Walsingham and Cecil believe "the real animus" is John Ballard. Described as a "militant, somewhat megalomaniac, chameleon-like" individual who, when in England, disguise[d] himself as a swashbuckling courtly soldier under the pseudonym "Captain Fortescue." A former prison mate and long-time acquaintance of Ballard portrayed him to Cecil as "a man vainglorious and desirous of his own praise, and to be meddling in things, above his reach. . . . Babington described him [Ballard] to Queen Mary as 'a man of virtue and learning and of singular zeal to the Catholic cause and your Majesty's service'"[3] Walsingham considers Ballard different from the rest of the Catholic opposition. He believes him to be an individual who likes to work in the trenches and believes him to be a man of action, "a front-line Catholic in constant motion, living a life of total commitment: a true field agent, [who makes] others feel like spoilt dilettantes."[4]

## Charles Paget (Liaison to Mary, Morgan, and Mendoza)

With his flight from England and self-imposed exile, Paget now seeks ways to recoup his financial losses.[5] Walsingham, ambassador to France at the time, notes Paget's financial predicament. The First Secretary will later exploit Paget's and other exiled Catholics' financial vulnerabilities to the English Crown's advantage. Paget also appears to be at the center of numerous anti-Protestant activities. His direct access to Catholic conspiracy planners also makes him a source of sensitive, valuable information.[6]

## CENTERS OF GRAVITY

### Mary's Communication Systems

Cecil and Walsingham have come to appreciate Mary's means of communicating with her supporters as a vital center of gravity to be seriously probed. If Cecil and Walsingham succeed in penetrating the Scottish Queen's communication network, they stand to gain tremendous insight into the Catholic's current intentions, plans, policies, and strategies against Protestant England. Depending on the degree of infiltration, understanding of critical communication nodes, and identification of specific information couriers, English control of Mary's network offers Cecil and Walsingham the potential to significantly influence future Catholic decisions and courses of action.

### Foreign Embassies in London

Both men's experience in combating and countering the Ridolfi Plot activities in the early 1570s provided them a greater appreciation of how the Catholic opposition used foreign embassies and diplomatic channels to mask and transmit information between the imprisoned Scottish Queen and her outside world. Finding a way to neutralize the effectiveness of their adversaries' use of foreign embassies as sanctuaries, free of host country interference, is an essential element of information. Therefore, identifying agents in those embassies most responsible for ensuring communication flow to and from Mary's incarceration location will become a top collection priority when the deception plan transitions to its implementation phase.

### Institutions of English Jurisprudence

The First Secretary and Lord Treasurer know full well that the concept of the rule of law and the importance of legal justification to punish English subjects regardless of status or economic station permeates all levels of English society. By the time of Elizabeth's reign, the idea of having personal legal protections against arbitrary punitive actions is already part of every English subject's DNA.[7]

Throughout her reign, Elizabeth was committed to ensuring her actions were based firmly on legal precedence. She sought legal arguments to justify the Duke of Norfolk's execution, punish those responsible for the Northern Rebellion, expropriate Catholic landholdings, clarify the legal definition of a "just" war, treat the increasing anti-Protestant activities as acts of treason and not heresy and requested that her subjects be legally authorized to occupy America in her name. Cecil and Walsingham would have to make sure that the rule of law was part of their operational plan should they have to force Elizabeth to decide Mary's fate.[8] However, they know that Elizabeth and her English subjects were not ready to support or condone regicide. Therefore, Cecil and Walsingham choose to delay the idea of legally legitimizing Mary's execution until foundational statutory measures are enacted.

## PROTECTING THE CRITICAL SECRET

At this point in the process, the plan transitions from an intellectual exercise to a more tangible implementation and execution of observable events. Therefore, Walsingham and Cecil must now decide how to protect their sensitive, clandestine planning from public exposure. However, after determining that observable deception activities would not occur for at least another year, the First Secretary and Lord Treasurer augment their initial target and pattern assessments with second-tier collection strategies to identify logistic support lines, infiltration ports of entry and exit, and safe house locations. They will also begin developing physical and operational security tactical, technical, and procedural guidelines to protect their sensitive endeavor from compromise.

To protect their increasing tempo of sensitive work from being noticed by the curious, Cecil and Walsingham will conduct most of their deception-related business at Barn Elms or Seething Lane—Walsingham's two domiciles located some distance from Elizabeth's court. Since their primary governmental duties make it difficult to involve themselves in the actual analysis and production of baseline target assessments, they select trusted intelligence agents and task them to collect, consolidate, and analyze the newly collected data. To cover this phase of the planning process, the First Secretary and Lord Treasurer send all support requests through routine communication channels devoid of any signs revealing a sense of urgency or short suspense requirements. Instead, plausible cover stories are used to explain tasking requirements, thus keeping their agents from discovering the overall deception plan and its objectives.

Regardless of their effort to put security guardrails in place, the First Secretary and Lord Treasurer continue to be concerned that Elizabeth may discover their covert activity at some point during the operation. While a final decision to determine the extent and role they wish Elizabeth to play in their scheme will remain in limbo, they will begin to seriously address the pros and cons of making her aware of their plan. That decision will ultimately depend on how confident they are in their ability to interpret and control Elizabeth's moods, behavioral inclinations, and their own situational awareness sensitivities.

---

### Recap of Phase 1: Concept of Operations

The Throckmorton Plot will enable Cecil and Walsingham to lay the foundational framework for a deception operation. In creating this initial planning platform, they...

1.) Identified potential individual targets and locations for future intelligence collection and analysis activities

2.) Developed baseline psychological profiles and behavioral pattern assessments of specific Catholic conspirators

3.) Addressed concerns about operational security measures to protect English deception planning activities from being compromised

---

**Figure 7.2.**
Source: R. Kent Tiernan

## NOTES

1. Information provided by Mr. William A. Parquette, former Strategic Planner for the Office of the Secretary of Defense for Policy/OSD(P).

2. Army Field Manual, Chapter 4, *Deception Planning*, 90–92; Joint Publication 3–13.4 (formerly JP 3–38), Military Deception, Director for Operations, United States Joint Forces Command, Joint Warfighting Center, Suffolk, Virginia, July 13, 2006.

3. Pollen's take on Ballard is much more critical. He writes, "Like so many priestly politicians, he was deficient in practical common sense, and the victim of theorists and extremists . . . and incapable of measured judgment, of facing the truth, [and] of sober thought" *Mary Queen of Scots and the Babington Plot*, Introduction, Pages lxxix–lxxx.

4. Charles Nicholl, *The Reckoning: The Murder of Christopher Marlowe* (Harcourt, Brace and Company, 1992), 148; John Hungerford Pollen, *Mary, Queen of Scots and the Babington Plot*. Edited from the original documents in the Public Record Office (T. and A. Constable for the Scottish History Society, 1922), Introduction: "Ballard's Character," lxxviii.

5. John Cooper, *The Queen's Agent: Sir Francis Walsingham and the Rise of Espionage in Elizabethan England* (Pegasus Books, 2012), 172.

6. Stephen Alford notes that "The two men met in Paris in August 1581 when Secretary Walsingham was in the city as a special envoy . . . he (Paget) offered himself as a spy . . . Sir Henry Cobham, English Ambassador in Paris, made it plain to Walsingham that Paget was "a practiser against the estate and a known supporter of Mary, Queen of Scots." *The Watchers: A Secret History of the Reign of Elizabeth*

*I*, Page 156. *Calendar of State Papers-Domestic Series*, 23 October 1582, Page 73, #79 notes that in a letter sent from Paris to Walsingham, Paget professes allegiance to Elizabeth and his readiness to be employed in any service, except in his matter of conscience in religion.

Responding to Paget's offer of service to Elizabeth, Sir Francis wrote to Charles Paget: "I have of late gotten some knowledge of your cunning dealing and that you meant to have used me for a stalking horse. Master Paget, a plain course is the best course. I see it very hard for men of contrary disposition to be united in good will. You love the Pope and I hate not his person but his calling. Until this impediment be removed, we two shall neither agree in religion towards God nor in true and sincere devotion towards our prince and sovereign. God open your eyes and send you truly to know him." Stephen Alford, *The Watchers: A Secret History of the Reign of Elizabeth I*, Page 157.

7. A.L. Rowse, *The England of Elizabeth: The Structure of Society* (PAPERMAC, 1950), 261–262.

8. Alison Weir, *The Life of Elizabeth I* (Ballantine Books, 1998), 210, 214; John Cooper, *The Queen's Agent: Sir Francis Walsingham, and the Rise of Espionage in Elizabethan England* (Pegasus Books, 2012), 100–101, 260–261; Antonia Fraser, *Mary, Queen of Scots* (Delacorte Press, 1969), 530.

# Chapter 8

# Looking Ahead

The First Secretary and Lord Treasurer must have had a sense of pride and satisfaction for what they had accomplished in seven short years. Their actions successfully weathered the disruptive 1570s storm. Had it not been for their early, prescient realization that England didn't have the capabilities to fight a unified Catholic force, they might have discovered too late that Protestant-controlled England was on a sure path to mayhem and destruction. Now, with the underlying deception framework in place, they once again turn their attention to domestic and foreign activities that could potentially impact their ongoing deception activities. In so doing, Cecil and Walsingham begin a second more comprehensive internal reassessment and prioritization of concerns that, if not soon resolved, could jeopardize the ability of Protestant England to staunch the rising Catholic tide.

Paradoxically, the turmoil of the 1570s created a tighter bond between the two men than ever before. By 1580, Cecil and Walsingham's sphere of governmental influence encompassed their kingdom's most critical subject areas and State interests, solidifying them in purpose, scope, and common cause. Moreover, the urgency to act boldly against the rising Catholic threat of the 1570s further strengthened what had now become a dynamic and symbiotic relationship.

On nearly a daily basis, intelligence reports repeatedly reminded Elizabeth's chief advisors that the challenges that lay ahead of them would only intensify without innovative countermeasures. Sir Christopher Hatton's[1] 26 April 1580 letter to Sir Francis Walsingham best summarizes England's increasingly precarious position.

> My good Mr. Secretary, my zealous care for her Majestie's safetie now fearfully stirred up, with this evill newes of affaires in Ireland, doth give me dutifull occasion in my absence to write some little of my simple opinion . . . The long-expected mischief, maliciously conspired by the greate and most dangerous of her Majestie . . . is now in action . . . wherein there remayneth,

that her Highness . . . should timely and victoriously resist this rabble of rebells and traytours, and to let nothing be spared either of treasure, men, munytion or whatever els, to save that Kingdome . . . The best counsel is . . . to resist . . . to ende this mischief, before her potent enemyes might find opportunitie to work their malice upon us.[2]

## REASSESSING THE SITUATION

### What to do about Mary—Final Resolution

By now, there is little question that Cecil and Walsingham believed that only aggressive, intelligence-based countermeasures would successfully remove Mary, Queen of Scots, from England. They also agreed her removal must occur before the Spanish Armada launched its invasion fleet. The fear of what the Catholics would do to English Protestants should the invasion succeed subsequently raised the sense of urgency to an unprecedented level.

From the very beginning of Mary's initial request for Elizabeth's protection, "Cecil and others [possibly including Walsingham] believed it to be no more than a feint, and that at the first opportunity she would show herself the true product of her Guisan genes by seeking to overthrow her English cousin." When Mary first arrived in England, "Walsingham more than once proposed that the real solution to that problem [Mary's presence] was to arrange to have the lords of Scotland request Mary's transfer to their custody, followed by her prompt execution; but the lords balked at shouldering all the blame themselves for so drastic a step, while Elizabeth was insistent that her hands must be kept at least superficially clean in any such transaction. And so dangerous limbo had continued."[3]

Walsingham was not alone in his thinking. Growing public demand for Mary's death was called for as early as the Ridolfi Plot (the early 1570s) when Mary's role in the conspiracy resulted in an overwhelming call for the Scottish Queen and Duke of Norfolk's heads. However, both senior advisors were unable to uncover evidence of her direct complicity in the plot. While irrefutable evidence later led to the Duke's execution, Mary remained free to continue her disruptive activities. Even the discovery of new plots failed to reveal direct evidence of Mary's desire to kill Elizabeth. However, the longer her imprisonment, the greater the demand for Mary Stuart's life grew.

> . . . they [many of Elizabeth's ministers] were keen to deny Mary the queenship altogether, and they were watching for the occasion to kill her . . . In March 1585, while Mary was incarcerated in her much hated Tutbury Castle, one of Mary's custodians reported if any danger had been offered, or doubt suspected, the Queen's body should first have tasted of the gall.[4]

Adding to their rationale of using extreme measures to remove Mary were the unrelenting Catholic demands that Spain and France invade the English kingdom with naval and ground forces. Finally, Cecil and Walsingham concluded that physically removing Mary "with extreme prejudice" was the best solution for England to redirect its resources exclusively on a future invasion scenario. Not surprisingly, both men discovered that as the years of Mary's incarceration increased, the idea of disposing of her became more feasible and justifiable to their way of thinking.

Therefore, Cecil and Walsingham began work on two mutually supportive initiatives to lay the groundwork for Mary's eventual execution. The first was a parliament-supported initiative that would provide the cautious Elizabeth with the legal statute necessary for approving Mary's execution. Second, " . . . [their] most urgent task was to discover the secret means she [Mary] used to communicate with the world outside her various prisons, so that [they] could tap into her correspondence and monitor what [they] saw as treasonous machinations."[5]

Cecil and Walsingham's successful penetration of Mary's communication network will become a driving force in the development of their plan to influence and eventually control the content and exchange of information between Mary and her supporters. The result of this effort will successfully play out during the Babington Plot in 1586.

## What to do about Elizabeth—Final Resolution

Another factor complicating Cecil and Walsingham's decision to strike at the Catholics using their unprecedented, offensive-oriented intelligence operation was Elizabeth's refusal to believe her life was in jeopardy. Elizabeth's almost nonchalant attitude toward such warnings left them frustrated and more determined than ever to take actions preventing direct threats to her person. Robert Beale, Chief Secretary to Walsingham and the Privy Council, best described how virtually impossible it was to manage Elizabeth when she was personally involved in State matters.

> A great deal depended on her emotional state. If she was well disposed, a secretary had a good chance of getting her signature. If she was not—and Elizabeth was notorious for her explosive temper and bouts of depression—then the government could simply grind to a halt. . . . When she was angry, the Queen should not be approached unless extreme necessity urge it.[6]

Walsingham and Cecil must have experienced many sleepless nights thinking about how they could best move forward without Elizabeth's interference. "It is not surprising that in Walsingham's vast correspondence, there are numberless sighs about Elizabeth's peevish and pinched inability to act decisively for the National good—there are numerous versions in his letters of hope that God will open her eyes."[7] It was, therefore, apparent to both Cecil and Walsingham that inserting Elizabeth into such a complex and time-sensitive endeavor, especially during its seminal stages of development, was out of the question.

> "If Elizabeth would not or could not take the decisions necessary to ensure national security, then there were those in authority who judged it their duty to act without her." John Cooper, *The Queen's Agent*, Page 93.

After years of seeking ways to accommodate the "Elizabeth factor," both men reluctantly concluded that involving Elizabeth in any aspect of their planning process would be too risky and decided to act independently of her. This decision proved to be the right one. Elizabeth's independent actions during the soon-to-be-discovered Throckmorton Plot nearly exposed and jeopardized their ongoing secret deception planning activities initiated two years earlier.

By summer 1582, the die was irretrievably cast, and the successful removal of Mary from England now rested on their shoulders alone. All that awaited their final move was a valid reason, or catalyst, to transition their deception planning process to the final implementation and execution phases—that reason fortuitously materialized when a seemingly minor and somewhat mundane incident occurred at the English-Scottish border. A Catholic courier, disguised as a barber, was caught carrying incriminating documents among his "tooth-pulling" equipment.[8, 9]

## NOTES

1. Sir Christopher Hatton (1540–1591) was a favorite of Queen Elizabeth I and the Lord Chancellor of England from 1587–1591. Handsome and accomplished, he impressed Elizabeth with his talent for dancing and quickly won her affection. In 1577, he became Vice-Chamberlain of her household and Privy Councilor. Hatton became a principal interrogator of Sir Anthony Babington and commissioner during the trial of Mary, Queen of Scots.

2. Thomas Wright (Editor), *Queen Elizabeth and Her Times: A Series of Original Letters Vol. II* (London: Henry Colburn, Publisher, 1838), 106.

3. Stephen Budiansky, *Her Majesty's Spymaster: Elizabeth I, Sir Francis Walsingham, and the Birth of Modern Espionage* (Penguin Books, 2005), 105; Anne Somerset, *Elizabeth I* (Anchor Books, 1991), 203.

4. John Hungerford Pollen, *Mary, Queen of Scots and the Babington Plot.* Edited from the original documents in the Public Record Office (T. and A. Constable for the Scottish History Society, 1922), Introduction: "Loyalty to Queen Mary," xiv.

5. Robert Hutchinson, *Elizabeth's Spymaster* (St. Martin's Press, 2006), 87.

6. John Cooper, *The Queen's Agent: Sir Francis Walsingham and the Rise of Espionage in Elizabethan England* (Pegasus Books, 2012), 93–94.

7. Alan Haynes, *Elizabethan Spymaster & Statesman* (Sutton Publishing, 1992), 240.

8. Information gleaned from the *Calendar of State Papers-Domestic Series, 19 April 1582*, Page 51, #14 indicates that an agent informed Walsingham that there was a probability of rebellion because the Papists had no hope of aid from the Pope or King of Spain. However, the King of France and the House of Guise wanted England defeated. The next month, another report provides information on seminaries and Papists in the North counties, reference to the invasion of England via Scotland, the re-establishment of the Romish religion, and deposing Elizabeth and replacing her with Mary. *Calendar of State Papers-Domestic Series*, Page 57, #78/79.

One could infer from these two reports that Walsingham may have known of the Throckmorton Plot well before the May 1582 "tooth-puller" incident.

9. Alison Weir, *The Life of Elizabeth I* (Ballantine Books, 1998), 345–346; Hutchinson, 101.

# Chapter 9

# "A Sign from God"

*London—Salisbury House (French Embassy)*
*"From a Discrete Distance"*
*May 1583*

As Walsingham positions his surveillance team at strategic points around Salisbury House to monitor Francis Throckmorton and other suspects' activities, he believes that "God truly works in mysterious ways." Thus, he refuses to accept that information collected from his intelligencers abroad and the recent discovery of evidence hidden behind a tooth-puller's mirror implicating Mary in another conspiracy was simply good luck, coincidence, or fate. Instead, he fervently believes the English-Scottish border incident is a God-sent sign that he and Cecil must seize the moment and exploit the opportunity handed them.

Upon returning to Seething Lane later in the day, Walsingham plans to reassure Cecil that their earlier decision not to inform Elizabeth of their deception scheme was the right one. For just this morning, he received a report from a sensitive source inside the French embassy that Elizabeth had recently opened a secret communication channel of her own with the French ambassador. The report indicated that Elizabeth told the ambassador she was aware of the Throckmorton Plot and demanded the names of Mary's couriers.[1]

Walsingham, now aware of Elizabeth's recent unilateral actions, had proof to confirm what they feared would happen should she ever discover their ongoing deception plan. Based on this revelation, the First Secretary will recommend to the Lord Treasurer that they immediately commence the plan's implementation phase. He is also intrigued by the idea that they could use the newly discovered Throckmorton Plot as an opportunity to accomplish two mission objectives simultaneously. Why not use the existing plot as cover for their rapidly developing and soon too-difficult-to-hide deception activities? Yes, the more he reflects on what has brought him to this moment, the more convinced he is that the deception scheme begun almost two years earlier was foreordained by "the Almighty."

He reflects how fortuitous he was chosen and then mentored by a person similarly dedicated to protecting their Protestant faith, country, and Queen. Under Cecil's tutelage and protective shield, Walsingham's involvement in countering the Ridolfi Plot, his vivid memory of the horrors of the St. Bartholomew Day massacre, and experience gained through years of rebuilding and reorganizing a dysfunctional body of intelligencers have prepared him well to be the sword of English vengeance.

It does not surprise Walsingham that Ambassador Michel de Castelnau, at the French embassy, is directing this newly identified Throckmorton Plot. English intelligence surveillance of earlier attempts to overthrow Elizabeth had already identified foreign embassies as centers for conspiratorial activities. However, what alarms him is the extent of Castelnau's cooperation with the meddling Spanish Ambassador, Bernardino de Mendoza.

Before leaving his observation post for the day, the First Secretary reminds himself that Pope Gregory XIII altered the Julian calendar in 1582, thus creating a ten-day difference between England and the continent (8 July in England becomes 18 July in Paris).[2] This new Gregorian calendar will pose timing and coordination problems for future intelligence activities. Therefore, when meeting with Sir William, he will recommend to the Lord Treasurer that, henceforth, all intelligence they receive from the continent will require date adjustments to reflect England/Julian, not the revised Gregorian calendar dates.

## NOTES

1. Stephen Budiansky, *Her Majesty's Spymaster: Elizabeth I, Sir Francis Walsingham, and the Birth of Modern Espionage* (Penguin Books, 2005), 124–126.

2. In 1582, when Pope Gregory XIII introduced the Gregorian calendar, Europe adhered to the Julian calendar, first implemented by Julius Caesar in 46 B.C. Since the Roman emperor's system miscalculated the length of the solar year by 11 minutes, the calendar had since fallen out of sync with the seasons. This concerned Gregory because it meant that Easter, traditionally observed on 21 March, fell further away from the spring equinox with each passing year. Although Pope Gregory's papal bull reforming the calendar had no power beyond the Catholic Church, Catholic countries—including Spain, Portugal, and Italy—swiftly adopted the new system for their civil affairs. European Protestants, however, largely resisted the reform. It was not until 1700 that Protestant Germany switched over. An act of Parliament in England accepted the Gregorian calendar in September 1752.

*Chapter 10*

# It's About Time!

## THROCKMORTON PLOT (1582–1584)

In May 1582, " . . . a Catholic conspiracy involving the Guise family of France, the Pope, Philip of Spain, and the Jesuits was hatched in Paris against Elizabeth, its object being to place Mary Stuart on the English throne . . . indicating that the Scottish queen was involved in some new conspiracy. From then on, her correspondence was carefully vetted, and her servants watched more closely . . . "[1]

The following year, "a Catholic named Francis Throckmorton was arrested. Papers in his study and confessions extracted on 'the rack' furnished Walsingham with evidence of a planned Franco-Spanish invasion and a list of English Catholics ready to assist them."[2] Throckmorton also divulged that the Duke of Guise was leading the French invasion force. And, the Spanish ambassador, Bernardino de Mendoza, provided critical information to the French from his embassy in London.

## PHASE 2—CONCEPT OF OPERATIONS

Little did the Catholic survivors of the failed Throckmorton Plot realize that Cecil and Walsingham's immediate counter-response would prove catastrophic to their future conspiratorial planning. The Plot's defeat was the catalyst that accelerated the implementation and execution phases of the Lord Treasurer and First Secretary's stratagem begun over two years earlier. Ironically, the lessons learned from the Catholic's failure to unseat Elizabeth would prove, in the end, more significant to Walsingham and Cecil than to their conspiratorial adversaries.

## Refining the Plan

By the time of Francis Throckmorton's execution on 10 July 1584, the English counter conspiracy architects had a more in-depth, comprehensive knowledge of who would be involved in the next attempt to remove Elizabeth from her throne and how they would execute their plan. Anticipating future attacks, Walsingham refined his deception initiatives by developing new, more substantive courses of action.

Comparing the early 1570s Catholic conspiracy template to the lessons learned from the Throckmorton, and later, Parry Plots, the First Secretary and Lord Treasurer were now able, with a high degree of confidence, to predict more accurately that:

1. Future conspiratorial plans against England would continue to originate from Europe, likely Paris, and Thomas Morgan would be the planning effort's focal point.
2. Key agitators would no doubt be disaffected, exiled Englishmen initially from outside England. As the conspiracy progressed, they would be infiltrated into the country to foment discord, gather invasion information, and assist in coordinating and implementing the plan with English Catholic sympathizers. Charles Paget and Don Bernardino de Mendoza, both now in Paris, would play important supporting roles.
3. Foreign invasion forces would continue to be the source of military interventionism, with the bulk of that support from the French Guise faction. Spain would also continue to be a vital source of military assistance. Once the invasion occurred, the Earl of Northumberland and other sympathetic English Catholic nobles would supply military support from within England.
4. English anchor groups would continue to be responsible for in-country coordination and support of conspiratorial plans and activities.
5. London's French and Spanish embassies would remain critical Catholic conspiracy centers of gravity moving sensitive communications between Europe, Mary's supporters, and her incarceration location. Knowledge gained from the Throckmorton Plot confirmed that the French embassy would be the critical node for conspiratorial activities in Mary's secure communication network.
6. The use of trusted couriers to move sensitive information from one point to another would remain a salient consideration and factor in all future actions designed to penetrate and neutralize Catholic communication networks.
7. Catholic conspirators would severely deal with the English Queen.[3]

Armed with this updated information, Walsingham will increase surveillance of Catholic plotters still at large,[4] reevaluate individuals already being monitored,[5] commence infiltration activities against key opposition centers of gravity,[6] and address their Catholic counterparts' operational "known unknowns."[7]

## PROTECTING THE CRITICAL SECRET

Before the Throckmorton Plot, Elizabeth appeared relatively blasé about earlier threats to her life. However, her attitude immediately changed upon learning that the Protestant leader, William of Orange, had been assassinated by a religious dissident. Using that shocking event as cover, Cecil and Walsingham will use the Throckmorton Plot to hide their deception activities (e.g., the employment of specifically deception-designed and tailored operation security tactics) "in plain sight." Thus, for the next two years, the Throckmorton Plot will be used to divert attention away from their sensitive deception implementation activities.

The Throckmorton Plot will also lead to a discernible shift in Cecil and Walsingham's deception operation command and control responsibilities. Decisions relevant to operationalizing their deception plan will now become the sole responsibility of the First Secretary. As Lord Treasurer and chief advisor to Queen Elizabeth, Cecil will transition to an advisory and support role, ensuring that resources—primarily money—are made available to Walsingham as needed. Cecil will now be in a better position to shield his and Walsingham's clandestine activities from Elizabeth. It will also permit him to coordinate deception-related political and security activities involving Thomas Morgan and Mary Stuart more effectively—actions that will become paramount to the future entrapment of the Scottish Queen.

## Recap of Phase 2: Concept of Operations

Due to the growing sense of urgency in England to counter attempts on Elizabeth's life, the 1582–1585 years proved efficacious in rapidly transitioning Walsingham and Cecil's Phase 2 Concept of Operations to a more robust series of implementation-focused courses of action. For example, during this unusually pressure-filled three-year period, the two men...

1.) Experienced additional pressure from Elizabeth to take more dynamic action against increasing Catholic attempts to dethrone her

2.) For the first time received Elizabeth-directed funding for intelligence counter-Catholic activities

3.) Employed lessons learned from the Throckmorton Plot to refine their understanding of how Catholics construct their conspiracies

4.) Channeled the extra funding to support deception initiatives

5.) Used the Throckmorton Plot as cover to hide, "in plain sight," deception-associated implementation activities

6.) Clearly defined their deception command and control responsibilities and strengthened the principle of centralized control and decentralized execution

7.) Increased the number of individuals aware of the deception plan

8.) Developed, coordinated, and deconflicted specific implementation courses of action

9.) Commenced specific deception implementation and execution activities

**Figure 10.1.**
Source: R. Kent Tiernan

## NOTES

1. Alison Weir, *The Life of Elizabeth I* (Ballantine Books, 1998), 345–346; Francis Edwards S.J., *Plots and Plotters in the Reign of Elizabeth I* (Four Courts Press, 2002), 128.

2. Charles Nicholl, *The Reckoning: The Murder of Christopher Marlowe* (Harcourt, Brace and Company, 1992), 198.

3. During the period between December 1583 and April/May 1584, Walsingham received information from the French embassy that a Dr. William Parry had vowed to the Pope that he would personally assassinate Elizabeth. This was the same William

Parry, who later became the center of another controversial plot that ultimately led to his execution in March 1585.

4. Key Throckmorton plotters still at large: Thomas Morgan, Charles Paget, Ambassador Don Bernardino de Mendoza (declared *persona non-grata* on 19 January 1584—moved to Paris and the French court), Ambassador Michel de Castelnau (recalled to Paris and later replaced by Châteauneuf), and Mary Stuart (under custody and control of Elizabeth and her senior advisors).

5. Persons of interest requiring further evaluation: Anthony Babington (identified by Henry Fagot as assisting in selling Catholic-inspired books out of the French embassy), Dr. William Parry (agent allegedly working for English intelligence), Thomas Paget (brother of Charles); Guise faction, Lord Talbot, Earl of Shrewsbury (responsible custodian for Mary Stuart's incarceration and a number of Catholic sympathizers once in his household), and Sir Edward Stafford, English ambassador to France (questionable relationships with members of the Guise faction).

6. Centers of gravity requiring further evaluation: Thomas Morgan's planning cell/location, the French Embassy in London (Salisbury House), English legal framework protecting Elizabeth, security around Mary Stuart, and Mary's secure communication network.

7. Known unknowns—essential elements of intelligence (questions still unanswered): When, where and how would the next Catholic conspiracy be executed, what was the status and timing of the planned operation, who would fill the key operational positions (e.g., agitators, enforcers, English sympathizers and in-country coordinators, key message couriers, etc.), who would provide the military forces, how many would be involved, where would the invasion forces land, and what do they plan to do with Elizabeth?

## Chapter 11

# "Devil in the Details"

As the flaming logs in the fireplace at the end of the great hall begin to transform into pockets of embers, the flickering light silhouettes two figures bent over a large, candlelit table. Both seem to be intensely concentrating on what looks like a pile of puzzle pieces haphazardly strewn across the velvet-covered tabletop. A closer look reveals that each piece has a number on it, and each number corresponds to a vertical column of numbers designating discrete deception actions to be executed. That list is lying prominently on a smaller table that stands between the two men. While the table physically separates them, they appear unified in their secret meeting's purpose and objective.

After more than seven years of rebuilding an intelligence service designed to take offensive actions against Catholic aggression and four years of planning to eliminate Mary, the time had finally arrived to unleash the "hounds of indirect warfare." However, both Cecil and Walsingham are unexpectedly experiencing the whole gamut of seemingly contradictory emotions. There is the thrill of activating the final phase of their plan, adrenaline-stoked exhilaration, and nervous anticipation associated with directly confronting the enemy. But, there is also the shared fear that their tedious and time-consuming preparations could lead to abject failure.

They brush aside their emotional concerns and refocus their attention on the numbered puzzle pieces before them and what other pieces might be needed to assure the deception execution is flawlessly deconflicted, coordinated, and synchronized in a time-sequenced fashion. They know that if all the pieces are not accounted for and do not seamlessly fit together, their future deception operations against the next group of conspirators and, ultimately, Mary Stuart will fail miserably.

However, their agreement of the steps to make the puzzle pieces coalesce into a cohesive whole is only part of the many complex and challenging problems confronting them this night. Once they solidify their shared vision of how each deception part fits with the other parts, they will turn their attention to some of the most critical activities they both know fall outside their control. Both realize that these specific factors or unknowns will become their most worrisome and perplexing problems from this point onward.

Late into the night and early morning hours, Cecil and Walsingham will spend the remainder of their time determining the what-ifs and potential unintended consequences of situations that could potentially threaten the smooth flow of their planned deception activities. This evening, the topic for consideration and discussion primarily focuses on the unpredictable behavior of their sovereign, Elizabeth I. They ask themselves the following questions:

- What if their unwitting Queen refuses to approve the relocation of Mary Stuart to two different locations during the next year?
- What should they do if Elizabeth is unwilling to pressure the French King into extraditing Mary's chief intelligencer to England for traitorous acts?
- How should they proceed if Cecil and Walsingham's efforts to widen the estrangement between Mary and her son, James VI, King of Scotland, fail to materialize?
- What if Elizabeth rejects the idea of executing Mary even if the evidence shows Mary approves of Elizabeth's assassination? What can they do to change her mind?

As the evening proceeds into the early morning hours, both men realize that their ability to anticipate and counter future situations will make or break their efforts to bring Mary Stuart to justice. This stark reality will monopolize their remaining waking hours for the operation's duration as they execute their deception activities.

Cecil and Walsingham are physically and mentally exhausted before the cock's crow signals the dawn of a new morning. They agree to continue their brainstorming exercise at their next *sub rosa* meeting. Then, bidding each other a safe return to their private domiciles, they stagger the timing of their departures, don their disguises, and take different routes back to London under cover of darkness.[1, 2]

## NOTES

1. The narrative accurately represents a typical, deliberate planning process that contemporary planners use when they address various aspects of deception planning and operational event executions.

2. Michael Hayden, former head of the National Security Agency and later Central Intelligence Agency, in his book *Playing to the Edge*, Page 101, stated that "Good intelligence is like a tapestry with multiple threads woven into a beautiful whole." As early as 1580, Walsingham and Cecil were poised to masterfully apply their significantly improved intelligence capabilities to the construction of a similarly beautiful interwoven deception operation.

# PART THREE

# (1583–1585)

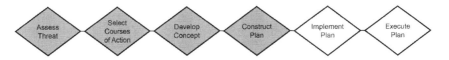

Deception Planning Phases.

## Chapter 12

# Fired Up and Ready to Go

While the Throckmorton Plot was pivotal in moving the deception plan forward, the planning tempo was further accelerated by three random yet perceived by Elizabeth's Privy Council as interrelated anti-Protestant events. These events (Somerville assassination scare—October 1583,[1] the assassination of William of Orange—June 1584, and Parry Plot—1584/1585) all centered on the violent removal of Protestant leaders. After the Prince of Orange's murder, the Elizabethan political establishment feared that Elizabeth was more vulnerable than ever to future assassination attempts. "William Parry made that fear real and tangible,"[2] and the sense of urgency to act more aggressively became palpable.

### PHASE 3—CONCEPT OF OPERATIONS

#### Key Implementation Activities

*Tightening Security around Mary*

#### January to December 1585

The First Secretary and Lord Treasurer believed their decision to restrict Mary's access to her supporters and stifle her communication would likely be viewed as a natural reaction in countering the Throckmorton Plot. They also saw it as an excellent opportunity to hide their future deception activities. So, in August 1584, while the Throckmorton Plot investigation progressed, they transferred Mary's custody from the accommodating Earl of Shrewsbury to Sir Ralph Sadler.

Then, in January 1585, she was moved to the damp and dilapidated Tutbury Castle, now under the control of the extreme anti-Catholic Sir Amyas Paulet. This marked the start of Walsingham and Cecil's strategically designed deception implementation and execution activities. From this point forward, the tightening of security around the Scottish Queen and restriction of information to and from her incarceration location would stymie future Catholic attempts to kill Elizabeth and lay the groundwork for Mary's eventual execution.

By the time of her relocation from Tutbury Castle to Chartley Hall on Christmas Eve 1585, English security actions had degraded Mary's ability to communicate not only with her son, the King of Scotland, but also with her vast array of supporters in England and abroad. As planned, the tightening of security caused the Scottish Queen a significant level of frustration and stress. It also created an urgent need for Morgan and Paget to develop a new, secure communication system as quickly as possible—a situation purposely designed and exploited by Walsingham.[3]

*Creating a Breach Between Mary and James VI*

**November 1584 to March 1585**
Employing a "divide and conquer" strategy, Walsingham and Cecil embarked on an initiative that would ultimately destroy France and Scotland's auld alliance. Walsingham and Cecil knew that key supporters of James VI were crucial to determining the future religious and political direction of Scotland. Therefore, to bring Scotland into England's sphere of influence, Elizabeth's two senior advisors identified those responsible for the young Scottish King's welfare and protection and commenced encouraging and facilitating a closer relationship between James VI and Elizabeth. This critical component of Walsingham and Cecil's plan significantly diminished Mary's participation and influence in the negotiations clearing the way for how Scotland, and even England, would be governed once James VI reached his majority.

To promote this desired situation, Elizabeth, still unwitting to the evolving deception plan and with the probable urging of Cecil, refused to let Mary represent herself during negotiations with young James's "protectors/guardians" and rejected the Scottish Queen's request that Castelnau, the French ambassador to London, convey her interests in the process. Elizabeth also delayed responding to Mary's requests that her secretary present her case at court. Amidst the delaying tactics emanating from London, Mary's attempts to be formally represented were also undermined by one of her son's primary emissaries to London—Patrick Gray.[4]

Familiar with Gray's background, Sir William Davison, Elizabeth's envoy to foreign courts, suggested that after Gray presented his credentials to Elizabeth, Walsingham should seriously consider exploiting Gray's greed and avarice.

So, as by qualitie of the person, with other circumstaunces, your honour may ghess what fruicte is to be gathered of his ambassage, and what respect they have here (in Scotland) for religion that employe men so qualified. He maketh great preparation, and taketh with him divers yonge gentlemen as vayne as himselfe.[5]

Having extraordinary insight into the human psyche, Walsingham recruited Patrick Gray and used him to widen the split between Mary and her son. To that end, Gray excelled at his task. At the end of his tenure at court, Gray provided valuable information about James VI, his mother, and Catholic initiatives to liberate the Scottish Queen. Gray was instrumental in creating discord and alienation between Mary, her son, and her Scottish Catholic supporters.[6]

## Legal Justification for Mary's Execution

### Late Summer 1584 to March 1585

In the past, Elizabeth was reluctant to make decisions of strategic importance, especially if there were no legal statutes or precedents to support her actions. Therefore, Walsingham and Cecil knew the only way their deception plan could succeed was if they presented Elizabeth with a legal document justifying her royal cousin's execution.

Exploiting the growing sense of urgency that Elizabeth's physical well-being was at risk, Cecil sent a series of recommendations to Parliament that, if enacted, would create an additional layer of security around their Queen. Through Cecil's persistent encouragement, "the Protestant factions of the English nobility and gentry drew up a Bond of Association[7] pledging all good citizens to slay, without scruples, any conspirator who plotted against the Queen. Furthermore, 'pretenders to the throne in whose favor these men conspired' were 'to be deprived of all rights as claimants to the succession' and were to be held personally responsible for such plots. The Bond of Association was confirmed by statute (27 Elizabeth 1585) entitled *An Act for the Security of the Queen's Royal Person, and the Continuance of the Realm of Peace* . . . This gave Mary Stuart [and her supporters] irrefutable notice of two facts: first, that her royal status would no longer protect her from public trial; second, that even a successful attempt on Elizabeth's life would bring her no advantage, but instead would cost her own head . . . Ambiguities between Elizabeth Tudor and Mary Stuart were over and done with."[8]

"The Elizabethan oath imposed sacred duties, publicly sworn on a copy of the gospels: constant vigilance, being prepared to inform on others without regard to friendship or community, and personal commitment to take up arms to defend the sovereign. The bond of 1584 was a masterstroke of propaganda . . . Although the bond was aimed initially at the gentry, thousands of citizens also queued to add their names . . . it reveals just how skilled Burghley [Cecil] and Walsingham had become in the art of manipulating public opinion . . . "[9]

When Walsingham showed Mary the Bond of Association document, "If he hoped she would be disconcerted by this very public vow of vengeance, Mary did not display it. She, without hesitation, signed the document on 5 January 1585."[10] Her signing of the pledge to protect Elizabeth from bodily harm surprised both senior advisors since it, in effect, played right into their hands.[11] However, despite their good fortune, both men realized that even if they successfully proved Mary's treachery, Elizabeth might still refuse to approve the Privy Council's demands to execute her royal cousin. Anticipating this worst-case scenario, Walsingham and Cecil developed a contingency plan that, if required, would add more pressure on Elizabeth to approve Mary's execution.[12]

## PLAN B—A 'PSYOP' CONTINGENCY OPTION

The First Secretary, Lord Treasurer, and most of the Privy Council agreed Mary's execution was the correct course of action. Still, they knew without additional pressure, Elizabeth would never consent to such a drastic step. Instead, she typically preferred easier, less controversial solutions. With that in mind, Walsingham and his fellow planners decided to manufacture an illusionary "sham plot"[13] as a contingency course of action to influence their hesitant Queen should she, predictably, resist condemning Mary Stuart to death.

The sham plot's storyline focused on the growing animosity between Walsingham and Sir Edward Stafford, English ambassador to France. The two men disagreed over several significant philosophical and policy matters. Their differences of opinion and dislike for each other were further aggravated by the First Secretary's growing suspicion that the French Guise family members were blackmailing Sir Edward because of his growing gambling debts. By 1585, the relationship between the two men had become irreconcilable. The toxic environment enveloping them will provide the ideal backdrop for the soon-to-be written contingency plan.[14]

### Isolating Thomas Morgan

*February/March 1585*

Thomas Morgan's long association with Mary was well known.[15] New evidence that he was a key player in the Throckmorton Plot and a likely participant in another scheme to kill Elizabeth[16] reinforced their belief that Morgan, like Mary, must be denied communication with each other. With Elizabeth's unwitting support of her top advisors evolving deception operation, Walsingham and Cecil decided to take a series of deliberate actions that would make Morgan, Mary's chief intelligencer, vulnerable to future influence activities.

Enraged by Morgan's double-dealings, Cecil suggested to Elizabeth that Morgan face justice for his constant attempts to encourage her assassination. In turn, Queen Elizabeth requested that King Henry III of France arrest, imprison, and extradite Morgan to England. Morgan was subsequently arrested on 9 March 1585 and taken to the Bastille two days later. Elizabeth's demand for his incarceration and extradition to England provided excellent cover for Cecil and Walsingham's multi-pronged scheme to physically isolate Mary's chief intelligencer to gain direct one-on-one access to him.

By early summer 1585, Morgan, like Mary, is isolated from the outside world. Yet, it is critical that he find a way to restore Mary's communication system, significantly degraded since her confinement at Tutbury Castle. Walsingham's plan has Poley, a recently recruited agent, contact Morgan to offer help re-establishing communication with Mary.

Walsingham and Cecil's actions leading to the isolation of their opposition's two top-priority targets provide them the opportunity to exploit the contrived situation to their advantage. Both men concur that if they are to succeed in their efforts to entrap Mary, it is of utmost importance that they strategically position themselves to infiltrate, penetrate, influence, and eventually control Mary Stuart's communication with her Catholic supporters. By late spring 1585, the First Secretary's intelligencers are ready to do just that.

## PROTECTING THE CRITICAL SECRET

At this point in the deception plan, English officials and subjects alike believe that Walsingham and Cecil's actions to protect Elizabeth are still a direct reaction to the Throckmorton and, later, Parry Plots. Likewise, Elizabeth remains unwitting to the real purpose of her two senior advisors' intent to entrap Mary. However, both Walsingham and Cecil are aware that using the Throckmorton and Parry Plots as justification to hide their sensitive venture would last only so long. Therefore, it quickly became time to move the deception plan forward.

Completely out of character, Elizabeth was so alarmed by her court's heightened sense of concern for her safety that she agreed to allocate an unprecedented level of funding to support Walsingham's efforts to protect her. The initial 750 pounds budgeted in 1582, while a meager amount to support intelligence activities, was, by the mid-1580s, significantly increased to approximately 2,000 pounds per annum.[17]

> Money was paid to such as Sir Francis Walsingham appointed, whose privy seal from time to time went without prest or account and without showing the cause of the employment of the same, which were sometimes for French causes and otherwise, to us unknown as to the employment hereof.[18]

As long as money continued to flow from Elizabeth's coffers to support intelligence activities outside the scrutiny of her Privy Council, Walsingham would take advantage of this unexpected fiduciary windfall to accelerate the deception plan's timetable. The challenging tasks that now lay ahead would put Walsingham and his coterie of intelligence's special talents and unique skills to the ultimate test.

## NOTES

1. Notations in Queen Elizabeth's *Calendar of Domestic State Papers* indicated that Catholic, anti-Catholic, and English military preparedness activities rose at a steady rate from January 1581 through September 1586. For example, in 1581, of the 410 total calendar notations, approximately 34% reflected concerns with matters related to Catholic, anti-Catholic activities, and English military preparedness issues. In April/May 1582, a significant spike of interest in those same issues accounted for approximately 40% of the calendar notations. This spike in interest may have been due to the discovery of early conspiratorial developments that later became known as the Throckmorton Plot.

Data for the years 1583 through the first nine months of 1586 reveals a steady rise of interest in matters affecting England's national security. Of the 590 calendar notations made in 1583, the interest level associated with Catholic, anti-Catholic, and English military preparedness subjects rose approximately 40%. The following two years, 1584 and 1585, of the 695 and 740 total calendar notations respectfully, the combined interest level associated with Catholic, anti-Catholic, and English military preparedness subjects climbed to 45% and 50% respectively. From 1586 to the capture of the Babington conspirators and removal of Mary Stuart from Chartley Hall to Fotheringhay Castle for trial in September, approximately 48% of the year's calendar notations referred to those same concerns. The First Secretary and Lord Treasurer could have taken advantage of the growing public paranoia, fear, and clamor for action using it as cover while moving their 1580 planned offensive operation into its implementation and final execution phases.

2. Stephen Alford, *The Watchers: A Secret History of the Reign of Elizabeth I* (Bloomsbury Press, 2112), 192.

3. Perhaps Walsingham was applying lessons learned about Mary's behavior displayed at Lochleven Castle in 1567 and 1568.

4. Patrick Gray, educated at Glasgow University and raised as a Protestant, had traveled to France, and developed friendships with many of Mary Stuart's friends. While in France, he became a Catholic and an avid supporter of the Duke of Guise's foreign policy, especially as it directly impacted Scotland's future interests. Upon his return to Scotland in 1583, he quickly gained favor with the young King James VI, was sent to London as his ambassador in 1584 to effect a treaty to quell the unrest along the English-Scottish border and strengthen the relationship between the Scottish King and Queen Elizabeth. In a message sent from Sir William Davison to Francis Walsingham in August 1584, Davison described Gray as a papist, devoted servant of Mary, Queen of Scots, and friend of France. Davison also intimated that Gray had been heavily compensated financially by the Duke of Guise and Spanish ambassador in Paris. However, at the same time, the English envoy pointed out that Gray's handling of monies designated to support Mary's cause was regularly "being pocketed" by Gray or redirected to his King or other greedy royal councilors. *Letters and Papers relating to Patrick Master of Gray*, Page 4. Gray's recruitment occurred sometime during the November–December 1584 time frame.

5. *Letters and Papers relating to Patrick Master of Gray*, afterward Seventh Lord Gray, Presented to the Bannatyne Club by Lord Gray (Edinburgh Printing Company, 1835), 5.

6. Gray, while assuring Mary of his devotion to her cause, was able to convince Elizabeth that his true allegiance was to her when he came to London. The Queen [Mary] was not gullible, but it was evident where Gray's true material interests lay. Francis Edwards, *Plots and Plotters in the Reign of Elizabeth I*, Page 131.

7. The Bond of Association condemning to death anyone conspiring to murder Elizabeth became official law in March 1585. Robert Poley, one of Walsingham's key double agent/provocateurs during the Babington Plot, was recruited during the April/May 1585 time frame. It was Poley who made the first one-on-one contact with Morgan on or about 26 June approximately a month and a half after he began working for Walsingham. The timing of Morgan's incarceration in the Bastille and Poley's contact with him in late June was arguably the result of Walsingham, Cecil, and Thomas Phelippes's time-phased execution of deception-related events (e.g., tightening security around Mary, isolating Morgan from his intelligence apparatus, and officially making the Bond of Association the law of the land).

8. Stefan Zweig, *Mary, Queen of Scotland and the Isles* (Lancer Books, 1935), 302–303.

9. John Cooper, *The Queen's Agent: Sir Francis Walsingham and the Rise of Espionage in Elizabethan England* (Pegasus Books, 2012), 194–195.

10. Robert Hutchinson, *Elizabeth's Spymaster* (St. Martin's Press, 2006), 118.

11. Had Mary refused to sign the legal document, it would have implied that she supported efforts to remove Elizabeth as Queen of England. However, by signing the document, Mary is agreeing that anyone threatening Elizabeth is liable to extreme retribution.

12. Years after Walsingham's death, Thomas Harrison, an alleged friend and servant of the First Secretary, "avowed that the plot [Parry] was 'wrought by them'" (Walsingham, Phelippes, and Harrison). L. Hicks, *An Elizabethan Problem*, Page 69.

While Hicks only suggests that English Intelligence was possibly behind the Parry Plot, he does point out that "the government certainly used the Parry Plot as a good propaganda tool" that encouraged a legal, punitive course of action (e.g., the Bond of Association).

Cecil and Walsingham, early in their deception planning process, had already anticipated that Elizabeth would require a legal justification to act with extreme prejudice against Mary should she be accused of treasonous acts. The Parry Plot, among other events (e.g., Throckmorton Plot, Summerville Incident, and murder of William of Orange), provided the First Secretary and Lord Treasurer the opportunity to lay the legal foundation via the Bond of Association to satisfy their and Elizabeth's political and legal sensitivities and concerns.

13. In Charles Nicholl's *The Reckoning: The Murder of Christopher Marlowe*, Page 154, he writes that "the so-called Stafford Plot . . . has all the markings of a Walsingham sham plot, the chief purpose of which was to embarrass the French ambassador and render him incommunicado during the trial and execution of Mary Stuart."

14. Hutchinson, 176–179; Alan Haynes, *The Elizabethan Secret Services* (Sutton Publishing, 1992), 95–96; Antonia Fraser, *Mary Queen of Scots* (Delacorte Press, 1969), 525.

15. William Cecil had, in fact, recommended Morgan to act as secretary for Lord Shrewsbury, who was ordered to act as Queen Mary's custodian. Running afoul of authorities by providing Mary sensitive information about events impacting her incarceration, Morgan was imprisoned by the Elizabethan government. Once freed, he left England for France in 1575. L. Hicks, *An Elizabethan Problem,* Page 5.

16. The scheme involved "Parry, a distributor of Catholic pamphlets and a former servant to the Earl of Pembroke. Parry had married into money that he eventually squandered. He was jailed but released after convincing Cecil he would spy for him. However, Parry joined the enemy as a convert during an intelligence-gathering trip in Europe. Returning to England, he won a seat in Parliament in 1584, where he betrayed himself by vehemently criticizing anti-Catholic legislation. During one of Walsingham's rare interrogations, Parry admitted he had plotted, while in Rome, to assassinate Elizabeth. He was executed in March 1585." Alan Haynes, *Walsingham: Spymaster & Statesman,* Pages 89–90.

17. Cooper, 182.

18. Charles Nicholl, *The Reckoning: The Murder of Christopher Marlowe* (Harcourt, Brace and Company, 1992), 110.

# Chapter 13

# Unleashing the "Leash"[1]

Having a comprehensive knowledge of his opponent's centers of gravity and now total access to his own agents who were previously responsible for countering the Throckmorton Plot, the First Secretary will redeploy these newly available assets to advance his rapidly evolving deception plan. To support the realignment of these human assets, Walsingham, with Cecil's assistance, will develop procedures to 1) monitor agent activities and their current locations, 2) systematically track the source and date of the collected information, and 3) consolidate information at a central location—probably Seething Lane. These new procedures, coupled with the anticipated benefits of a communication network under development at Chartley Hall in early fall 1585, will enable the First Secretary to accurately monitor and assess the status of Catholic targets and his own agents' surveillance activities. Thus, by January 1586, Walsingham will be capable of responding rapidly and effectively to ongoing Catholic conspiratorial activities.

## FINAL TARGET ASSESSMENTS/
## ENGLISH AGENT ASSIGNMENTS

### Mary Stuart

Since the Scottish Queen's flight to England in 1568, Walsingham had been moderately successful in blunting incessant Catholic attempts to spread discord by controlling Mary's location of confinement, thus limiting contact with her supporters. As the threat of Catholic intervention increased, Elizabeth, fortunately, had given Cecil *carte blanche* to move Mary to increasingly restrictive locations making it more difficult for the Catholic conspirators to free her.[2] By the end of 1584, and with the control he held over Mary, the First Secretary began to use her as a "stalking horse" to influence and manipulate Catholic conspirators' decisions and courses of action. Not

surprisingly, the many years of incarceration and numerous stressful relocations had not treated Mary well. Mary would soon be forty-three years old.

> Beneath all her regal poise and charm lay the harsh medical and psychological
> impact of almost two decades of captivity at the hands of Elizabeth . . . She
> knew that her beauty had been blurred by years of boredom and sedentary
> life: she was now double-chinned and stood painfully with stooped shoulders,
> her legs swollen and crippled with arthritis . . . she [Mary] had suffered from
> a veritable medical lexicon of afflictions—a gastric ulcer, dropsy, headaches,
> constipation, neuralgia, viral fevers, and rheumatism. Some may have been
> psychosomatic causes; others such as vomiting, abdominal pain, and weakness
> in the arms and legs, may have been symptoms of the hereditary metabolic
> disorder porphyria.[3, 4]

At the same time, Mary was still reeling from knowing that her son had
abandoned her in favor of Elizabeth, who bribed James VI with an annual
pension of 4,000 pounds. Until then, Mary had a flicker of hope that James
might repent of his behavior toward her, but the final arrangement between
Elizabeth and James extinguished the captive Queen's last hope of reconciliation. Her secretary subsequently deposed that the news afforded her "the
greatest anguish, despair, and grief with which I have ever seen her seized,
and her tormented state of mind made her more inclined to sanction the desperate measures that Babington had delineated."[5, 6]

Another significant factor was that her new jailor, Sir Amyas Paulet,
monitored the Scottish Queen's every move while at Tutbury Castle on a
twenty-four basis. In turn, Paulet provided Walsingham with frequent updates
about the Scottish Queen's physical and mental health. Such near-real-time
access to this type of valuable information will later permit Sir Francis
the opportunity to manipulate and exploit Mary's growing psychological
vulnerabilities.

## Sir Amyas Paulet—Mary's Last Custodian

Sir Amyas Paulet assumed custodial responsibilities for Mary's safekeeping
from the Earl of Shrewsbury and Sir Ralph Sadler in early 1585. At the time,
many rumors were sweeping through Elizabeth's court about the somewhat
abrupt transfer of responsibilities to Paulet—a love affair between Shrewsbury
and Mary, sympathy for Catholics and Mary's situation, and personality conflicts between Mary, Elizabeth, and Shrewsbury's wife. Regardless of the
exact reason for the move, the timing coincided with the deception plan's
transition from implementation to the execution phase, increasing Mary's isolation from her supporters and further degrading her communication network.

Figure 13.1. Sir Amyas Paulet (left) and George Talbot, 6th Earl of Shrewsbury. Artist: Ronda Penrod. Reproduced by permission of Ronda Penrod

From this point hence, Sir Amyas Paulet will prove to be an ideal choice to participate in the final execution phase of Walsingham's gambit.

> . . . he [Paulet] had been specially selected by Walsingham for the task in hand, because all his contemporaries agreed, he was not only a prominent Puritan but also a mortal enemy of the Queen of Scots and all she stood for. Walsingham understood his man; Paulet was quite immune to the charms of the Queen of Scots and found her irritating and even tiresome as a character . . . Paulet's Puritan conscience allowed him to hate her in advance. When they actually met, Paulet was able to transform charms into wiles in his own mind . . . Paulet's instructions were clear: Mary's imprisonment was to be transformed into the strictest possible confinement.[7]

In addition to keeping Mary under ever-tightening confinement at Tutbury Castle, Paulet would also play a significant role in installing a communication intercept system at Chartley Hall. When completed, this system will monitor and control Mary and her supporters' information flow after her arrival in late December 1585.

## Thomas Phelippes—Master Cryptographer and Forger

Thomas Phelippes, a Master of Arts graduate from Trinity College, Cambridge, and fluent in French, Italian, and Latin, was recruited by Walsingham in 1578 and assigned to the then English ambassador to France, Sir Amyas Paulet. Initially providing encryption and decryption services for Paulet, he was responsible for running high-value agents out of the English embassy and distributing cash to French Protestants (Huguenots) to support their resistance to French Catholic demands for national religious orthodoxy. Phelippes was sent back to France in July 1582 for approximately eight months.[8]

By the mid-1580s, Thomas Phelippes becomes Walsingham's *de facto* deputy for intelligence operations and undisputed go-to person for England's most sensitive intelligence operations. In autumn 1585 and before the announcement about Mary's relocation from Tutbury Castle to Chartley Hall, Cecil directs Phelippes and Paulet to surveil the area around Chartley Hall. The fruits of that trip will result in what would later be known as the "beer keg" plot and will, in the end, help provide evidence proving Mary directly participated in treacherous acts against Elizabeth.[9]

## Thomas Morgan

By the early 1580s, Thomas Morgan had become one of the most influential figures in the Catholic English-exile community. He was also considered Mary's chief factotum and a central figure behind the effort to remove Elizabeth from her throne. The First Secretary and Lord Treasurer believe that gaining direct access to Morgan will also put them in an ideal position to influence and manipulate Mary through her chief intelligencer.

Pursuing that objective, Cecil and Walsingham convince Elizabeth that Morgan is the primary culprit behind the Throckmorton and Parry Plots and cajole Elizabeth to issue an extradition order to bring Morgan back to England for prosecution. In March 1585, Morgan is arrested and held in the Bastille while legal arguments for extradition begin.

Two months later (May 1585), "Walsingham order[s] Paulet to open the letters sent to Mary by Castelnau the French ambassador in London, to read them and deliver them opened to his prisoner [the Scottish Queen] being held at Tutbury Castle."[10] Morgan expresses great concern over Walsingham's order and its implications. Faced with the responsibility of protecting Mary, yet physically isolated and unable to direct day-to-day Catholic activities, he waits for the right opportunity to reconstitute secure communications with her.[11]

## Robert Poley and Gilbert Gifford—Double Agent/Provocateurs

The opportunity Morgan is seeking arrives in the persons of Robert Poley and Gilbert Gifford. Consummate confidence artists, both men play significant roles in the eventual entrapment of Mary Stuart. Using cover stories to explain their presence in Parisian circles, Walsingham tasks them at different

Figure 13.2. Thomas Morgan. Artist: Ronda Penrod. Reproduced by permission of Ronda Penrod

times between late summer 1585 to late summer 1586 to exploit Morgan's difficulty communicating securely with Mary. First, from the summer of 1585 to early December of that same year, Poley will assist in reconstituting the means to communicate with Tutbury Castle.[12] Then, from January 1586 until the Babington conspirators' capture in the late summer, Gifford will carry messages to and from Mary's new place of incarceration, Chartley Hall.

Robert Poley earned his reputation as a prison informer in the early 1580s. Walsingham believes Poley has the potential to be an intelligence agent and recruits him in April/May 1585. While Walsingham is never entirely comfortable with Poley, he uses him to effectively gain access to two vital conspiratorial centers of gravity—the communication system from Paris to Tutbury

Castle via the French Embassy in London, and later, Anthony Babington's group of conspirators in London.

Poley's future success in influencing and manipulating those he encounters results from Walsingham's ingenious plan that will place him in direct contact with Mary's chief intelligencer languishing in the Bastille. At first, "Morgan [does not] trust Poley, the man's demeanor [is] unsettling, and in recommending him to Mary, he propose[s] that she should test Poley's loyalty."[13] Initially, Poley will act as an intermediary between Morgan and one of his old Catholic acquaintances. However, after convincing Morgan of his loyalty to Mary's cause, Morgan accepts Poley into the Catholic conspirators' fold. Winning Morgan and Mary's trust by establishing a more secure communication link between Paris and Tutbury Castle, Walsingham will give Poley an even more sensitive mission once Mary and her entourage move to Chartley Hall.

Gilbert Gifford had a much different background from Robert Poley. He was part of a well-known Catholic family, a kinsman of Francis Throckmorton, and cousin to Dr. William Gifford, a lecturer at a Catholic seminary in Rheims. Gifford traveled to Rome in the late 1570s, entered a seminary for English priests, was expelled for bad conduct, wandered around Paris, and in 1585 met Thomas Morgan and John Savage. It is Savage who later volunteers to assassinate Elizabeth. Gifford eventually attains a letter of introduction to Mary Stuart and agrees with Morgan to support the Scottish Queen.

Unbeknownst to Morgan, Walsingham co-opts Gilbert Gifford, who then offers to assist Morgan as a courier for Mary's new secure communication network at Chartley Hall. In the end, Morgan's acceptance of Gifford as the primary message carrier between the conspirators in Paris and the Scottish Queen's new place of imprisonment is a situation that even Walsingham thinks is too good to be true.[14]

## John Ballard

"But [there was] another man as important as Babington in what became the greatest of Elizabethan conspiracies, and the one that in the end destroyed the Queen of Scots. What historians know as the Babington Plot could so easily have been called the Ballard Plot instead." Stephen Alford, *The Watchers,* Page 208

After the failure of the Throckmorton Plot, Ballard replaces Charles Paget as the primary Catholic field agent in England and Scotland. Armed with an earlier papal approval to assassinate Queen Elizabeth, Ballard will return to Paris and meet with Thomas Morgan, Charles Paget, and Spanish Ambassador Bernadino de Mendoza to discuss new plans to invade England. With their tacit approval, Ballard will begin recruiting a coalition of like-minded supporters dedicated to overthrowing Protestant rule in England. An earlier event will also play a significant role in this most recent attempt to develop a post-Throckmorton Plot conspiracy. Ballard will witness a series of exorcisms conducted outside London. At one of these religious rituals, he will meet a young man named Anthony Babington.

## Bernard Maude—Double Agent/Provocateur

Bernard Maude is "cut from the same cloth" as Robert Poley. No stranger to impoverishment, he is drawn to exploiting people to enhance his economic status. Maude received his Bachelor of Arts degree from Trinity College, Oxford, in 1566. As a servant in the Archbishop of York's household, Maude falsely accuses the archbishop of religious unorthodoxy. He threatens to divulge that information if the prelate refuses to give him money. Much to Maude's chagrin, his blackmail attempt fails, and Maude is sentenced to three years in prison in the summer of 1582.[15]

While scouring the numerous prisons searching for informants to support his expanding intelligence capabilities, Walsingham finds Maude a likely candidate for his intelligence operation against a new conspiracy forming in Paris. As a result, Walsingham releases Maude before his sentence is completed and brings him into his intelligence service c. 1585.

## Anthony Babington

Like Thomas Morgan before him, Anthony Babington spent time in the Earl of Shrewsbury's household before traveling to France in 1579. During this trip, he impressed Morgan and agreed to spread Catholicism and liberate Mary from prison. Upon his return to England in 1582, Babington carried letters to Mary from the French embassy in London and assisted in distributing prohibited Catholic literature during the height of the Throckmorton Plot. Babington was identified by Giordano Bruno alias Henry Fagot (a Walsingham mole in the French embassy in London) as a Catholic sympathizer and letter courier. In late 1584, John Ballard,[16] who begins spearheading the new conspiracy's development, observes Babington and several of his fellow companions while attending a Catholic exorcism in England.[17]

## Robert Poley—Babington's "Iago"[18]

Although never fully trusting Poley, Walsingham values his extraordinary ability to exploit opportunities as situations quickly change. As the Babington Plot matures, a new communication system at Chartley Hall is activated. Because Poley's role in supporting Mary's ability to communicate from

**Figure 13.3. Anthony Babington. Artist: Ronda Penrod. Reproduced by permission of Ronda Penrod**

Tutbury Castle is no longer necessary, Walsingham redirects Poley to penetrate the coterie of Anthony Babington in London. Poley accepts the challenge, and by the spring of 1586, becomes a trusted confidant of Babington.

## John Savage

Savage, a former law student at Barnard's Inn, joined other English Protestant exiles at the Jesuit seminary in Rheims, France, between 1581 and 1585. Before his seminary studies, he was a soldier in the Duke of Parma's army fighting Protestant resistance in the Low Countries. According to a colleague at Barnard's Inn and the Spanish camp, "he [Savage] was an excellent soldier, a man skillful in languages, and learned besides." [19]

While at the Catholic seminary, he becomes a fanatic believer in the idea of regicide espoused by Dr. William Gifford—a popular lecturer at the seminary.[20] Gilbert Gifford, a fellow student, described Savage as "one of the best companions, and best conditioned, besides a very good scholar, practical and pliant in company as ever I knew." [21]

While attending classes in Rheims, Savage is exposed to the growing student interest in the subject of regicide and embraces Dr. Gifford's philosophy that killing royal tyrants was a legal, justifiable act. During the summer of 1585, Savage swore an oath in front of the two Giffords—William and Gilbert—that he would serve the Catholic cause by killing Queen Elizabeth. Returning to London in autumn of that same year, Savage begins additional legal studies at Barnard's Inn and waits for further directions from Paris. He receives instructions in March 1586 when John Ballard commences a series of trips between Paris and London, furthering the new conspiracy's cause.

## Gilbert Gifford—"Jack of all Trades"

Like his fellow partner in crime, Robert Poley, Gilbert Gifford will play a significant role by using his unique versatility in executing activities critical to Cecil and Walsingham's deception operation's success. Throughout the Babington Plot evolution, Gilbert Gifford juggles an array of challenging tasks with the aplomb of a master deceiver and manipulator.

Having established credibility with Thomas Morgan, Ambassador Châteauneuf, John Ballard, and Mary Stuart, Gifford freely roams various Catholic centers of gravity in Paris and London. He delivers Mary's messages, visits the residences of key Catholic supporters and sympathizers, cajoles John Savage to adhere to his vow to assassinate Elizabeth, intermingles with Babington and his devoted followers, and coordinates events with John Ballard. He even finds time in Paris to write an anti-Jesuit pamphlet with another Walsingham agent, Edward Grately.

Gilbert is a ubiquitous character whose presence in both Protestant and Catholic circles is accepted by friends and foes alike. Like Poley, Walsingham and Cecil consider Gifford's access to information and the numerous Catholic centers of gravity a truly fortuitous situation.

## Charles Paget

A close friend of Thomas Morgan, Paget, like Morgan, believes it is his duty to support all activities associated with the liberation of Mary Stuart. "What is more, there was growing evidence of the part Paget had played over some years in the carrying of letters between the French and Spanish ambassadors in London and Mary, Queen of Scots, in Derbyshire and Staffordshire."[22]

Charles Paget was also directly involved in other plots against Queen Elizabeth and Protestant control of England. The Guise faction in Paris and Spain's King Phillip II supported his efforts.

During the Throckmorton Plot, Paget secretly traveled to England to gather information on potential invasion landing sites and assess Catholic support for the planned Guise/Spanish invasion. However, before the Throckmorton Plot's collapse, Paget returned to France to design another similarly constructed conspiracy later called the Babington Plot. In that effort, Charles Paget will play a significant role in planning and coordinating new attempts to unseat Elizabeth.

### Thomas Rogers (alias Nicholas Berden)— Collector/Watcher

Nicholas Berden is one of Walsingham's most prolific producers of "actionable" intelligence. He is a Catholic convert who worked for Walsingham in Rome. Berden was in a Roman prison for a short time due to suspicions by fellow students who questioned his commitment to Catholic orthodoxy. However, after declaring his renewed dedication to the old faith, Berden was released and returned to London in late 1583. By the summer of 1584, Walsingham employed Berden as a prison informer to determine the extent of Catholic resistance in England and abroad.

During his time in prison, Berden befriends numerous Jesuits. Following his release, he returns to France in August 1585, where the exiled English Catholic community readily accepts him because of what they perceive to be his strong Jesuit connections. He writes his first report from Paris in early August 1585, noting the theological and philosophical divisions in the English Catholic exile community. Berden's most significant contribution provides Walsingham with the names of refugees favorable to Catholicism and those with access to the English court. He also discovers that Catholic exiles, with support from the new French ambassador in London, have created a postal arrangement that circumvented English letter inspection and censorship protocols.

While in Paris, Berden is introduced to Morgan, who asks for help to open a secret correspondence channel with Mary.[23] Morgan then sends Berden back to London to further promote the Catholic cause. But, hoodwinking Morgan, Berden instead provides Walsingham critical information that will assist the First Secretary in keeping track of conspiratorial activities in and around London.[24, 25]

## THE COURSE IS SET

The development of Walsingham and Cecil's Indirect Preemption strategy during the 1570s provided the First Secretary with the means to respond to this new Paris-based conspiratorial threat. By January 1586, Walsingham's deception implementation plans were effectively in place.

First, Cecil's efforts beginning in September 1584, coupled with the officially sanctioned Bond of Association by Parliament in March 1585, provided the legal means to execute anyone, including Mary Stuart, guilty of activities intended to harm Queen Elizabeth.

Second, by March 1585, Mary's exclusion from negotiations determining Scotland's future government caused a complete break in relations with her son, James VI. As a result, Scotland remained under England's sphere of influence, with Protestantism becoming Scotland's official religion. As a consequence, Mary's stature in the eyes of Scottish Catholics was significantly diminished.

Third, key Catholic conspirators and their centers of gravity in England and Paris had been identified, penetrated, and unknowingly compromised.

Fourth, in March 1585, while awaiting extradition back to England, Thomas Morgan was successfully isolated from his intelligence support structure due to his imprisonment in the Bastille.

Fifth, security around Mary was tightened, making it nearly impossible for her supporters to communicate with her. As a result, by the end of December 1585, Mary, like her chief intelligencer Thomas Morgan, was virtually isolated from the outside world.

And last, by the end of December 1585, Cecil and Walsingham's successful employment of deception tactics, techniques, and procedures against the Babington conspirators was about to reach fruition. With the Scottish Queen and her entourage now securely ensconced at Chartley Hall, little did she realize that her English captors were already in total control of her communications system. How ironic that in mid-January 1586, as the Scottish Queen expresses joy and a sense of newfound freedom after receiving her first secret communication in over a year,[26] Walsingham's intercept of those comments confirms that the system ("beer keg" scheme) designed to entrap Mary in treasonous acts is an unqualified success.

## NOTES

1. A group of foxes is called a leash or a skulk.
2. Mary Stuart was moved approximately twenty times before her execution in 1587.

3. Porphyria is an extremely rare blood disease caused by an overaccumulation of a protein in hemoglobin that carries oxygen in the blood.

4. Robert Hutchinson, *Elizabeth's Spymaster* (St. Martin's Press, 2006), 146–147.

5. By March 1585, Mary's letters to the French ambassador Mauvissière (Castelnau) confirmed her awareness of being excluded from the right to rule Scotland with her son James. *Letters of Mary Queen of Scots, Vol. II* (Henry Colburn Publisher, 1844), Pages 136, 143–144.

6. Anne Somerset, *Elizabeth I* (Anchor Books, 1991), 427.

7. Antonia Fraser, *Mary Queen of Scots* (Delacorte Press, 1969), 475–476.

8. It is possible Phelippes's return to the continent was due to Walsingham's concern that the Catholics were planning another attack on Protestant-governed England—rumors of the Throckmorton Plot. Phelippes, therefore, may have been sent to gather information related to the Catholic centers of gravity and fill intelligence gaps concerning the opposition's intelligence organization.

9. Charles Nicholl, *The Reckoning: The Murder of Christopher Marlowe* (Harcourt, Brace and Company, 1992), 106–108.

10. Hutchinson, 119.

11. By deliberately leaving the letters open, Morgan and Mary were purposely made aware that their "secure" communication channel to and from Tutbury Castle was compromised. Imprisoned and isolated in the Bastille, Morgan's ability to create a new, secure means of communicating with Mary was severely constrained.

12. This is the same communication channel that earlier in the year Walsingham not so subtly informed Mary and Morgan that Paulet was opening their letters.

13. Alan Haynes, *The Elizabethan Secret Services* (Sutton Publishing, 1992), 63–64; *Calendar of the Cecil Papers in Hatfield House: Vol. 3 (1583–1589)*, (Originally published by the Majesty's Stationary Office, 1889), Cecil Paper #170, 10/20 July 1585.

14. Cecil Paper #202, 5/15 October 1585.

15. Alan Haynes, 69–70; Alan Haynes, *Walsingham: Elizabethan Spymaster & Statesman* (Sutton Publishing, 2004), 153–154.

16. Anthony Babington described Ballard as "a man of virtue and learning and of singular zeal to the Catholic cause and your majesty's service." John Hungerford Pollen, *Mary, Queen of Scots and the Babington Plot*. Edited from the original documents in the Public Record Office (T. and A. Constable for the Scottish History Society, 1922), Introduction: "Ballard's Character," lxxix.

17. Ballard arrived from Rouen, France, in late 1584 and met Jesuit Father William Weston, who had become involved in a series of exorcisms. Protestants claimed that such actions were intended to convert people seemingly possessed with demons or mental issues to the Catholic faith. Weston's first exorcism was on William Marwood, a servant of one Anthony Babington of Derbyshire. This exorcism took place in the home of Sir John Peckham of Denham, Buckinghamshire, England. In attendance were Ballard, Babington, and several of Babington's friends who will later become involved in the Babington Plot. On 4 August 1586, Denham House was raided by Walsingham's agents, with most of its occupants arrested. Alan Haynes, *The Elizabethan Secret Service*, Pages 69–70.

18. In Shakespeare's *Othello* play, written c.1603–c. 1604, Iago is the main antagonist. A constant companion and friend of Othello, he is considered trustworthy, honest, and plain speaking. People around him call him honest Iago, but he really believes in cheating and lying to advance his self-interest. Motivated by underlying jealousy and hatred, Iago fabricates a story that will cause Othello to take actions that will eventually lead to his downfall and destruction. Although predating Shakespeare's play, Robert Poley proves to be the quintessential Iago to Anthony Babington.

19. John Hungerford Pollen, *Mary, Queen of Scots and the Babington Plot* edited from the original documents in the Public Record Office (T. and A. Constable for the Scottish History Society, 1922), Introduction: "Dupes," xliv.

20. William Gifford was a cousin of Gilbert Gifford who was also attending the seminary at the time. Francis Walsingham probably recruited Gilbert in 1585.

21. Pollen, xliv.

22. Alford, 173.

23. Poley had already gained access to Morgan in the Bastille and had offered his services to carry messages securely to Mary. Morgan may have been trying to expand his communication capabilities by also using Berden to assist Poley in solving his Paris to Tutbury Castle communication problem.

24. The fact that Berden managed to avoid arrest by one of Walsingham's leading priest hunters in London attests to the success of his cover story and operational tradecraft.

25. Stephen Budiansky, *Her Majesty's Spymaster: Elizabeth I, Sir Francis Walsingham, and the Birth of Modern Espionage* (Penguin Books, 2005), 150; Haynes, *Elizabethan Secret Services*, 47–49; Pollen, xl–xli.

26. Fraser, 482.

## Chapter 14

# "Only Time Will Tell"

*Tutbury Castle, Staffordshire*
*Christmas Eve, Pre-dawn hours*
*24 December 1585*

Everything appears to be in readiness as Sir Amyas Paulet surveys the bustling activity that is taking place in the torch-lit courtyard. The horse-drawn royal coach and other modes of transportation are in line waiting to take Mary and her retinue to Chartley Hall about fifteen miles west of Tutbury Castle.

For months Paulet has been working with Thomas Phelippes, Walsingham's right-hand man, preparing Chartley Hall for Mary's arrival. Both Paulet and Mary are relieved to be leaving the depressing confines of Tutbury Castle with its drafty rooms and odiferous halls that seem to create a cloying miasma that envelops everyone who lives inside its walls. However, Paulet feels a sense of disquiet that relocating Mary might have the unintended consequence of Elizabeth's rage against them if their plans to entrap Mary fail. Even worse would be Elizabeth discovering she was manipulated to act as an unwitting participant in a deception activity, thus jeopardizing her reputation. He fears Elizabeth's reaction could quickly become a tragic reality.

Nonetheless, he takes solace in knowing Elizabeth accepted the Lord Treasurer and First Secretary's cover story explaining why Mary should be moved from Tutbury Castle to the more accommodating Chartley Hall in Staffordshire. Cecil told Elizabeth that Tutbury Castle was long overdue for thorough cleaning after housing Mary and her people for over ten months. Elizabeth also sees Mary's relocation as a public relations move that will please both Protestant and Catholic subjects. Furthermore, it will portray Elizabeth as a merciful, tolerant, and forgiving Queen willing to overlook Mary's transgressions against her.

What Elizabeth and Mary believe regarding Mary's relocation no longer matters to Paulet at this point. Instead, his immediate concerns are about the new communication penetration capability he and Phelippes had

**Figure 14.1. Chartley Manor House; engraving, nd [1653–1686] (print). The William Salt Library, Stafford, UK © William Salt Library / Bridgeman Images**

developed earlier at Chartley Hall and whether their efforts will achieve the desired outcome.

If successful, this new capability will penetrate, control, and exploit Catholic message traffic between the French embassy in London and Mary's new location of incarceration. It had taken Paulet and Walsingham's intelligencers nearly a year's worth of valuable resources and numerous deception executions to come to this crucial point in the evolution of Walsingham's deception plan. Paulet, aware that his new communication system at Chartley Hall was untested under actual conditions, fears that if it proves to be unreliable, the years spent preparing for Mary's demise will be for naught.

Mary, with her staff and their baggage, slowly departs from Tutbury Castle. Paulet draws his horse alongside his royal prisoner's coach to set the pace of travel to Chartley Hall. In the rhythm of his mount's measured gait, Paulet has many questions on his mind that will, hopefully, have answers once Mary settles into her new place of residence. But, as Tutbury Castle fades from view, Paulet knows the die is cast, and only time will tell if his all-consuming worries about failure are justified.

*Chartley Hall, Staffordshire*
*Christmas Eve, Sunset*
*24 December 1585*

Mary stands at the window gazing at the unfamiliar countryside below from her new, comfortable accommodations. She has difficulty believing that she is finally free from her past year's loathsome residence at Tutbury Castle. It is almost too good to be true. When told by her jailor, Sir Amyas Paulet, she would temporarily reside in Chartley Hall while Tutbury Castle undergoes a yearly "airing," Mary immediately has a new sense of hope and optimism.

Unbeknownst to Mary, Walsingham intentionally made her recent imprisonment at Tutbury Castle a purgatory-like environment to further erode her already failing health, morale, and psychological stability. Moreover, her sense of physical isolation, deprivation of basic amenities, and loss of royal privileges had significantly increased with each passing month.

Mary reflects on the many indignities she has endured. For months, she has suffered a vise-like constriction in her daily life. Intrusive security measures, reduced servant staff, restricted access to anyone not approved by her custodian, and total control over her activities have all created a living hell. She feels she is suffocating and at her wit's end!

As the waning winter sun begins to set in the West, Mary muses that perhaps this unexpected move to Chartley Hall will be the ideal location from which to seek revenge on her royal cousin for the injustices she has had to endure. Should the opportunity arise, payback will indeed be sweet!

*Chapter 15*

# Points of Failure

"The best laid schemes of mice an' men, gang aft agley. An' lae'e us nought but grief an' pain, For promis'd joy!"

—Robert Burns ("To a Mouse, on Turning Her Up in Her Nest With the Plough," November 1785, Stanza 7)

## WEAK LINKS

Sir Francis Walsingham knew his plan to establish an effective message intercept operation at Chartley Hall depended entirely on the credibility of the information flowing through that system. Given the responsibility to develop a means of intercepting communications before Mary's move from Tutbury Castle to Chartley Hall, Phelippes and Paulet—architects of the intercept system—were sent on a fact-finding mission to Staffordshire in autumn 1585. They discovered that Chartley Hall lacked its own beer brewing facility and, therefore, required a weekly delivery of that libation from Buxton upon Trent, a small village located approximately ten miles from Chartley Hall. Based on that serendipitous revelation, an ingenious plan unfolded.[1]

### The "Honest Man" and the Double Agent

Gifford, earlier in the year, had been recruited to work for the English. In early December, Walsingham briefed Gifford on the new intercept system's status and assigned him the role he would play when the system became fully operational. Following his meeting with the First Secretary, Gifford met with Thomas Phelippes, who provided more details about the beer keg scheme. Phelippes then directed Gifford to contact the brewer from Buxton.[2]

Phelippes and Paulet found that the Buxton upon Trent brewer was reputed to be a Catholic sympathizer and could easily be bought for a price to carry letters to and from Chartley Hall.[3] Gilbert Gifford contacted the brewer and convinced him he (Gilbert) was working for Morgan. Subsequently, the brewer agreed to seal all messages in a waterproof pouch and place them in the bunghole of a beer keg. When a message transfer cycle was activated, the brewer was told he would be contacted by a "secret party" (Gilbert Gifford) that a message would be forthcoming.[4]

## First Signs of Trouble

Paulet's disdain for Catholics combined with Walsingham and Phelippes's experience dealing with the vagaries inherent in the bribing and "running" of adversarial sources, especially double agents, had undoubtedly harbored grave concerns about the trustworthiness of both the brewer and Gifford. However, considering the importance of the mission and the irreplaceable role that each would play in the critical intercept process, they initially chose to take the risk of relying on these two dubious characters.[5]

Nevertheless, Paulet's concerns persisted. Sir Amyas opined that "The brewer, in his new position of importance, was taking full advantage of the situation behaving in a thoroughly offhand manner—calling for more money and then breaking appointments." Mary's jailor was also irked "by [the brewer's] breezy attitude."[6] Voicing his growing concern about the brewer's questionable reliability, Paulet wrote:

> The 'honest man' plays the harlot with this people egregiously, preferring his particular profit and commodity before their service . . . The house where he dwells is distant from here only ten miles, and yet, I do not remember that he has delivered at any time any packet to this queen until six or seven days after the receipt . . . He appoints all places of meeting at his pleasure, wherein he must be obeyed, and has no other respect that he may not ride out of his way, or at the least, that his travel for his cause may not hinder his own particular business.[7]

Paulet's misgivings about Gilbert also grew as the tempo of activity increased between the French embassy in London and Chartley Hall. Given the current "chain of custody" message flow, Sir Amyas suspected that messages Gifford was assigned to carry from the French embassy to Phelippes and then on to the brewer were very susceptible to information tampering. In addition, Paulet informed Walsingham that Gifford occasionally gave him contradictory answers about certain aspects of a particular message.

To assuage Paulet's concerns,[8] Walsingham, Paulet, and Phelippes jointly conducted a baseline assessment of the message traffic through the Chartley

Hall communication system. They identified a glaring weak link during that process, potentially making the entire scheme vulnerable to compromise and Catholic manipulation. They determined that messages to and from Chartley Hall changed hands nine times in each direction. One of those nine transfers involved a direct exchange between Gilbert Gifford and the Buxton brewer. To reduce the risk of Gifford and "the honest man's" possible chicanery, Walsingham and Phelippes added a tenth and eleventh risk-mitigating exchange. Paulet would now review all messages before being passed from the brewer to Mary. Alternatively, Paulet would read Mary's messages immediately before the brewer passed it to Gifford. As a result, Paulet and Phelippes were always in position to verify the authenticity of the messages forwarded by Gifford and the brewer.

## The Unwitting Cousin

By April 1586, with message traffic between the French embassy and Chartley Hall accelerating, Gifford was no longer able to devote all his time as Walsingham's letter courier to and from Chartley Hall while fulfilling myriad other tasks Walsingham had assigned him. Accordingly, Gifford requested that Paulet provide him an assistant to carry the letters when Gifford was out of the country. Gifford recommended his cousin, Thomas Barnes, be his stand-in.

Bowing to the importance of keeping their intercept mechanism running without interruption, Walsingham, Phelippes, and Paulet reluctantly agreed to Gifford's request. Avoiding the potential risk of compromising the entire intercept system at this critical moment, Gifford received approval to contact Barnes who agreed to act as a proxy for Gifford sometime between 20 April and 16 May 1586.[9] With the extra chain of custody security measures integrated into the "beer keg" system sometime earlier, no discernible problems occurred.

## Chain of Custody

*From the French Embassy in London to Chartley Hall*

- Gilbert Gifford picks up encrypted letters at the French embassy in London and delivers them to Thomas Phelippes for decryption. After the hand-off to Phelippes, Gifford then proceeds to a designated location in Staffordshire. If Thomas Barnes is the courier, he delivers the letters to a "trusted intermediary" who then passes the letters to Phelippes for decryption. Like Gifford, Barnes will immediately proceed to a designated location in Staffordshire to await the letters' return.

- After Phelippes decrypts the letters and makes copies for Sir Francis Walsingham, Arthur Gregory[10] reseals the original encrypted letters and returns them to Phelippes. Phelippes then sends the resealed letters via express rider to Gifford or Barnes in Staffordshire.
- Upon receipt of the resealed letters, Gifford or Barnes passes them to "the honest man" who, in turn, shows them to Sir Amyas Paulet.[11]
- After carefully examining the letters, Paulet returns them to "the honest man" who then inserts them into a secret compartment in the beer keg. Upon delivery of the keg to Chartley Hall, one of Mary's secretaries retrieves the letters, decrypts the original encoded contents, and then gives the letters to Queen Mary.

# Chain of Custody Message Flow

(*Number of Times Message Changes Hands)

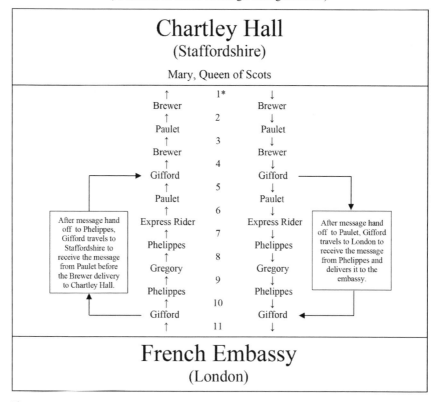

**Figure 15.1.**
Source: R. Kent Tiernan

## From Chartley Hall to the French Embassy in London

Generally, the same process occurred in reverse. However, in this case, once Gifford or Barnes passed the letters from Chartley Hall to their designated point of contact, they immediately proceeded to a predetermined location in London. After Phelippes completed decrypting the letters, copies were made for Walsingham. Gregory resealed the original letters handing them back to Phelippes who forwarded them via express rider to Gifford or Barnes waiting in London. Gifford or Barnes then delivered the resealed original letters to the French embassy.

## NOTES

1. Stephen Budiansky, *Her Majesty's Spymaster: Elizabeth I, Sir Francis Walsingham, and the Birth of Modern Espionage* (Penguin Books, 2005), 154–155.

2. Gifford will not return to Paris and report to Morgan on his task carrying letters to Mary from the French embassy in London until late January/early February 1586.

3. Based on his venal vulnerabilities, Paulet sarcastically referred to the brewer as "the honest man."

4. Robert Hutchinson, *Elizabeth's Spymaster* (St. Martin's Press, 2006), 121; Alan Haynes, *Walsingham: Elizabethan Spymaster & Statesman* (Sutton Publishing, 2004), 150.

5. Stephen Alford writes: "They [Walsingham and Phelippes] knew how valuable this operation was in divining the true intentions of the Queen of Scots." Therefore, the key to keeping their intercept mechanism secure would depend on how well they would be able to manage and monitor the suspect individuals responsible for moving communications to and from Chartley Hall. *The Watchers*, Page 203.

6. Alan Haynes, *Elizabethan Secret Services* (Sutton Publishing, 1992), 70; Haynes, *Elizabeth's Spymaster & Statesman*, 152.

7. Hutchinson, 125.

8. Gifford made his first message delivery to Chartley Hall on 16 January. Alison Plowden, *The Elizabethan Secret Service*, Page 94.

9. Stephen Alford, *The Watchers,* Page 203, states that the courier system proved remarkably successful—"somehow the system held together. More than this, in fact, it worked beautifully."

10. Robert Hutchinson writes that Gregory was adept at opening and resealing intercepted letters in such a way that the addressee would be unaware they had been tampered with. *Elizabeth's Spymaster*, Page 98.

11. Haynes, *Walsingham: Elizabethan Spymaster & Statesman* (Sutton Publishing, 2004), 158.

# PART FOUR

# (1585–1586)

Deception Planning Phases.

## Chapter 16

# Preparing the "Coup de Grace"

*"Man's mind is so formed that it is far more susceptible to falsehood than to truth."*

—Desiderius Erasmus (1466–1536), Dutch humanist and theologian.[1]

Being men of extraordinary foresight, Walsingham and Cecil knew from the very beginning that the success of their elaborate deception scheme was dependent on causing Mary and her Catholic conspirators to take actions that would ultimately lead to their demise. Thus, in pursuing an advantage over England's mortal foes, the First Secretary's emphasis on specific manipulative tactics shifts when the operation transitions to its final influence/provocation phase in early 1586.

For more than five years, Walsingham and Cecil have spent considerable time, effort, and government treasure allocating resources and identifying and penetrating the Catholic opposition's centers of gravity to gain access to key decision-makers. By this point in the evolution of the planning process, it is clear to both men that gaining access and then convincing those targets that their English agents are legitimate and loyal to the Catholic cause is essential to achieving the objectives they have set before them.

## JANUARY 1586—SETTING THE SCENE

"A strange circle of conspirators was formed, including a fanatical priest named Ballard, a desperado aptly called "Savage," and various young gentlemen with more money than brains. . . . The latest adherents to the plot, and the most ardent among the conspirators, were, it need hardly be said, Walsingham's spies, insinuated among the young idealists as provocative [influence] agents; for Walsingham designed, not only to keep himself fully informed as to what was

going on, but also, and above all, to jog the elbow of Babington the enthusiast."
Stefan Zweig, *Mary Queen of Scotland and the Isles*, Page 311.

By late January 1586, Thomas Morgan's isolation from his fellow Catholic exiles is now in its tenth month. Nevertheless, he is still considered the *de jure* coordinator and focal point for the Catholic secular, anti-Jesuit faction's more moderate stance against Elizabeth and personally responsible for the support and well-being of Mary Stuart. However, Morgan knows he must find a way to deal with two incredibly challenging situations—his inability to communicate securely with Mary and the rising tensions between the Jesuit and secular Catholic factions in Paris. Morgan undoubtedly must have felt some relief after learning that Mary was moving to what appeared to be a less restrictive location with more secure access to communications with the outside world.

(Walsingham's Agents in the narrative below are shown in brackets {})

The solution to Morgan and Mary's earlier communication blackout at Tutbury Castle was {Robert Poley}, primarily responsible for reconstituting the severely degraded communication system. "In January, Morgan and Paget wrote directly to {Poley} from Paris. They asked him to organize the delivery of a packet of letters to Mary, contact Lord Seton as a channel of communication to the Scottish King, and generally ensure that the Catholic party in England 'be encouraged and put to hope.' Also, "Morgan recommended {Poley} to Ambassador Châteauneuf as the 'fit man' to deliver a certain 'packet' to Scotland."[2]

By mid-January 1586, {Gilbert Gifford} delivers secret letters sent from Morgan and the French ambassador, Châteauneuf, to Mary at Chartley Hall—letters piling up at the French embassy in London for the past year. Gifford is freely moving between and within Catholic circles in London and Paris by the end of January.

Because of Morgan's incarceration, Charles Paget, by default, is considered by many English exiles to be the *de facto* clearinghouse for anti-Protestant activities emanating from Paris. With greater freedom of movement, Paget has more direct influence implementing Morgan's top three priorities: liberating Mary, replacing Elizabeth, and diminishing Jesuit influence on the current and future English Catholic activities.

Upon her relocation to Chartley Hall, Mary Stuart is overjoyed with her new communication system and commends Morgan for his outstanding work. At the same time, she expresses sorrow over his detention in the Bastille. However, Mary cautions all her supporters about the importance of protecting the integrity of her "new" communication capability at Chartley Hall. She also informs them that "she would accordingly communicate nothing of importance until she was sure the ambassador had received a new cipher, which she was enclosing . . . she begged him [Châteauneuf] too, to be on strict guard against the spies who, under cover of the Catholic religion, would be assiduously working to penetrate his house, and her secrets, as they had under his predecessor [Michel de Castelnau]."[3]

John Ballard, the driving force behind a revitalized conspiracy drawn from the remnants of the failed Throckmorton Plot, is in the process of whipping up enthusiasm and support for his new conspiratorial initiative. Upon learning that Dr. William Gifford refuses to return to England to coordinate the conspiracy from London, Ballard, with the concurrence of Morgan and Paget, is considering Anthony Babington as William Gifford's replacement to lead the plot from London.

Babington is back in London and often seen engaged in philosophical conversations with his coterie of similar-minded friends. They are frequently observed in public discussing the best way to serve the cause of freeing Mary Stuart from English imprisonment.

During summer 1585, after swearing an oath in front of Thomas Morgan, Charles Paget, and {Gilbert Gifford} to assassinate Queen Elizabeth, John Savage returns to London and takes up legal studies at Barnard's Inn. In January, Savage awaits further orders from Paris.

Since his humiliating expulsion from London due to his involvement in the Throckmorton Plot, the Spanish ambassador, Bernardino de Mendoza, is reassigned to the French court in Paris. In his new position, Mendoza's machinations against Elizabeth and her Protestant government become even more intense. The Spanish ambassador will liaise between the conspirators and King Philip II of Spain in the months to come.

From January 1586 onward, Sir Francis Walsingham, while sharing responsibilities with Sir William Cecil in developing and implementing their deception plan, masterminds the operation's final phase. An undisputed genius at manipulating human behavior, Walsingham will become personally involved in keeping Babington in place as leader of the London conspirators. Moreover, his in-depth knowledge of the Babington conspirators and their psychological vulnerabilities will give him significant leverage in exploiting future Catholic actions, behaviors, and decision-making processes.

## EXPLOITING PSYCHOLOGICAL VULNERABILITIES

"How Mary had pinned her hopes and prayers on the empty promises. [France, Spain, and Rome] had planned her escape, as well as how all these schemes had failed, were laid before Walsingham. He could see with absolute clarity where the chinks in Mary's armor were: whom she trusted and how she thought over the past two years." Francis Edwards, *Plots and Plotters in the Reign of Elizabeth I,* Page 254.

Harkening back to the writings of Thomas More and Niccolò Machiavelli, the First Secretary and Lord Treasurer know their endeavor will require an in-depth understanding of their opponent's psychological inclinations and manipulation vulnerabilities. In concert, their agents will also have direct, sustained access to their designated targets. Walsingham learned from his past experiences that access, proximity, and time are critical, interdependent variables of manipulation activities. He is also keenly aware of how difficult these variables are to control.

## The Static Targets

Both Mary and Thomas Morgan find themselves physically isolated from the general population, captive to the whims of their jailors, and severely limited when attempting to communicate with their fellow compatriots. Walsingham and Cecil were undoubtedly pleased with the results of their cleverly designed plan to create, manipulate, and exploit Mary and Morgan's increasingly fragile mental states.

Mary and her entourage's constant relocation during nearly twenty years of incarceration has taken a heavy toll on her physical and mental health. In addition, {Sir Amyas Paulet's} custodianship still constrains her even with her relocation to the more comfortable Chartley Hall.

Mary also reels from discovering that her son James VI renounced her and formed an alliance with Elizabeth. Considering her declining stamina, the Scottish Queen knows the chances of freeing herself from Elizabeth's clutches are becoming less likely. The endless cycles of exhilarating highs and devastating lows are increasingly making Mary desperate to escape.

Morgan's sequestration makes it difficult for him to find time-sensitive solutions to the critical challenges facing him and the Catholic exile community. His arrest in Paris and imprisonment in the Bastille could not have come at a worse time. Still recovering from the Throckmorton and Parry Plot failures, a growing split in the anti-Protestant community in Paris, and the lack of secure communications with Mary, Morgan's situation is about to be significantly improved by the very person who put him into prison, Francis Walsingham.

Walsingham, according to plan, presents both captives with ways out of their dilemmas. Mary's "out" is her unexpected relocation to Chartley Hall and access to a new communication network to the outside world. Morgan's "out" is twofold. First, {Robert Poley} offers to help him set up a new communication system for Mary at Tutbury Castle. Second, several months later,

{Gilbert Gifford} offers his assistance to help coordinate the new developing plot against Elizabeth. Both "offers" exemplify the genius of these two masters of deception, Cecil and Walsingham, proficient exploiters of human behavior and psychological vulnerabilities.

However, none of these psychological acts of jujitsu would have been possible without Walsingham and Cecil having convinced Elizabeth that Catholic threats were reaching critical mass, requiring more aggressive security countermeasures. And, without Elizabeth's support, Mary would not have been moved to Chartley Hall, and Morgan would not still be sitting in the Bastille awaiting extradition to England.

## The Wild Card

Following his self-imposed exile to France in 1581, Charles Paget becomes a target of interest for Walsingham. As co-leader of the Welsh—more secular, anti-Jesuit—faction, Paget looked to reconcile differences between recusant, moderate-leaning Catholics and Elizabeth's government. However, Paget's involvement in the Throckmorton Plot brought accusations from the Jesuit faction that Paget was trying to ensure the plot to invade England would fail. As a result, rumors surfaced he was in the employ of Walsingham.

On at least three occasions, Paget had contacted the First Secretary and the English ambassador to France. Each time he proposed that he return to England to serve the Crown. However, in each case, agreement on the terms of Paget's return to England failed to materialize.[4] These unusual *sub rosa* attempts by either party to reconcile Paget with his Protestant detractors, coupled with Paget's urgent need to recoup his sizable tax revenue losses caused by leaving England without a travel license, exposed both financial and psychological vulnerabilities that Walsingham could later potentially exploit.

## The Useful Idiot

New information received from {Gilbert Gifford} in late 1585 significantly changes Walsingham's focus on who will likely lead the London-based conspirators to support the planned Spanish invasion and subsequent removal of Elizabeth. The exiled English Catholic leadership in Paris initially chooses Dr. William Gifford, a distinguished professor of Philosophy at the English College in Rheims, to lead the dissidents in England. However, when confronted with the leadership opportunity, he fears his life will be forfeited should he return to England and adamantly rejects the offer. Gifford's refusal leads to a second choice, Anthony Babington, who Walsingham considers a better fit for his deception objectives. In his mid-twenties, Sir Anthony is "attractive in face and form, quick of intelligence, agreeable, and facetious.

But was inexperienced in the ways of the world and an unlikely man of action."[5, 6]

Walsingham knew of Anthony Babington's involvement to free Mary as early as the Throckmorton Plot in 1582. Identified by Walsingham's agents as a message courier to and from Salisbury House (French embassy in London) and a distributor of banned Catholic literature in England, the First Secretary chose not to arrest Babington. Instead, Babington was permitted to go free, unaware that he would be kept under constant surveillance by English intelligencers henceforth.

Failing to recruit Dr. William Gifford, Ballard, with Morgan and Paget's support, will begin pressuring Babington to be the London-based point of contact for coordinating future in-country conspiratorial operations.

### The Doctrinaire Firebrand

"With an unerring eye of a conspirator, John Ballard picked Sir Anthony Babington . . . as the catalyst by which the plot might be forwarded. Babington was rich, well-educated and well-traveled, as enduring a Catholic as he was an idealistic dreamer. The personable Babington was an easy prey for Ballard . . . "[7]

Having observed Ballard's activities since 1581, Walsingham and Cecil consider him a person of many moods and vulnerabilities. Through the iterative process of psychological profiling, the First Secretary concludes that Ballard is prone to believing only the information that supports his irrefutable commitment to advancing Catholic invasion plans. Consequently, he dismisses information contrary to his anchored biases out of hand. Walsingham will later successfully exploit this insight by influencing and manipulating Ballard's behavior.

Even as late as 9 July when the plot began to unravel and faced with "the unlikelihood of Elizabeth's Catholic subjects joining an open rebellion, [Ballard] 'with the terrible certainty of a religious zealot, perhaps as a result of an unrealistic believer in miracles, he refused to read the writing on the wall for his grand conspiracy.'"[8]

## PLACEMENT OF KEY ENGLISH DOUBLE
## AGENTS/PROVOCATEURS

By late 1585, the First Secretary had already positioned his three double agents near the key Catholic conspirators and their centers of gravity. Walsingham's skillful use of the {Poley}, {Gifford}, {Maude} triad will prove invaluable in sealing Mary Stuart's final fate.

## {Robert Poley}

After {Poley} successfully convinces Thomas Morgan that he, {Poley}, is committed to the cause of freeing Mary and provides a temporary communication fix at Tutbury Castle, his original mission for Walsingham is complete. Ironically, Mary's relocation to Chartley Hall offers both Morgan and Walsingham the opportunity to advance their conflicting objectives by putting {Poley's} talents to better use. Both chief intelligencers order {Poley} to stand down and await further instructions.

With the Babington Plot gaining momentum in March 1586, Morgan and Walsingham reactivate {Poley}, tasking him to become a member of Anthony Babington's inner circle. Unaware that {Poley} is working for Walsingham, Morgan believes {Poley's} presence in Babington's coterie will assist in advancing the conspiratorial effort while providing another means of keeping Morgan apprised of the London group's activities. At the same time, Walsingham believes {Poley's} penetration of the Babington group will give him near real-time information and insight into Anthony Babington's future decisions. As a result, each opposing leader now thinks he has gained a significant advantage over his counterpart.

## {Gilbert Gifford}

During the critical late 1585 to August 1586 time frame, {Gilbert Gifford's} work furnishes Walsingham with crucial information about the fluid situations in Paris and London. Gifford also provides detailed information about the opposition's decision-making processes and future intentions. Directly involved in a risky, stressful environment that both Catholics and Protestants scrutinize, Gifford manages to accomplish the following:

- Carried messages between Mary's supporters and Chartley Hall
- Convinced his English employers to accept his hand-chosen assistant who will move messages when {Gifford} is dealing with other more pressing tasks
- Attended sensitive Catholic planning meetings both in Paris and London
- Worked closely with members of the French embassy in London
- Encouraged the assassination of Elizabeth within the Babington group
- Liaised with the conspiracy agitator John Ballard while in England
- Carried out the wishes of Morgan, Paget, and Mendoza while in Paris

{Gifford} even finds time to travel between London and Paris to co-author an anti-Jesuit pamphlet with {Edward Grately}.[9] Ironically, Francis

Walsingham and the person Gifford has recently betrayed, Thomas Morgan, support Gifford's activity.[10]

## {Bernard Maude}

While searching the numerous prisons for informers to support his expanding intelligence network, the First Secretary spots {Bernard Maude} as a likely candidate to join his operation against the new conspiracy forming in Paris. Walsingham releases {Maude} before his sentence is complete and recruits him sometime in 1585.

By March 1586, {Maude} regularly mingles with Catholic dissidents at the Plough Inn in London, their pub of choice. Among those dissidents is Anthony Babington and his select group of *bon vivants*. When Ballard shares information on the plot with the Babington group during his first visit to the Plough Inn that March, {Maude} is also in attendance. "Ballard [is] completely taken in [by {Maude}]."[11] Consequently, he becomes Ballard's regular traveling companion and, in May 1586, accompanies Ballard to Paris via Rouen. In Paris, Ballard holds meetings with Paget, Morgan, and Mendoza to discuss the invasion of England.

By January 1586, Francis Walsingham holds a distinct advantage in understanding the Catholic planners' intentions, planning status, and operational focus. Aside from the fortuitous windfall of penetrating this important "center of gravity" with the recruitment of {Gilbert Gifford}, the First Secretary also successfully infiltrates Morgan's inner sanctum with three other well-placed double agents—{Robert Poley}, {Bernard Maude}, and {Nicholas Berden}.[12] These four in-place intelligencers provide Walsingham with valuable information about the conspirators' future actions.

Figure 16.1 shows the extent of English agent access to key Catholic conspirators. Walsingham's agents are now intercepting messages to and from Chartley Hall and reacting with countermeasures to Morgan's initiatives.

Now having the means to track, and in some cases, anticipate and co-opt Catholic conspirators' activities, Walsingham commences the penultimate phase of his deception operation—inducing the Catholic conspirators to unwittingly implicate Mary Stuart in a plan to kill Queen Elizabeth. England's chief intelligencer and his handpicked group of collectors, watchers, and double agent provocateurs will diligently work to attain that desired objective for the next nine months.

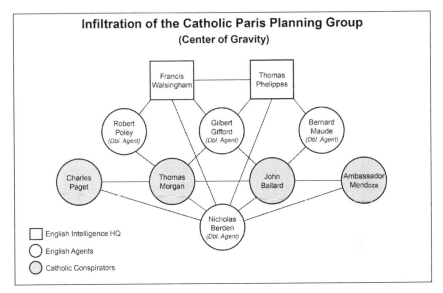

**Figure 16.1.**
Source: R. Kent Tiernan

## The "Influence" Attack Plan

Sir Francis Bacon, one of Walsingham's more famous intelligencers, is reputed to have observed that "people prefer to believe what they prefer to be true." Through his past experiences, Walsingham has also discovered that it was much easier to reinforce a person's preconceived notions and biases than change them. That combined insight will prove invaluable to his success in exploiting, controlling, and manipulating Catholic behaviors and actions. Possessing the means to track Catholic conspiratorial activities via the beer keg scheme, Walsingham launches his deception operation's most nuanced stage—introducing and reinforcing specific ideas into the Catholic conspirators' thought processes.

Based on his past personal experiences, Walsingham discovered that storylines must be believable, verifiable, and consistent over time to successfully influence his opponents into taking actions that would benefit the storyteller.[13] With this lesson in mind, the First Secretary directs {Gifford}, {Poley}, and {Maude} to advance and reinforce the following "stories" among the Babington plotters.

1. Babington's leadership is key to the conspiracy's success, and Mary depends on him to free her from English captivity. [*Objective:* Recruit Babington to lead the London group]

2. Mary's freedom and Elizabeth's demise depend on the steadfast support of the conspiracy's rank and file. Mary, without qualification, must approve and support the conspiracy. [*Objective:* Commit Mary to the plot]

3. The conspiracy will succeed because support for the scheme by English Catholics, Spain, France, and the Pope is overwhelming. [*Objective:* Inflate support for the plot]

4. Any delay in executing conspiracy activities will cause irreparable harm to the plot and the plotters' success. [*Objective:* Ensure the plan's momentum moves forward—Walsingham's most significant personal challenge]

The deception plan's success will depend, in no small part, on the storytelling skills of the puppet master himself, Sir Francis Walsingham, and his English double agent/provocateurs, {Robert Poley}, {Gilbert Gifford}, and {Bernard Maude}.

## NOTES

1. Source: Desiderias Erasmus Quotes, BrainyQuote.com, www.brainyquote.com/quotes/disiderias-erasmus-148976, accessed July 30, 2021.

2. Charles Nicholl, *The Reckoning: The Murder of Christopher Marlowe* (University of Chicago Press, 1992), 144–145; *Calendar of the Cecil Papers in Hatfield House: Volume 3, (1583–1589)*. (Originally published by the Majesty's Stationary Office, 1889), Cecil Paper #170, 10/20 July 1585.

3. Stephen Budiansky, *Her Majesty's Spymaster: Elizabeth I, Sir Francis Walsingham, and the Birth of Modern Espionage* (Penguin Books, 2005), 152–153.

4. One school of thought posits that direct contact between Paget and Elizabeth's senior officials is proof that Paget (and for that matter Morgan) was controlled by Walsingham [e.g., L. Hicks, S.J. *An Elizabethan Problem*; Francis Edwards, S.J. *Plots and Plotters in the Reign of Elizabeth I*; Patrick H. Martin, *Elizabethan Espionage*, et al.].

However, there are other plausible alternative explanations: 1) Paget's communications with Walsingham et al. may have been a contrived Catholic "dangle" operation designed to infiltrate Protestant English intelligence, 2) Walsingham may have attempted to "pitch" or recruit Paget to work for him; even if the recruitment failed Catholic knowledge of his communications with Walsingham would throw doubt on Paget's loyalty to the Catholic cause, or 3) Paget may have honestly offered himself as a double agent to the First Secretary, but was rejected. Regardless of the real purpose of the suspicious one-on-one contacts, by January 1586, Walsingham possessed the required insight into Paget's psychological proclivities to manipulate him to the deception operation's advantage.

5. Alison Plowden writes that Babington was "fatally lacking in the qualities which made a successful conspirator." *The Elizabethan Secret Service*, Page 97.

6. Robert Hutchinson, *Elizabeth's Spymaster* (St. Martin's Press, 2006), 125–126; Nicholl, 148.

7. Mary M. Luke, *Gloriana: The Years of Elizabeth I* (Coward, McCann & Geoghegan, Inc., 1973), 497.

8. Hutchinson, 137.

9. {Grately} entered the English college in Rome in 1579 and, while there, was recruited by English intelligence. During his time in France, he co-authored a book/ pamphlet of anti-Jesuit slanders with {Gilbert Gifford}. Walsingham, aware of the split within the exiled English Catholic anti-Protestant community, sought to further aggravate the tension between the two factions.

10. Cecil Paper #202, October 1585.

11. Hutchinson, 126.

12. Fearing that {Berden's} cover was about to be compromised, Walsingham recalled his double agent to England during the May–June 1585 time frame. Given a new responsibility for conducting surveillance of Catholic conspirators and their activities in London, he continued to receive English Catholic exile reports relevant to counter-Protestant intentions and courses of action.

13. Mr. William A. Parquette, Professor of Practice, Penn State University, former Strategic Planner for the Department of the Army, G3 Operations.

## Chapter 17

# Running the Conspirators to Ground

"War is first and foremost a psychological contest—specifically a mind game between a deceiver and a dupe. To play the game and win, one must be a con artist, a magician, or a deception analyst. To even understand this mind game, one must at least have a strong grasp of cognitive psychology, information warfare, intelligence analysis, or the like." Barton Whaley, 37th translation of Sun Tzu's *Principles of War*, Page 8.

In addition to successfully disseminating the four storylines designed to influence the Babington conspirators' behavior, the effectiveness of Walsingham's covert communications intercept system at Chartley Hall is the other critical factor that will determine Mary, Queen of Scots' final fate. This intercept system allows Walsingham to monitor the four narratives' degree of influence on the plotter's actions and intentions, including details concerning the conspirators' invasion plans.

Exploiting the advantage gained through his system's ingenious feedback loop,[1] Walsingham can quickly respond to unanticipated adversarial activities that fall outside the purview of his intelligencers' specific areas of responsibilities. On more than one occasion, from March through early August 1586, Walsingham will encounter unanticipated situations with consequences that, if not quickly addressed, will undoubtedly derail the last and most critical phase of the deception operation. Through it all, Sir Francis proves adept at keeping his influence/manipulation activities on track.

(Walsingham's agents in the narrative below are shown in brackets {})

Figure 17.1 depicts the importance of {Gilbert Gifford's} role and Thomas Barnes's unwitting assistance in ensuring that all communications with Mary

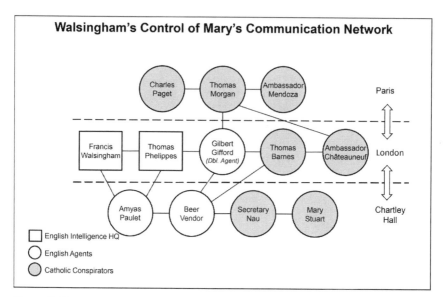

**Figure 17.1.**
Source: R. Kent Tiernan

Stuart from January to mid-August 1586 are delivered (via the beer keg vendor) and subsequently filtered first through Walsingham's intercept network. This ingenious system, developed by {Thomas Phelippes} and {Sir Amyas Paulet} several months before Mary's arrival at Chartley Hall, proves to be the crucial deception component that will implicate her in plans to assassinate Elizabeth I.

Walsingham knows that if he can monitor the Catholics on a near real-time basis, he will be one step closer to achieving his goal of entrapping the Scottish Queen. Imperative in making this happen, he creates the means to influence Catholic behaviors and activities that will ultimately condemn Mary by using her words against herself. To assist the First Secretary with this final influence phase objective, Walsingham calls upon his expert double agent/provocateurs to carry this effort to its successful conclusion. The message traffic on the following pages shows how Walsingham's ability to intercept Mary's correspondence and access to information from agents placed within the conspirators' centers of gravity will eventually lead to her indictment for high treason.

## OPERATIONAL EMPHASIS I: INFLUENCE

### 1. Recruit Babington to lead the London group

*September 1585*

With the last phase of the deception operation about to commence, Dr. William Gifford refuses to act as the conspiracy's London coordinator.[2] Walsingham's agents penetrate Thomas Morgan's Paris-based planning group and pass this information to Francis Walsingham. Walsingham, who has been collecting information on Babington since his involvement in the Throckmorton Plot, believes the impressionable, young, Catholic nobleman can be easily influenced and is vulnerable to manipulation, especially under pressure. Therefore, he concludes that the naive young man would be an ideal replacement for William Gifford.

{Gilbert Gifford} refuses Morgan's offer to replace the reluctant Dr. Gifford, but Gilbert agrees to assist the conspiracy in some other capacity.[3] As a valuable agent in place, {Gilbert Gifford} convinces Morgan it is more important that he, {Gifford}, supports the secure flow of message traffic to Mary's new location at Chartley Hall. {Gifford's} relatives also reside near Chartley Hall, making his suggestion to Morgan even more attractive.

*March 1586*

John Ballard travels to England to meet with Anthony Babington and some of his fellow compatriots. {Robert Poley} and {Bernard Maude} are present at the meeting. Ballard informs Babington and his group that there will be an invasion of England by Catholic forces and asks Babington and his friends to support it. Encouraged by Morgan and {Gilbert Gifford}, Ballard tours England's North counties to generate more Catholic support.[4]

By the end of March, a plethora of opportunities exist for Walsingham's agents to influence the selection of Anthony Babington as the leader of the London-based conspiracy. {Bernard Maude} is John Ballard's permanent traveling companion, {Robert Poley} is now Anthony Babington's closest friend and confidante, and {Gilbert Gifford} moves freely among Catholic conspirators in England and Paris.

*April 1586*

Morgan and James Beaton[5] send their endorsement of Babington as a loyal English supporter and recommend him to Mary.[6]

*May 1586*

Ballard returns to London after his trip to the North counties and Paris, where he assesses Catholic support for the invasion of England. Ballard discusses the invasion plan with Babington and pressures him into accepting the conspiracy leadership role in London.[7, 8]

## 2. Commit Mary to the Plot

*February 1586*

{Thomas Phelippes} is already intercepting and deciphering Mary Stuart's messages to and from Chartley Hall.[9]

*March 1586*

Morgan informs Mary Stuart about the conspiratorial plan designed to liberate her from her English captors. Morgan warns Mary to avoid doing anything that would cause her removal from Chartley Hall. He even advises her to strike up a more accommodating relationship with her jailor, {Sir Amyas Paulet}.[10]

Charles Paget provides Mary with more details about the invasion plan and vouches for {Robert Poley}. Paget and Morgan consider {Poley} a "loyal, trusted agent."[11]

Morgan receives new ciphers from Mary. She instructs him to send the ciphers to the Guise family, who will provide resources to augment the invasion forces. Morgan asks Mary to make funds available to advance her cause and compensation for her London-based supporters. In her message, Mary states that while she trusts {Gilbert Gifford}, she fears he might be discovered, "so great was {Paulet's} vigilance."[12]

*April 1586*

Morgan informs Mary of a new penetration technique to infiltrate Walsingham's activities and recommends {Gilbert Gifford} as a loyal subject who will assist in freeing her from English captivity.[13] {Gifford}, in turn, writes to Mary's personal secretary, Gilbert Curll, and affirms his loyalty to the Scottish Queen.[14]

*May 1586*

Mary Stuart receives planning details about the invasion force structure and logistics.[15] Paget sends a letter to her and commends Ballard's efforts to rally

English Catholic forces to take up arms should the foreign troops invade the kingdom.

In late May, Mary expresses her chagrin over the long delays between messages sent and received from those who wish to free her from captivity. She complains that the most recent message packet contained letters written between December 1584 to January 1586.[16, 17] Mary assures Mendoza of her support for the invasion of England, "promising to enlist her son, James VI's, help." She also urges Paget to remind the King of Spain to take immediate actions to launch the invasion.[18]

By the end of the month, Walsingham possesses evidence that Mary, Queen of Scots, is committed, in principle, to the invasion plan. However, he still lacks direct evidence that she supports the assassination of Elizabeth.[19]

*June 1586*

Morgan sends Mary a letter officially approving Babington as a reliable contact.[20]

## 3. Inflate Support for the Conspiracy

*April 1586*

With his traveling companion, {Bernard Maude}, Ballard returns to Paris and meets with Paget, Morgan, and Mendoza to determine the best plan for a successful invasion. After the conference, Ballard returns to London to talk to Babington and "begins constructing a new invasion plan." By this time, {Poley} is closely watching Babington.[21]

*May 1586*

During his visit with Anthony Babington, John Savage, {Bernard Maude}, {Robert Poley}, and Babington's circle of fellow conspirators, Ballard informs the group the invasion will commence in the summer and that Elizabeth will be assassinated.[22] He also informs the plotters that Mendoza promises to send sixty thousand Spanish troops to support the invasion. He conveys to Babington, Savage, and the other conspirators that he believes the Dukes of Guise or Maine would conduct the enterprise for France. For the Italian and Spanish forces, the Prince of Parma.[23, 24]

After his discussion with Babington, Ballard returns to Paris and provides Charles Paget his assessment of English support for an invasion. Paget takes Ballard to meet the Spanish ambassador, Bernardino de Mendoza.[25]

Mendoza informs the King of Spain about Ballard's belief that the time is right for an invasion of England, and the English Catholics in Paris are requesting military support from Spain. The Spanish ambassador assures Ballard of Spain's goodwill but asks Ballard for more details.[26]

Paget sends a letter to Mary and commends Ballard's efforts to rally English Catholic forces to take up arms should the foreign troops launch the invasion. Paget reports that Bernardino de Mendoza asks for a list of principal noblemen and knights in the north who will support the invasion and the best ports for landing troops.[27]

While Mendoza's request for more information is cautionary in tone, Paget conveys a much more enthusiastic position.[28] The disparity and diverse views of the two men allow Walsingham to leverage and reinforce Ballard and Paget's more optimistic assessment of English Catholic support.

John Ballard returns to Paris to discuss the plot in more detail. Ballard tells Mendoza that he has learned that Elizabeth is to be assassinated and wants to know the extent of Spain's assistance in supporting the invasion plan. Ballard believes Mendoza's reply is very supportive and encourages Mendoza to accelerate Spain's planning.[29]

Morgan and Paget reaffirm their support of Ballard's optimistic assessment of the magnitude and scope of English Catholic and Spanish support for the invasion.[30]

Ballard goes back to England, seeks out Babington, and begins modifying the plan's basic structure.[31]

At this point in the conspiracy, Walsingham's agent provocateurs have proven adept at taking advantage of Ballard's unshakeable belief (confirmation bias) that English Catholic and Spanish support for the conspirators' plan to invade England and liberate Mary is real and growing. Even though Mendoza is still not satisfied with Ballard's optimism concerning support from the North counties, Ballard, with {Maude} in tow, leaves London to reconfirm his earlier assessment of the situation.

## 4. Ensure the Plan's Momentum Moves Forward

Walsingham believes that success in achieving this pivotal objective will require the utmost delicacy and precision in his employment of the psychological manipulation tradecraft. He fears that failure to do so could appear that he is complicit in the Catholic conspirators' plan to assassinate Elizabeth.

To achieve Walsingham's ultimate objective of preventing Mary Stuart from usurping Elizabeth's throne, he must encourage the conspirators to assassinate Elizabeth: a disconcerting paradox certainly not lost on the First Secretary. His success in this precarious balancing act will depend on his situational awareness, sense of timing, and ability to react quickly to the information he receives on the plotters' intentions via his controlled "beer keg" communication system. He also knows that any misstep could have dire consequences for him personally (e.g., Elizabeth's death or her discovery that he had knowingly encouraged her assassination).

## April 1586

John Ballard becomes aware of John Savage's vow to assassinate Elizabeth and shares that information with Thomas Morgan, Charles Paget, and Spanish Ambassador Mendoza. Savage is in London, awaiting further instructions from Paris. Rumors abound that Savage's commitment to assassinating Elizabeth is wavering. {Gilbert Gifford} contacts Savage and pointedly reminds him of the vow he took a year earlier in front of Thomas Morgan and Charles Paget.[32]

At the Church of St. Giles-in-the-Fields in London, Savage conspires with Ballard to stir up sedition in the realm and murder Elizabeth. Savage again receives letters of encouragement from Thomas Morgan and {Gilbert Gifford} to act resolutely.[33]

## May 1586

Morgan and Paget continue the drumbeat of encouragement and urge Savage to remain steadfast in his commitment to the assassination.

While {Gifford} and Morgan urge Savage to fulfill his sacred vow,[34] Ballard addresses the issue of killing Elizabeth with Babington and proposes that Savage be the instrument to see it done. However, both men agree that the plot will have a better chance of succeeding if Savage is assisted in the task by five other gentlemen.[35, 36]

## June 1586

Babington enlists a group of associates he believes to be reliable. They discuss the best way to dispatch Elizabeth.[37]

By the beginning of June, Walsingham had to be pleased with his double agent provocateurs' results. At this point in the counter-conspiracy activities, all four influence actions were accomplished and in a relatively short period of time.

Catholics view Babington as the leader of the London-based conspirators. Mary is receiving updates about the conspiracy and associated invasion plans. Morgan, Paget, and Ballard believe that Spain, France, and English Catholic nobles located in the country's north are firmly behind the invasion. The momentum of the conspiracy itself appears to be moving forward at a steady pace.

Nevertheless, by late May 1586, events begin to show that a sense of doubt over the invasion plan surfaces among some conspirators and rank and file supporters in London.

## Early Signs of Skepticism

During their first meeting in May, Ballard attempts to convince Babington to lead the cause from London by sharing details of the invasion plan. Babington informs Ballard that he believes support for the invasion is weak.[38] At their second meeting later that month, Babington, after receiving assurances that support from English Catholic nobles and Spanish military forces can be counted upon, again voices his skepticism and states the following: 1) Catholics in northern England are too busy with their own affairs, 2) the invasion plan is a logistical nightmare, and 3) few Englishmen will rally against Elizabeth. Later, Babington shares information about the plot with his friends, who also voice their reservations.[39, 40]

## OPERATIONAL EMPHASIS II: CONTROL AND MANIPULATION

June marks a turning point in how the First Secretary will conduct the final phase of his deception operation against the Babington conspirators. In response to Babington and his supporters' noticeably diminishing enthusiasm, Walsingham is forced to do an about-face and adjusts and refocuses his intelligence assets.

From June onward, Walsingham will stay directly involved in manipulating the one individual who communicates details of the plan to Mary, Queen of Scots. That hapless, indecisive person, increasingly uncomfortable with his role in the conspiracy, is Anthony Babington. Walsingham's earlier decision to have his intelligencers encourage the conspiracy leadership to choose Babington as a plan coordinator from London is about to pay huge dividends.

In late June, Mary writes the following to Babington: "I have understood that upon the ceasing of our intelligence, there were addressed unto you from France and Scotland some packets for me. I pray you, if any, have come to your hands and be yet in place to deliver unto the bearer thereof who will make them be safely conveyed to me."[41]

Regardless of Mary's ego-stroking recognition of Sir Anthony's importance to her well-being, Babington begins to share his uncertainty about the plot with his new confidante and companion, {Robert Poley}. Aware of Babington's increasing desire to remove himself from the role he believes he had thrust upon him, {Poley} provides Babington with a solution, or an out, from his tenuous situation. {Poley} offers to use his connections to relieve him of his worries and concerns for a sizeable remuneration. He tells Babington that he worked in the household of Walsingham's daughter and son-in-law in his youth, and through the daughter, they ({Poley} and Babington) could secure a travel license from Sir Francis Walsingham to leave the country. Warming to the offer, Babington asks {Poley} to tell Walsingham that he (Babington) is willing to do Queen Elizabeth some service "by way of discovery in his travels." Walsingham replies with "many honourable speeches." Several days later, Babington asks {Poley} if he could help him "obtain a license for traveling." He also makes "general offers of service."[42]

{Robert Poley} arranges a meeting between Babington and Walsingham. Babington asks for a travel license to leave the country to pursue his personal interests.[43]

{Gifford} meets Babington to discuss the reliability of John Savage. Then, the conversation turns to the subject of Ballard's activities. Babington informs {Gifford} that his friends have "various hesitations"[44] about the conspiracy.[45] Based on his meeting with Babington, {Gifford} tells the First Secretary that Babington has two primary concerns. First, he is nervous about the very idea of killing Queen Elizabeth. Second, he is also uncertain about the other conspirators' level of commitment to carrying out such an act.

Figure 17.2 shows that double agents {Poley}, {Gifford}, and {Maude} have a tight interconnection with Babington and his supporters. These three

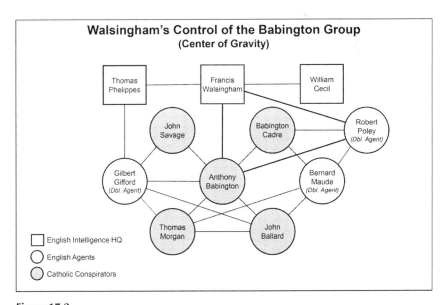

**Figure 17.2.**
Source: R. Kent Tiernan

double agents now provide Walsingham with up-to-date information about the Babington group's link to the conspiracy command and control center in Paris. The dark line between Walsingham, {Poley}, and Babington reflects the significant role that {Robert Poley} plays in bringing Babington to Sir Francis Walsingham. Babington is now in a "no-win" scenario, a situation that will ultimately lead to his execution and the execution of thirteen of his conspirators and friends, and Mary, Queen of Scots.

*July 1586*

## 1. Sir Anthony Babington—Puppet on a String

July proves to be an extremely unsettling month for Sir Anthony Babington. Believing that his life depends on aligning himself with the winning side, he knows he stands on shaky ground. His inability to choose to remain with the Catholic conspirators or offer his services and allegiance to Elizabeth leaves him in an uncomfortable state of limbo. However, little does he realize that the decision was never his to make. Babington's fate was decided for him long ago when he first got involved in the conspiracy and subsequent meetings with Walsingham. Hence, every action Babington takes will be under the manipulative control of Sir Francis Walsingham and his cadre of double agent provocateurs. Consequently, he finds himself pulled deeper into the quagmire of a conspiracy/counter-conspiracy life-or-death struggle.

On 3 July, through {Poley's} urging, Babington meets Walsingham at Barn Elms, the First Secretary's private residence. During this meeting, Walsingham implies he is aware of Babington's secret activities and encourages him to serve Queen Elizabeth. Afterward, Babington tells {Poley} that he is considering three options. He could 1) continue supporting the conspiracy, 2) withdraw from the conspiracy, or 3) leave the country. {Poley}, at first, vows his allegiance to his friend regardless of his final decision but then urges Babington to continue supporting the conspiracy.[46]

Walsingham calls {Gilbert Gifford} in for a crisis meeting with {Phelippes} and directs him ({Gifford}) to meet with Babington to encourage him to write in detail the invasion plan.[47]

That same day {Gilbert Gifford} visits Babington at the safe house kept by {Poley}. {Gifford} tells Babington that the invasion is now a certainty, and there is no time to consider leaving England. He insists that Babington must tell Mary about their plans to free her. {Gifford} reveals that Thomas Morgan is urging Mary to open a dialogue with Babington and that he (Babington) will likely receive a letter from her soon.[48] {Gifford} then recommends that

Babington prepare a ciphered response in advance, providing details of the invasion plan.[49]

Little did Babington know that the moment his letter to Mary leaves his hands, his usefulness as Walsingham's unsuspecting foil to undermine the Catholic conspiracy hangs in the balance. Babington's fate and that of his supporters are inexorably wedded to Mary's response to a message hastily written by Babington under pressure applied by {Gifford} and {Poley}. As Walsingham awaits Mary's reply from Chartley Hall, the First Secretary continues to dangle the lure of a travel license in front of Babington.[50, 51]

On 6 July, Walsingham reads Babington's letter to Mary. {Thomas Phelippes} forwards it to Mary two days later via the beer keg network. Walsingham then requests Babington to come to court to explain what services he could render the Crown if granted a travel license. They meet for the last time on 13 July.[52]

Four days later, Mary receives a letter from Morgan informing her that {Robert Poley} is providing him with information on activities designed to support Mary's liberation.[53]

On 13 July, Walsingham offers his possible approval for Babington to travel if he (Babington) agrees to serve against the Catholic dissidents. Babington leaves the meeting and seeks advice from a respected Jesuit priest, Father William Weston,[54] who cautions that "if you yield, you give up your religion, if you decline his offers, you inevitably incur the peril of death."[55]

## 2. Babington Buys Time

By mid-July, even after Babington informs Mary of the invasion plan and negotiates with Walsingham for his approval to leave England, he continues to "hedge his bets" over who he should support. He, like Walsingham, is trying to buy time. But unlike the First Secretary, he is waiting for the right moment to join the winning side. Knowing it will take him time to allay his concerns over the legality and moral certitude of conducting activities designed to assassinate a royal monarch, Babington commissions {Gilbert Gifford} to obtain answers "beyond the seas" to the following four questions:

1. Is the action of regicide directly lawful in every part?
2. Who will assure him of the legality of the act?
3. On whose authority is such an action granted?
4. Will those attempting such a dangerous act be rewarded?[56]

However, as fate would have it, Babington will never receive the clarification he requires. Overcome by unforeseen events, {Gilbert Gifford} leaves for Paris in late July but never returns to England.[57]

## 3. Walsingham Buys Time

If waiting for Mary's response to Babington's 6 July letter was not caus-
ing enough tension and impatience among Walsingham, {Phelippes}, and
{Paulet}, several unanticipated and potentially catastrophic events in early
July force the First Secretary to take remedial actions on-the-fly.

Three days later, Ballard returns from the North counties and Scotland with
discouraging news that Elizabeth's Catholic subjects are not likely to support
the rebellion. To make matters worse, the First Secretary learns {Maude's}
cover is compromised. The disclosure that he works for English intelligence
threatens to shut down the entire Catholic conspiracy.[58]

The next day, Ballard seeks out {Gifford} and asks for his counsel on
how to best deal with the issue of {Maude's} betrayal and lack of guidance
from Paris.[59]

On 12 July, {Gifford} reports to Walsingham that Ballard is angry about
Morgan and Paget's lack of communication. He threatens to return to France
at once, but {Gifford} convinces Ballard to remain in England.[60]

By mid-month, Ballard receives a letter from Morgan putting the conspiratorial plan on hold, especially the planned assassination of Elizabeth. In
frustration, Ballard procures a license from the French embassy to return to
France but changes his mind. {Gifford}, once again, convinces him to stay
in England.[61]

## 4. Delaying Mary's Response to Babington

Mary takes almost ten days deliberating on Babington's 6 July letter. On 17
July, she encourages Sir Anthony to proceed with the plan and asks him to
inform the Spanish ambassador in Paris of her decision. She also instructs
Babington to destroy her letter after reading it: "fail not to burn this present
quickly."[62]

{Thomas Phelippes}, via the "beer keg" communication intercept system,
receives Mary's reply the next day and makes a copy for Walsingham, who
informs Elizabeth about the particulars of Mary's response. From 22–28 July,
Walsingham puts a temporary hold on any further actions against the Catholic
conspiracy while he, {Phelippes}, and {Paulet} develop a plan to arrest the
key plotters.[63]

Meanwhile, Mary and Babington are unaware of Walsingham's decision
to delay Mary's response to Babington's 6 July letter. Mary writes Mendoza
of her communication with Babington. Previously informed by Morgan that
the conspiracy's success was possible if the Spanish moved quickly, Mary
tells the Spanish ambassador that she is fully aware of the invasion plan and
discusses ways to escape from Chartley Hall. Mary also laments past failures

to free her had dampened her enthusiasm, but she is now more optimistic that success is attainable.[64] However, Walsingham is now in possession of Babington's 6 July letter, Mary's 17 July reply, and her 27 July message to Mendoza. Walsingham finally has the "smoking gun" evidence required by English law to indict Mary, Queen of Scots, for traitorous acts against Queen Elizabeth I!

While Walsingham's team deliberates on how best to widen the net to capture as many Catholic traitors as possible, Babington finally receives Mary's response, sent eleven days earlier. She instructs him to destroy the letter, but he fails to do so. Babington later shows Mary's letter to {Poley}.[65, 66]

During the last two days of July, Walsingham instructs {Poley} "to move [encourage, persuade] Babington to deal with the principal practisers in the state," essentially telling the hapless leader to get actively involved with the plotters to kill Elizabeth. {Poley} and Babington discuss the plot in greater detail, and {Poley} advises Babington to visit the First Secretary and disclose the entire plot. He argues that if Sir Anthony reveals the conspiracy himself, he stands the best chance of receiving Elizabeth's pardon and Walsingham's favor. {Poley} informs Babington that Walsingham cannot see him right away but would make time for him several days later. However, Babington never receives an invitation to see the First Secretary again.[67]

## 5. Termination

Walsingham learned from his earlier involvement with the Ridolfi and Throckmorton Plots that timing is everything when closing down a counter-conspiracy operation. In the Babington Plot case, he understands many plotters will escape along with critical, incriminating evidence needed for legal prosecution if he shuts the operation down too soon. Thus, success will depend solely on Walsingham's intuitive sense of timing.

### August 1586

On 2/3 August, {Phelippes} asks Walsingham if Babington should be apprehended or "otherwise played with." Walsingham tells {Phelippes} "to wait one more day but no longer before moving against Babington." {Francis Mylles}, Walsingham's assistant and key surveillance officer (Watcher), and {Phelippes} receive information that Babington and others have taken new lodgings in London for operational security reasons. They prepare a warrant for their arrest.[68]

On 4 August, {Poley's} safe house is surrounded, and Ballard is arrested, yet Babington is free to leave. A round-up of the other conspirators ensues. {Poley} assures Babington that his earlier meetings with Walsingham will protect him from Elizabeth's retribution. {Poley} tells Sir Anthony that he will plead his case in front of Walsingham if he (Babington) offers his services to the Crown. However, hours later, {Poley} is also arrested.[69] Unnerved by Ballard's and now {Poley's} arrest, Babington finally realizes his close friend and confidante, {Poley}, has betrayed him and writes him a final letter:

> Robin . . . I am ready to endure whatsoever shall be inflicted . . . What my source hath been towards Master Secretary you can witness; what my love towards you yourself can best tell. Proceedings at my lodgings have been very strange. I am the same I always pretended. I pray God you be, and ever so remain towards me . . . The furnace is prepared to try my faith. Thine how far thou knowest.[70]

On 5 August, Walsingham updates Elizabeth on his counterplot against John Ballard and Anthony Babington.[71]

The conflicted, confused, and frightened leader of the London-based conspirators now joins his panicked band of English supporters and compatriots and flees for his life.[72] As for the main target of Walsingham's entire operation, Mary Stuart, while she is riding through the Staffordshire countryside under the watchful eye of {Sir Amyas Paulet}, is detained by the Crown's military guard and charged with treasonous acts against Elizabeth. They escort her to a nearby manor for further questioning before returning her to Chartley Hall. Shortly after that, Mary is transferred to Fotheringhay Castle, where she is tried, condemned, and executed on 8 February 1587.

## NOTES

1. A feedback loop is an integral part of a system where the process is analyzed, adjusted, reanalyzed, and readjusted as many times as necessary until the desired outcome is achieved. In this case, the Chartley Hall communication system is refined multiple times, discarding what does not work and making adjustments to achieve its operational functionality as intended by Walsingham.

2. John Hungerford Pollen, *Mary, Queen of Scots and the Babington Plot.* Edited from the original documents in the Public Record Office (T. and A. Constable for the Scottish History Society, 1922), Introduction: "Dupes," xlviii.

3. Pollen, Introduction: "Setting the Death Trap," xlix.

4. Alan Haynes, *The Elizabethan Secret Services* (Sutton Publishing, 1992), 70.

5. Beaton, the Archbishop of Glasgow, was an avid supporter of Mary and is her diplomatic representative in Paris.

6. Haynes, 74.

7. Under interrogation, Babington later claimed Ballard asked him to lead the conspiracy in early July. John Hungerford Pollen, *Mary, Queen of Scots and the Babington Plot.* II: Confessions and Examinations of Anthony Babington, Pages 56–57.

Babington's claim that he became the leader of the London conspirators in July is not accurate. Message traffic indicates he was the focal point of activity as early as the April–May time frame.

8. Pollen, II: Confessions and Examination of Babington, "Ballard Comes to Babington," 52–53.

9. Anne Somerset, *Elizabeth I* (Anchor Books, 1991), 426.

10. *Calendar of the Cecil Papers in Hatfield House: Volume 3, (1583–1589).* (Originally published by the Majesty's Stationary Office, 1889), Cecil Paper #256, 2/12 March 1586.

11. Cecil Paper #258, 31 March/10 April 1586.

12. Cecil Paper #260, 31 March/10 April 1586; Pollen, Introduction: "The Death Trap," lvii–lviii.

13. Cecil Paper #265, 14/24 April 1586.

14. Stephen Alford, *The Watchers: A Secret History of the Reign of Elizabeth I* (Bloomsbury Press, 2012), 202.

15. By the middle of May, Mary's replies were beginning to work their way through the system. Her initial responses made it clear that she sympathized fully with Queen Elizabeth's enemies.

16. This information confirms that Cecil and Walsingham's decision to tighten security while Mary was at Tutbury Castle beginning in January 1585 effectively delayed the flow of message traffic between Mary and her supporters. The letters are dated 7 December 1584; and 15 January, 20 February, 9 April, 20 July, and 28 July 1585; with the last letter dated 28 January 1586.

17. Cecil Paper #274, 10/20 May 1586.

18. Alison Weir, *The Life of Elizabeth I* (Ballantine Books, 1998), 363.

19. Cecil Paper #256, 31 March/10 April 1586; #260, 31 March/10 April 1586; #273, 19–29 May 1586.

20. Antonia Fraser, *Mary Queen of Scots* (Delacorte Press, 1969), 487.

21. Haynes, 70; Pollen, Introduction: "The Plotters Dispersed," cii.

22. Somerset, 427.

23. Many of the discussions are now taking place in {Poley's} living quarters, which acts as a safe house for the plotters.

24. Pollen, Introduction: "Ballard's Plotters," xcvii–xcviii.

25. Robert Hutchinson, *Elizabeth's Spymaster* (St. Martin's Press, 2006), 126.

26. Pollen, Introduction: "Ballard's Plotters," xciv.

27. Pollen, Introduction: "Ballard's Plotters," xcv–xcviii.

28. Cecil Paper #273, 19/29 May 1586.

29. Somerset, 426–427.

30. Pollen, Introduction: "Ballard's Plotters," xcv–xcvi.

31. Somerset, 427; Pollen, Introduction: "Ballard's Plotters," cii.

32. Haynes, 72.

33. Alford, 208.

34. Haynes, 77.

35. Given that {Maude} is in close contact with Ballard, and {Poley} is Babington's intimate companion, the decision to provide Savage with the assistance of five

other men was likely encouraged by the two agent provocateurs. They added this level of "insurance" to assure that the assassination would continue as initially planned regardless of Savage's wavering commitment.

36. Somerset, 427; Pollen, II: Confessions and Examination of Babington, "Dealings with Individuals," 58.

37. Somerset, 427.

38. Pollen, II: Confessions and Examination of Babington, "Ballard Comes to Babington," 53.

39. {Poley} and {Maude} were privy to these conversations and immediately relayed this information to Walsingham. Concerned that growing resistance and skepticism could derail his plan, Walsingham quickly realized that if the situation continued undeterred, the conspiracy's momentum could slow significantly, if not come to a complete halt. Should that happen before Walsingham received confirmation that Mary was complicit in a plan to assassinate Elizabeth, his primary objective would be seriously jeopardized. Paradoxically, by ordering his agent provocateurs to slow down the momentum of the Babington group's resistance to the original invasion plan, Walsingham kept their plan's momentum moving forward. This tactic would continue until 27 July when Walsingham finally acquires the irrefutable evidence that will eventually condemn Mary, Queen of Scots, for traitorous acts against England and the Crown.

40. Haynes, 76; Pollen, II. Confessions and Examination of Babington, "Ballard Comes to Babington," 53; Discussions with Salisbury, Tichborne, and Barnewell, 54–55.

41. Fraser, 487.

42. Stephen Budiansky, *Her Majesty's Spymaster: Elizabeth I, Sir Francis Walsingham, and the Birth of Modern Espionage* (Penguin Books, 2005), 162; Pollen, Introduction: "Babington's Plot," cxxiv.

43. Pollen, Introduction: "Babington's Activities," cxxiv.

44. Stephen Alford writes, "Babington's objections to the plan included the fear that an invasion would lead to either a massacre of Catholics in England or destruction of the Kingdom by foreigners." *The Watchers*, Page 208.

45. Haynes, 79.

46. Pollen, Introduction: "Babington's Activities," cxxv.

47. Alan Haynes, *Walsingham: Elizabethan Spymaster & Statesman* (Sutton Publishing, 2004), 159.

48. An English double agent provocateur alerting Babington to an event before the event occurs reveals how deeply penetrated the conspiratorial infrastructure had become. It also allowed Walsingham to anticipate and prepare countermeasures in advance of the actual event.

49. Haynes, 79.

50. John Hungerford Pollen, *Mary, Queen of Scots and the Babington Plot*. Introduction: "Mary's Letter Received and Answered," Page cxxxvii, points out a striking incongruity between what Mary wrote to Babington in her initial letter in late June and his unrelated response in early July. Pollen writes, "Babington's letter to Mary has no intrinsic connection with the letter from her. She had asked him to forward her

letters. He sends her a full plan of the campaign. It is indeed strange that a man, not very much used to writing in cipher, could have got this whole letter off during one day, having previously deciphered the letter from Mary." Yet, Hutchinson, *Elizabeth's Spymaster, Page 128 points out Babington's letter to Mary refers to details about force strength, ports of debarkation, forces required to defend those ports, and potential courses of action to free Mary and assassinate Elizabeth.*

If Pollen and Hutchinson's observations are close to the mark, perhaps what Babington wrote could very well have been influenced and dictated by {Gifford} or his not-so-close friend and confidante, {Robert Poley}.

51. On 5 July, Elizabeth and Mary's son, James VI, conclude a treaty between England and Scotland that will provide James a pension of four thousand pounds per annum. Francis Edwards, *Plots and Plotters in the Reign of Elizabeth I*, Page 133.

52. It is highly likely that by the time Mary responded to Babington's 6 July letter, she was aware of that political transaction. Her knowledge of that event may have been a key factor in Mary's decision to support the plan to assassinate Elizabeth. Alan Haynes, *Walsingham: Elizabeth Spymaster and Statesman.* Page 80, opines that Babington wrote a remarkable letter which on the wave of urgency, induced by his visitor ({Gilbert Gifford}), took him (Babington) further into a plot from which he hitherto held back through scruple and lack of powerful energy.

53. Cecil Paper #299, 10/20 July 1586.

54. Father Weston conducted an exorcism on one of Babington's servants in late 1585. After his arrest on 4 August 1586, Weston claimed that "many opportunities came in my way of conversing familiarly with this Anthony Babington, and of discussing affairs in general with him." His final conversation with Babington was immediately after Babington's 13 July meeting with Walsingham. While imprisoned and interrogated by his English captors, Weston was never indicted in the Babington Plot and died a free man in Valladolid, Spain, on 9 June 1615. *Two Missionaries Under Elizabeth,* edited by John Morris, Pages 183–186.

55. Pollen, Introduction: "Babington's Activities," cxxvi.

56. Pollen, Introduction: "Babington's Activities," clvii.

57. Upon his return to Paris, {Gifford} interviews Mendoza. While Walsingham and {Thomas Phelippes} later claim they did not know {Gifford} was in Paris, "Instead of inquiring whether Spain was ready, and showing that the English-Catholics could not rise til this was assured, he tells the Spaniard [Mendoza] that troops are not required, that the English are sure to rise, and inflames him [Mendoza] by every art to write to England in favour of the assassination. The letters, he [Gilbert] knew would be intercepted, and he, Gilbert, would secure a new triumph." Pollen, Introduction: "Gilbert and Mendoza," Pages clxxiii–clxxiv. The reason for {Gifford's} return to Paris remains a point of contention among historians. However, {Gilbert Gifford}, while in Paris, did continue to advance Walsingham's "influence" story about the English-Catholic nobles located in the north of the country and their strong support of the conspirators' objective to replace Elizabeth with Mary Stuart. Also, the fact that "Elizabeth and Walsingham promised in March 1587 to pension {Gifford} with 100 pounds annually for his loyal attention" supports the argument that he was still

working for Walsingham after his return to Paris in July 1586. Hsuan-Ying Tu, *The Pursuit of God's Glory*, Page 97.

58. When Walsingham writes Elizabeth telling her {Maude's} cover is compromised, he assures her that {Maude} had minimal impact on influencing Ballard's decisions. However, Edward Wyndsore (Windsor), during his conspiracy indictment, stated that when he decided to break with Ballard, {Maude} persuaded him to stay the course.

Walsingham's assessment of {Maude's} worth was probably an attempt to downplay the significance of his agent's "blown" cover to allay Elizabeth's concerns. John Hungerford Pollen, *Mary, Queen of Scots and the Babington Plot*. Introduction: "Babington Plot," Page cxviii.

59. Alan G. Smith, *The Babington Plot* (Macmillan & Co. Ltd., 1936), 156.

60. Pollen, Introduction: "The Catastrophe," cliv.

61. Pollen, Introduction: "The Catastrophe," clii–clviii.

62. Alford, 214.

63. Alford, 214–215, 217.

64. Cecil Paper #289, 29 June/9 July 1586, *Letters of Mary, Queen of Scots. Volume II* (Henry Colburn, Publisher, MDCCCXLIV, 1864), 178–179.

65. Mary's letter was delivered to Babington by a "homely man in a blue coat." Not surprisingly, that man worked for {Thomas Phelippes}.

The pressure on {Phelippes} to process message traffic accurately and expeditiously flowing to and from Charley Hall had to be staggering. Time once again became a critical factor as he, Walsingham, and {Paulet} had to quickly devise and employ tactics that would freeze the conspirators in place, unaware of their forthcoming arrests.

66. Alford, 214; Charles Nicholl, *The Reckoning: The Murder of Christopher Marlowe* (Harcourt, Brace and Company, 1992), 157.

67. Alford, 220; Haynes, *Elizabethan Secret Service,* 88.

68. Pollen, Introduction: "The Catastrophe," cl; Budiansky, 163.

69. {Poley's} arrest, combined with {Gifford's} unexplained escape to France in late July, could indicate these actions were part of a plan to maintain their cover stories. Later events would prove that they continued to work for English intelligence.

70. Nicholl, 158–159.

71. Hsuan-Ying Tu, *The Pursuit of God's Glory: Francis Walsingham's Espionage in Elizabethan Politics, 1568–1588* (Ph.D. Thesis/History, University of York, 93–94.

72. Babington is arrested on 14 August outside of London and executed on 20 September 1586.

# PART FIVE

# (1587–1590)

# Chapter 18

# "The End Is My Beginning"[1]

*Fotheringhay Castle*
*8 February 1587, 12:01 a.m.*

After months of unsuccessfully defending herself against accusations that she had approved traitorous activities to overthrow England's Protestant government and assassinate her royal cousin, Queen Elizabeth I, Mary Stuart awaits her fast-approaching execution at Fotheringhay Castle. Sleep eludes her as that fateful hour draws near. All she can do now is make peace with her God and prepare for the moment she will "slip the surly bonds of earth."[2] She also reflects on the recent events that condemned her to the executioner's block scheduled for 8:00 a.m.

Looking back, she never anticipated that escaping from the rebellious Protestant nobles in Scotland in 1568 and requesting sanctuary in England would condemn her to almost twenty long years of house arrest. Mary had always known that her relationship with Elizabeth was tenuous at best. Yet, she tried, albeit unsuccessfully, to negotiate an agreement with Elizabeth to safely return to Scotland, where she hoped to become her son's (James VI) regent. During her early imprisonment, Mary knew that her greatest nemeses, Sir William Cecil and Sir Francis Walsingham, were blocking her freedom from English control.

However, even at this late hour, Mary is steadfast in her belief that it was Walsingham and Cecil's unrelenting hatred of her and what she represented to Catholics in England and abroad that pushed her to the brink. The many years of manipulation, deception, and isolation took an emotional toll on her, eventually causing the catastrophic misstep of formally supporting a conspiracy to kill Elizabeth. Yes, her tacit approval of Babington's 6 July 1586 letter calling for Elizabeth's physical removal from governance was ill-advised. But, after nearly twenty years of confinement, failing health, and so many failed plots—Ridolfi, Throckmorton, and Parry—Mary believed her only hope for freedom rested with the Babington conspirators. Perhaps, if it were not for this one crucial misstep, she might have survived to fight another day for the return of Catholicism to England. In the end, she would never know that her trip to Fotheringhay Castle and rendezvous with the executioner's axe was not because of a poor, impulsive decision on her part. Instead, it resulted from Cecil and Walsingham's well-planned, strategic deception operation that began nearly seven years ago.

The time of her execution finally arrives. As she slowly walks with royal dignity toward the platform in the center of the Great Hall,[3] Mary wonders why, after the 20 November signing of her death warrant, Elizabeth persisted in displaying such hatred and contempt toward her. And, why, too, had Elizabeth kept her in such agonizing suspense for more than two and a half months only to divulge the execution date just hours before her execution.[4] Finally, she wonders why had Elizabeth and Amyas Paulet ignored her many pleas for mercy, disregarding her entreaties, and forbade any contact with senior members of her royal household, including, most importantly, her doctor and spiritual advisor.[5]

If Elizabeth's objective was to humiliate and hound her to the grave, Mary takes great comfort in knowing she never bowed to those cruel indignities. Instead, she would leave it to her God to judge Elizabeth's transgressions toward her.

Standing at the execution platform's bottom steps, Mary turns her thoughts from the temporal world to the spiritual paradise she is about to enter. In her heart, she hopes that her end will indeed portend a new beginning.

**NOTES**

1. Mary's royal motto.
2. From the sonnet, *High Flight*, written by John Gillespie Magee on 18 August 1941.
3. Robert Hutchinson writes "The scene that confronted her was dominated by the scaffold—a black draped, five-foot-high wooden stage, twelve feet wide, built alongside a large fireplace in which a huge log fire blazed against the raw, damp chill of the morning. A high wooden chair had been placed in one corner of the straw-strewn floor, but all eyes were quickly drawn to the squat block positioned at the opposite corner of the platform. The axe, the instrument of Mary's destruction, was casually propped up against the eighteen-inch-high rail that ran around three sides of the scaffold. The executioner Bull and his assistant, both masked and dressed in black gowns with white aprons, awaited their victim to one side. Despite the arrangements to keep the execution secret, word of what was happening had quickly spread locally. The hall was crowded with spectators of quality—the local gentry and their neighbors from adjacent counties—who came to see the morning's historical moment. The *hoi polloi*,

probably more than a thousand strong, waited shoulder to shoulder outside in the cold courtyard of the castle's lower bailey." *Elizabeth's Spymaster*, Page 191.

4. Hon. Mrs. Maxwell Scott, *The Tragedy of Fotheringhay founded on the journal of D. Bourgoin Physician to Mary Queen of Scots*, and unpublished MS. Documents (Sands and Company, 1912), 97.

5. Hon. Mrs. Maxwell Scott, 141–149.

# Chapter 19

# "The Queen Is Dead Long Live the Queen!"

*St. Olave Parish*
*Hart Street/Seething Lane, London*
*9 February 1587*

At last, it is done! Overwhelming relief washes over Sir Francis Walsingham as he gazes out the window of his house on Seething Lane, located within walking distance of the Tower of London. He thinks how ironic, yet how typically spiteful of Elizabeth, that she selected Lord Shrewsbury to inform the "monstrous serpent," Mary Stuart, of her execution date scheduled for the morning of 8 February. To further underscore her annoyance with Shrewsbury and his family, Elizabeth commanded Shrewsbury's younger son, Lord Henry Talbot, to deliver the news of Mary's execution at Fotheringhay Castle to her senior officials in London. Her vindictive actions simply reinforced his long-held belief that "the son inevitably bears the sins of the father."

A sardonic-like grin slowly spreads across the First Secretary's face as he recalls the gossip that spread through Elizabeth's royal court about the Earl of Shrewsbury's intimate relationship with that "devilish woman." There were also rumors that Shrewsbury's wife, Bess Hardwicke, was influenced by the very same person Elizabeth called "the worst woman in the world." It is now apparent to the First Secretary that Elizabeth believed these rumors. Moreover, her selection of the Earl and his son as her official "messengers of death" speaks volumes about the Queen's displeasure with the Shrewsbury family's past service to the Crown.

Upon further reflection, the First Secretary makes a mental note that unsubstantiated information, if repeated over an extended period and delivered from many different mouths, will eventually be treated as fact. He vows to fully integrate this valuable lesson of human behavior into his intelligencers' guidelines on deception tactics once he recovers from an illness that forced him from court to his country estate, Barn Elms, a month earlier.

Despite the uplifting news that his Queen and country's greatest domestic nemesis and beacon of hope for pro-Catholic forces is no more, Sir Francis remains emotionally conflicted. He feels a sense of overwhelming pride about accomplishing a unique and sensitive initiative that he and a small, select group of individuals developed almost six years ago. However, at the same time, Walsingham is experiencing pangs of uncertainty, unease, and concern. He wonders if the successful elimination of the most significant threat to the kingdom will create even more intractable problems at home and abroad that could threaten his status as First Secretary, Queen Elizabeth's reign, and England's Protestant religion.

He worries there could be dire consequences not only for himself but for Sir William Cecil and their other confederates should Elizabeth discover they had successfully carried out a deception operation against the Babington conspirators without her knowledge and approval. Unfortunately, Elizabeth's recent public display of unbridled fury over a separate but related issue has already resulted in Cecil's temporary banishment from court and Privy Council secretary William Davison's incarceration in the Tower of London. The First Secretary regrets not emphatically reminding them about Elizabeth's long history of vacillation and outright aversion to making high-risk/high-reward decisions, especially if she thought it could tarnish her reputation. Unfortunately, both Sir William Cecil and Mr. Davison are now paying the price for his forgetfulness.

Sudden panic grips him when he considers the possibility of what will happen if Elizabeth finds out about the existence of the deception plan. After taking a deep breath to calm himself, Walsingham makes it a top priority to reconfirm that the "Book of Secret Intelligences,"[1] containing detailed information of the counter-Babington plan, is still safe and secure from probing eyes.

Other questions begin to flood into the First Secretary's mind. For example, how will the English people respond to Mary, Queen of Scots' execution? Knowing that many English subjects are staunch Catholics, he wonders if Elizabeth's policy of compromise with the Catholics will be enough to continue to appease them, or would Mary's demise now lead to open rebellion?

There is also concern about Scotland, Ireland, Spain, France, and the Pope's reaction to Mary's removal from the world stage. Will the Catholic resistance threatening England since the Northern Rebellion increase in fervor and frequency, or will Mary's physical removal attenuate the clarion call to free the English kingdom of Protestant control? What effect will Mary's death have on the planned invasion of England by the Spanish Armada? How accurate are his secret service's intelligence reports that Spain's logistical support problems will delay the actual attack for at least another year? How much support can Elizabeth's government count on from the French Huguenots in repelling the Spanish when the invasion does come? Finally, how will Mary's elimination affect the future Tudor line of succession? With Elizabeth now well beyond her childbearing years, who will come forth as a viable, legitimate successor to ensure the Protestant faith's continuity in England and now, Scotland?

Despite the many unanswered questions, the First Secretary believes that the benefits gained by removing Mary Stuart—the *cause célèbre* for those wishing great harm to England—far outweigh the risk of inciting future attempts to assassinate his beloved Queen. He also takes great comfort in knowing that he plays a significant role in assuring Elizabeth and Protestant governance's survival and continuation.

Yes, the First Secretary is comfortable that history will affirm that his unswerving commitment to destroying the resurgent Catholic threat is right, honorable, and just. So, as Sir Francis Walsingham turns away from his window fronting Seething Lane, he silently prays that posterity will view his legacy in protecting his Queen, country, and religion in a favorable light. Moreover, he hopes future generations will judge his actions as an unequivocal endorsement of the Machiavellian principle—in matters of national survival, "the ends always justify the means."

## NOTE

1. "This [book] no longer survives, but from the other papers we know that it would have held the names of agents, the aliases, and the alphabets (or keys) to the codes and ciphers they used, and monies they were paid. These highly secret papers were locked away in the secretary's secure cabinets." Stephen Alford, *The Watchers*, Page 18.

# Chapter 20

# "Softly into the Light"

*Barn Elms*
*6 April 1590*

> "Tired with all these, for restful death I cry." William Shakespeare,
> Sonnet 66.

His time has finally arrived. The First Secretary has not felt such a sense of relief and personal calm for as long as he can remember. His frail body, racked with chronic ailments and energy-sapping pain, had been the reason for many of his absences from court.

As his mental clarity begins to fade, he reflects on the service he had provided his God, Queen, and country. Sir Francis takes solace in knowing that he and his friend and mentor, William Cecil, successfully defeated an implacable Catholic opposition whose objective was to extirpate Protestantism in England. Together they had taken on a multitude of national security initiatives and successfully deflected multiple attacks that unrelentingly threatened the gains they had worked so very hard to win. He was immensely proud and felt his God would judge him in a favorable light for that alone.

Throughout the years, Walsingham's relationship with Elizabeth was another matter that leaves him with a sense of discomfort bordering on resentment over how she treated him. While he always emphasized conducting his business based on principles rather than personalities, he wonders why Cecil appreciated his value and contributions to their kingdom's survival, but Elizabeth did not. She was an enigma, both frustrating to deal with and, at times, very infuriating during his time of service to the Crown. But he found ways to work around her indecisiveness, temper tantrums, and inability to act on essential matters with Cecil's help. However, there could have been additional accomplishments if she had been more flexible in her positions, especially when dealing with "matters of State."

What he could not countenance was Elizabeth's coldness and aloofness toward him. Even after he had taken to his bed for the last time, her note sent from court reminded him "to make speedy dispatch of [the] Irish business."[1] He would never truly comprehend why she had so often embarrassed him in court when she had the option of venting her displeasure with him in private. Why had she balked at approving his daughter Francis's marriage to Sir Philip Sydney when she considered Sir Philip one of her court favorites? Were his daughter and the Walsingham family not good enough?[2] Why had he never reaped the benefits of Elizabeth's royal patronage when others of lesser station and service to her realm had been given estates, land, and other lucrative gifts? Why had Elizabeth not forgiven the crushing debt of his son-in-law, Sir Philip Sydney, when Philip died supporting her war in the Low Countries? Didn't she know that her silence would leave him with an overwhelming debt obligation that could financially ruin him and the family he would soon leave behind?[3]

If she only understood that regardless of their differences, he had been unswervingly loyal and dedicated to protecting her and her reputation. Little did Elizabeth know that just several months earlier, with his health rapidly declining, he gave Cecil his official diplomacy papers, including specific information about England's relations with Spain. Simultaneously, to protect his sovereign from potential public and international ridicule and condemnation, he also gave *The Book of Secret Intelligences* to the Lord Treasurer for his safekeeping. This vital document contained detailed descriptions of the English intelligence organization's most sensitive, clandestine activities during Elizabeth's reign, including the Babington Plot. His sovereign would never fully appreciate that his and Cecil's long-range plan to execute her royal cousin, Mary, gave England the time to organize its military and limited resources to defeat the Spanish Armada a year and a half later.

Walsingham felt an odd sense of relief, knowing he had safely passed that information to his mentor and friend. This act alone lifted from his shoulders the onerous burden of hiding the fact that Mary was framed without Queen Elizabeth's knowledge.

Sir Francis suddenly feels himself being pulled into a gentle vortex with a bright light at the end of it. As he draws closer to that light, his thoughts about the long, troubling relationship he had with Elizabeth begin to fade. With each labored breath, Sir Francis realizes that it does not matter what people think of him. What is important is how he feels about himself and the service he rendered his Queen and country for so many years. As the warming light begins to envelop him, it becomes unquestionably clear that, in the end, his God alone will be the final judge of his actions. That merciful epiphany fills him with great comfort and peace as he loses consciousness.

At eleven o'clock on the night of 6 April 1590, those at his bedside recounted that it looked as if Sir Francis was serenely smiling as he drew his last breath.

## NOTES

1. John Cooper, *The Queen's Agent* (Pegasus Books, 2012), 322–323.

2. *Queen Elizabeth and Her Times,* a series of letters, Volume II, selected from the private correspondence of Lord Treasurer Burghley, the Earl of Leicester, the Secretaries Walsingham and Smith, Sir Christopher Hatton and most distinguished persons of the period (Henry Colburn publisher, 1838), 193–194.

3. Cooper, 228.

# Epilogue

## THE ENGLISH INTELLIGENCERS

Following Walsingham's death, William Cecil reluctantly assumed control of the intelligence service despite his other demanding government responsibilities.[1] However, the stressful years managing Queen Elizabeth's governance took a toll on his health. So, he transferred the sensitive documents entrusted to him by Walsingham to his son, Robert, enabling him to assume full control of the intelligence organization.[2] Faithful to Queen Elizabeth to the very end, Sir William Cecil collapsed at court and died a short time later at his London residence on 5 August 1598.

Francis Walsingham's passing left Thomas Phelippes—forger, cryptologist, and right-hand man—without direction and court sponsorship. Phelippes, essentially set adrift and economically insecure, was unnerved and disappointed, considering his vital role in ridding England of Mary Stuart. Two intelligence groups were now vying for Queen Elizabeth's favor. Phelippes decided to tie his future to Robert Devereux's (Earl of Essex) rising star at court by accepting a position on his burgeoning intelligence staff. A victim of poor judgment, bad luck, and Devereux's fall from grace, Phelippes not only lost his job as Essex's cryptologist but also forfeited his government pension. Penniless, he occasionally served time in various debtor prisons. When not in prison, Phelippes was employed by William Cecil from time to time to assist with intelligence tasks until Cecil died in 1598. With the ascension of Mary's son James VI, now called James I, to the English throne, William Cecil's son, Robert, continued to avail himself of Phelippes's services. However, because of alleged accusations that Phelippes was part of a plot to assassinate the King during a Parliament session, he spent four years in the Tower prison until he was finally cleared of all charges. Phelippes was the last living person directly responsible for Mary's execution. He died c. 1625.

Queen Elizabeth's pleasure with Sir Amyas Paulet's performance as Mary Stuart's jailor at Tutbury Castle, Chartley Hall, and Fotheringhay Castle did not go unrecognized. Less than two months after Mary's execution, Elizabeth appointed him to the prestigious position of Chancellor of the Order of the Garter. As a member of Elizabeth's Privy Council, he continued to support stringent actions against Catholic recusants. Between February and March 1588, he was one of four commissioners sent to the Low Countries to discuss relations with the Queen. Paulet died in London on 26 September 1588.

Gilbert Gifford's hasty departure to France several weeks before the arrest of the Babington conspirators garnered much speculation not only in Paris but London as well.[3] While outwardly continuing his support of the Catholic cause, Gifford also kept communicating with English intelligencers. However, as Mary's trial for treason unfolded, Morgan and Paget became suspicious of Gifford's loyalty. In late 1586, Gifford was ordained in the Jesuit order and officially entered the priesthood in March 1587. He was subsequently arrested in a brothel that same year and sent to the Bastille. However, when the Parisian authorities discovered he was a priest, Gifford was transferred six days later to the Bishop's prison, where he died in 1591 at the age of thirty-one.[4] The allegiance of Gilbert Gifford, the English double agent most responsible for the successful entrapment of Mary, Queen of Scots, remains a mystery today.

Robert Poley, unlike Gilbert Gifford, was swept up in the first phase of Babington conspirator arrests. After two years in the Tower prison, he was released.[5] From 1588 to 1601, he continued to be a prison informer and fulfilled duties as a special messenger to Denmark, the Netherlands, France, and Scotland. He was also implicated in the death of the poet and playwright Christopher Marlowe.[6] Robert Poley, the man instrumental in causing Anthony Babington and his cohorts' execution, faded into history. The date of his death is unknown.[7]

The ubiquitous Nicholas Berden returned to London several months before the Babington conspirators were "rolled-up" in August 1586 and frequently communicated with Catholic exiles until 1588. However, there is much speculation that he was forced to retire when his relationship with Walsingham became compromised in mid-March. "He [Berden] wrote the First Secretary to say he wanted to follow 'a more public course of life' and with Sir Francis's help, he seems to have secured a position at Elizabeth's court as 'Pourveyor of Poultrye,' for which he secured some kind of preferment."[8, 9] Like so many of his peers involved in Mary, Queen of Scots' demise, details of Berden's remaining years are unknown.

Thomas Barnes, the cousin of Gilbert Gifford and unwitting courier supporting the beer keg communication scheme, avoided prosecution for treasonous acts by agreeing to work as a double agent for Walsingham and

Phelippes. They tasked him to reestablish contact with Charles Paget and collect information on exiled English Catholic dissidents while feeding them disinformation about English political and military affairs. When not in London, Barnes also resided in Antwerp and Brussels. His last recorded contact with Phelippes was in February 1593. His final fate also remains a mystery.

## THE BABINGTON CONSPIRATORS

The first group of conspirators executed on 20 September 1586 included Anthony Babington, John Ballard, John Savage, Edward Abingdon, Charles Tilney, and Chidiock Tichborne. Those in the second group— Edward Jones, Henry Donne, Robert Gage, Thomas Salisbury, John Charnock, Jerome Bellamy, and John Travers—were executed the next day.

Thomas Morgan, Mary's former chief intelligencer, was released from the Bastille shortly after Mary's execution. Later, Morgan was expelled from France (believed to be an English spy) and fled to the Spanish Netherlands, where he was again imprisoned for another three years by the Jesuits who considered him a traitor to the cause. Released in 1593, Morgan drifted throughout Europe and eventually settled in Amiens, France. While there, he attempted to meet with the English ambassador in Paris to discuss reconciliation with the English Catholics but was rebuffed. He died in 1606.

Charles Paget moved to Brussels, where he provided services to King Philip II of Spain for eleven years. In April 1598, he contacted Thomas Barnes—now wittingly working for English intelligence—to discuss the possibility of returning to England should the political climate change with Elizabeth's passing. Following James VI's (Mary's son) accession to the English throne, Paget was permitted to return to England. Paget, considered by James to have been a loyal supporter of his mother, Mary, the newly anointed King, granted him a 200 pound per annum pension and repossession of his ancestral lands. Paget died at his Weston-on-Trent manor in 1612.

Bernardino de Mendoza, the Spanish ambassador who played an essential role in the Throckmorton and Babington Plots to remove Elizabeth from the English throne, remained in the French court until his resignation in 1591 due to ill health. By the time he returned to Spain, he had become completely blind and died in 1604 at the convent of San Bernardino in Madrid.

## NOTES

1. Sir William Cecil was the longest-serving minister of any Tudor monarchs, giving over forty years of his life to supporting that royal family's rule.

2. From the mid to late 1590s, Sir William and Robert would be seriously challenged by a new favorite in court, Robert Devereux, the 2nd Earl of Essex, who organized a competing intelligence organization. However, Devereaux's arrogance and insulting behavior finally led to his falling from the Queen's favor. Following a failed attempt to overthrow Elizabeth's supporters, he was executed at the Tower of London on Tower Green 25 February 1601.

3. Gifford's sudden departure from London has two possible explanations: 1) lacking a government warrant approving his double agent activities, Gifford feared he would be arrested as one of the conspirators and tried as a traitor for his role in advancing the Babington Plot, or 2) he was ordered to return to Paris before the arrests occurred to maintain his cover and continue to collect information on Catholic anti-Protestant activities.

4. Jesuits investigating Gilbert Gifford's activities after the failed Babington Plot found incriminating letters between Gifford and Thomas Phelippes. Father Robert Southwell, a Jesuit priest, was arrested by the English in 1592 and executed in 1595. He claimed the postmarks on those letters proved that Gifford was working for Walsingham well before the Babington Plot. John Hungerford Pollen, *Mary Queen of Scots and the Babington Plot.* III: Letters of Gilbert Gifford, Pages 118–130.

5. Walsingham had probably imprisoned his spy to maintain his cover for future purposes. However, as word of the failed Babington Plot reached Paris, suspicions of Poley's grew and his use as a double agent was lost.

6. In 1597, he was sent to Marshalsea to spy on the playwright Ben Jonson whose play *The Isle of Dogs* had upset his English leadership.

7. Charles Nicholl writes, "The last payment to him in the Chamber accounts is in 1601. At about this time, 'our well-beloved subject R.P.' was recommended for the post of yeoman-waiter at the Tower of London. This is perhaps Robert Poley, nearing fifty, being put out to grass. The post seems appropriate: a minor official in the enforcement business, comfortably quartered in his old haunt from the days after Babington." *The Reckoning: The Murder of Christopher Marlowe,* Page 337.

8. A poulter ran a large, important sub-department of the royal household. Berden's father, John, was a member of the Poulters' company before he died in 1591.

9. Stephen Alford, *The Watchers: A Secret History of the Reign of Elizabeth I* (Bloomsbury Press, 2012), 316; Robert Hutchinson, *Elizabeth's Spymaster* (Thomas Dunne Books, St. Martin's Press, 2006), 280.

# Postscript

Regardless of the vast separation of time between the Walsingham gambit, the successful Bolshevik "Trust" deception operation (1920–1927),[1] and post-WWI German rearmament (1919–1939),[2] the commonalities between these three operations offer a roadmap for creating and exploiting instability within an adversary's organizational infrastructure. Sir Francis Walsingham and Sir William Cecil's efforts to entrap and eliminate Mary Stuart and her conspiratorial supporters is an early historical example of a successful deception/influence operation against an existential threat. It is a cautionary tale relevant to today's world.

Elizabethan England, Bolshevik Russia, and post-WWI Germany, 1) faced existential threats to the future governance of their countries, 2) determined that non-kinetic approaches were the best courses of action to eliminate the threat, 3) identified, infiltrated, provoked, and influenced their opposition's priority targets and centers of gravity, 4) developed stories causing desired actions that would isolate and manipulate priority targets, and 5) used that the information collected from their target's responses to exploit and advance their primary goals and objectives. Elizabethan England and Bolshevik Russia also used the evidence collected on their targets' actions as justification to eliminate their priority target(s). (Mary and the Babington conspirators were tried and executed; the Bolsheviks conducted "show trials" followed by mass executions).

For a more contemporary strategic example, I highly recommend reading Thomas E. Mahl's *Desperate Deception: British Covert Operations in the United States, 1939–1944* and Jennet Conant's, *The Irregulars: Roald Dahl and the British Spy Ring in Wartime Washington.*

Finally, for those interested in examining more recent activities designed to deceive, influence, and provoke the United States at a strategic level, I suggest reading the Office of the Director of National Intelligence's 10 March 2021 public release of its Intelligence Community Assessment titled: *Foreign Threats to the 2020 US Federal Elections.* When more information is released to the public, it would not be surprising to find that much of today's adversarial deception, influence, and provocation tradecraft (excluding cyber tactics) will mirror similar activities used by Walsingham and English intelligence over 440 years ago.

## NOTES

1. For information on "The Trust," I refer you to three sources: 1) a document released under the Freedom of Information Act (FOIA) to the public by the Central Intelligence Agency titled *The Trust* edited and republished by the Security and Intelligence Foundation in 1989, 2) *Disinformation*, by Natalie Grant, Chapter 13, and 3) *Chekisty: A History of the KGB*, by Dr. John J. Dziak, Pages 47–50.

2. For detailed information on how Germany successfully violated the draconian restrictions imposed on the German military after World War I, Dr. Barton Whaley wrote an excellent study titled *Covert German Rearmament 1919–1939: Deception and Misperception.*

# Acknowledgments

I want to extend my gratitude and appreciation to the following people who provided me with the inspiration and encouragement that led to the completion of what I consider a more than eight-year "labor of love." Without their unswerving support, *"The Walsingham Gambit: Deception, Entrapment, and Execution of Mary Stuart, Queen of Scots"* would have only remained an idea. My sincere thanks to the following:

- Shirley Metcalf-Watkin who graciously introduced me to the beauty of England and its people. Charles and Daphne Henson, Chum, Tom, their wives, Doris and Mary, and Gregory Arms proprietors, Ruby and John, whose warm friendship and untold hours of conversation about the "Yank's" presence in Lincolnshire during World War II made me feel very welcome as a new student at Harlaxton Manor.
- Stanford University Overseas Program/Britain I Group—especially Ed Donaghy, Carolee Nance-Kolve, Don Cook, Dr. Karen Schweers-Cook, and Rick West. Through their friendship and mutually shared experiences, my love of England, its people, and my fascination with Tudor history took root.
- The late James Pfautz, Major General, USAF and Robert Lewis, Chief Master Sergeant, USAF, Ret., who, at a critical juncture in my life, supported me in leading a group of talented intelligence specialists responsible for identifying and analyzing foreign denial and deception activities.
- The late Dr. Barton Whaley, Dr. John Dziak, Dr. James Bruce, and Dr. David Thomas—friends, mentors, advocates, and trailblazers in the subject of deception; significant influencers in my interest in "the art."
- Dr. Lawrence Gershwin who gave me the opportunity to return to the United States Intelligence Community to continue my involvement in foreign denial and deception analysis and counter-deception tradecraft.
- A. Denis Clift, President Emeritus, National Intelligence University, who, in 2002, graciously accepted the idea of integrating a post-baccalaureate

Denial and Deception Advanced Studies Program (DDASP) into the university elective curriculum.

- Fr. Alexander R. Drummond who, when informed by Dr. John Dziak of my interest in the Babington Plot, provided his perspective on the subject and graciously sent me two books relevant to Mary Stuart's trial and final months at Fotheringhay Castle.
- William Parquette, colleague, confidante, and a loyal friend, who had a profound, positive impact on my tenure as Staff Director/Vice Chairman, Foreign Denial and Deception Committee (FDDC). His skillful management of the trailblazing DDASP significantly advanced the committee staff's educational outreach program and provided invaluable assistance in navigating this effort through the United States government pre-publication review processes.
- Debra Stanislawski and Michael Betts, two exceptionally talented FDDC staff deputies, who, from 2008 to 2014, successfully carried the FDDC "message" to the United States intelligence and national security communities.
- George Mitroka, James Anibal, and Dr. Warren Snyder, who, for twelve years, developed the DDASP into the most popular elective at the National Intelligence University.
- Randy Hack, a fellow aficionado of "the art," who could always be counted upon to support FDDC staff education and training initiatives, especially in matters relevant to the DDASP.
- Alberta Hickey, for eight years as my Executive Assistant, who kept bureaucratic and administrative distractions to a minimum so I could focus my energy and attention on the FDDC staff's mission objectives. Nona, you are the greatest!
- Richard Stimer, Colonel, USAF, Ret., and others dedicated to "the art" who graciously accepted me into their professional group of subject matter experts.
- Lee Livingston, who, when informed of my idea of applying a deception planning paradigm to the Babington Plot, encouraged me to turn that idea into a plan for action.
- Joel Thibault, daughters Erin Tiernan-Yeaman and Megan Tiernan-Porter, and son-in-law Brian Porter who patiently helped this seriously technology-challenged author.
- The North Preserve "Focus" Group hosted by Diana Edeline and attended by Tom McGoldrick, Susan Roth, George Sims, Joe Kowalsky, Neil and Phyllis Greenwalt, Sandy Heath, and John Thibault. This group participated in a brainstorming session to make the subject of an Elizabethan event and deception both engaging and readable for the general reading public.

- Dr. James Bruce, Dr. Michael Dues, Dr. Barbara McKay, Kim Pearce, David Bottini, Tom Smith, and Cherelle Power who encouraged me to continue with my literary endeavor suggesting subject areas requiring additional research and recommended several organizational changes to improve the manuscript's narrative flow.
- Ronda Penrod, who designed a unique book cover and artistic renderings of key people involved in the Elizabethan deception plan's evolution to destroy Mary, Queen of Scots. Her visual portrayals added greater context and human qualities to those individuals addressed in the narrative.
- Eugene Vamos who provided invaluable expertise when addressing copyright, public domain, and licensing issues.
- Michael Bayers for his unswerving support in editing and organizing my manuscript for the United States government pre-and post-publication review process, and his invaluable assistance in ensuring this manuscript complied with Lexington Book's publishing standards. As a result of our working together, we have become good friends from the very beginning.
- Lillian Grace Holechek-Tiernan, my loving mother, who was always proud of my life's achievements. If she were here today, I believe she would be pleased with my first literary endeavor, *The Walsingham Gambit*.
- Most importantly, my best friend, confidante, partner, and wife, Carole Sue, who has endured days and sometimes weeks of my emotional highs and lows as I wrote this manuscript over the past eight years. Through it all, she has been my rock and sounding board. She always brought me back to what I was trying to accomplish in the first place. I am and will be forever grateful for her calming influence, unswerving encouragement, and loving support.

# Appendices

"There is a principle which is a bar against all information, which is proof against all arguments, and which cannot fail to keep a man in everlasting ignorance; that principle is contempt prior to investigation."[1] Herbert Spencer, British Philosopher and Sociologist (1820–1903)

## NOTE

1. A fascinating study by Mr. Michael StGeorge titled *The Survival of a Fitting Quotation* argues that the true source is William Paley, English theologian and moral philosopher (1743–1805). StGeorge claims that the Spencer quote is a variant version of Paley's observation that "The infidelity of the Gentile world, and that more especially of men of rank and learning in it, is resolved into a principle which, in my judgment, will account for the inefficacy of any argument or any evidence whatever viz., contempt prior to examination."

# Appendix A

## *Deception Planner/Intelligence Analyst Insights*

Examining the events leading up to and during the Babington Plot through a deception planning and analysis lens leads to the following conclusions:

1. The threat of Elizabeth's removal from the English throne and reestablishment of the Catholic faith increased steadily from the late 1560s to the mid-1580s and created a heightened sense of urgency and forced Cecil and Walsingham to act aggressively against the threat both at home and abroad.

2. Protestant England's survival and ability to successfully defeat its Catholic opponents demanded an innovative change to its national security policy and reorganization of its intelligence service, especially after the Northern Rebellion of 1569, Pope Pius V's excommunication of Queen Elizabeth in 1570, and the St. Bartholomew Day Massacre in 1572.

3. Cecil and Walsingham were skilled intelligencers unequivocally dedicated to protecting their Queen, country, and religion. They were also ideally suited psychologically, emotionally, and intellectually to conduct a clandestine deception operation unbeknownst to Queen Elizabeth.

4. By the late 1570s to the early 1580s, Sir Francis Walsingham and Sir William Cecil accumulated a working knowledge of the Catholic conspiratorial "*modus operandi*." They discovered its critical centers of gravity (i.e., focal points of activity) and identified key opposition players in England and abroad.[1]

5. By the early 1580s, England's reformed intelligence organization had the capability to plan and execute a complex deception operation.

6. Concept development and planning phases of the English deception operation began in the early 1580s. Implementation and execution phases commenced c. 1583–c. 1584 using the Throckmorton and Parry Plots as "hiding in plain sight" cover.[2]
7. The scheme designed to entrap Mary required that Elizabeth be an unwitting participant in several key deception initiatives.
8. The official enactment of the Bond of Association, isolation of Thomas Morgan in the Bastille, tightening of security by moving Mary to Tutbury Castle, the irrevocable alienation of Mary from her son, James VI, and the successful control of her Chartley Hall communication network were tightly coordinated events designed to entrap Mary Stuart.
9. History recognizes Sir Francis Walsingham as the person responsible for Mary, Queen of Scots' demise, but facts tell another story—he had significant help from others.
10. Walsingham would not have succeeded in controlling the Babington Plot without the support of William Cecil, Thomas Phelippes, and Walsingham's three top double agent/provocateurs (Robert Poley, Gilbert Gifford, and Bernard Maude).

So, what was gained from such a bold deception/provocation operation whose sole purpose was to eliminate the symbol of Catholic resistance both in England and the European continent?

The idea's originators certainly understood that Mary's execution could have severe ramifications by potentially accelerating Catholic actions to replace Elizabeth and return the old faith to the English shores. However, given intelligence reports about significant delays provisioning the Spanish Armada and the lack of Catholic interest in using a retaliatory force for such an act, the First Secretary and Lord Treasurer determined the benefits of eliminating Mary far outweighed the potential negative consequences of such an action.

They also hoped that physically removing Mary would buy England the needed time to improve its military structure, readiness posture, and defensive capabilities before the Spanish invaded. Fortunately, England's marshaling its limited resources and the indecisiveness of Spain's leadership, coupled with some bad luck, were significant factors that led to the surprising defeat of the Spanish Armada in 1588.

As important to Cecil and Walsingham, Mary's removal and the successful defense of England against the Spanish invasion ensured that Elizabeth remained on her throne and Protestantism would continue to be the official state religion in the land. Yet, despite these highly satisfying victories, they proved to be short-lived.

**Figure Appendix A.1. Mary and son, James VI. Artist: Ronda Penrod. Reproduced by permission of Ronda Penrod**

Ironically, the negotiations that began with Scotland in 1584 to support the deception plan to entrap Mary by creating an irreconcilable rift between the young James VI and his mother laid the groundwork for James to assume the throne upon Elizabeth's death.

The fact that Elizabeth would be succeeded by the son of the very woman she had kept under lock and key for almost twenty years would have been a bitter pill to swallow had she known who would succeed her. With the passing of "Gloriana" in 1603, the Tudor dynasty would breathe its last and be replaced by Mary Stuart's ancestral line. Perhaps in a way, Mary, Queen of Scots, reigned victorious in England after all, and "The End Was, indeed, Her Beginning!"

## A Cautionary Tale: Deception Planner Perspective

For those countries that lack the ability to compete on an equal political, economic, and military footing, deception will continue to be their statecraft instrument of choice to level the playing field. Thus, it should be no surprise that the foundational knowledge required to apply such manipulative activities against a stronger adversarial opponent successfully has numerous historical precedents.

Walsingham's virtual hijacking of the Babington Plot is a poignant example of how an intelligence organization employing deception as the cornerstone of its operation successfully achieved its strategic objectives without firing a shot against an unsuspecting enemy. That favorable outcome resulted from Walsingham and Cecil's adherence to the following planning criteria developed during the 1570s to August 1586. As their deception planning evolved, they found that a successful outcome required at a minimum:

- A small, select inner circle of planners having a thorough knowledge of the deception plan (e.g., Walsingham, Cecil, and perhaps Phelippes and Paulet). A second tier of people implementing and executing specific parts of the plan but unwitting to their activity's actual purpose (e.g., Elizabeth I, Duke of Shrewsbury, Patrick of Grey, John Dee, and trusted intelligencers providing baseline target assessments and deception analysis). Finally, a contingent of people witting only to the purpose of their specific deception assigned tasks (e.g., Gifford, Poley, Maude, Berden)
- Restructured and expanded intelligence collection and analysis capabilities
- Clearly defined mission goals and objectives and "need to know" guidelines
- A bureaucracy-free command and control infrastructure that permits the deception leadership direct access to any person or situation involved in supporting the plan
- A strictly enforced physical and operational security plan
- Comprehensive enemy threat assessments and "friendly" deception planning and operational resource support capabilities evaluations
- An understanding of the target's focal points of planning activities and communication networks, identification of decision-makers, planners, and supporting players, the target's psychological vulnerabilities, and potential systemic points of failure
- Cover story development, event deconfliction, and coordination and centralized collected information focal points
- Extensive intelligence and subject matter expert support

## A Cautionary Tale: Intelligence Analyst Perspective

A conspiracy by its very nature is a deceptive activity. For intelligence analysts using multi-sourced information to determine truth, there is always the possibility that the acquired information has been manipulated to distort reality. If deception has historically provided an edge, or advantage, to the deceiver, what steps or measures can the targeted individual take to identify and counter such manipulation eventualities more effectively?

Detecting deception, like deception planning, is an artful endeavor. Unfortunately, no panacea will consistently uncover manipulative activities. However, there are various actions that, when focused on an opponent's "way of doing business," will significantly improve an intelligence analyst's ability to 1) determine what the adversary knows about your intelligence collection capabilities, 2) determine if deception is potentially at play, 3) if yes, characterize its construction, 4) identify exploitable vulnerabilities, and 5) take actions that will counter and mitigate the objective of the adversary's deception activity.

The development of deliberately structured analytical approaches to detect, characterize, and exploit deceptive activities simply did not exist in the 16th century. However, as Walsingham methodically organized his resources to confront the Babington threat, his requirements for comprehensive knowledge and insight into the plotter's "*modus operandi*" and exploitable vulnerabilities became his top analysis priority.

To meet Walsingham's mission goals, objectives, and deception planning requirements, his intelligencers provided the following information support and analytical products that significantly contributed to defeating the Babington Plot. In addition, Walsingham's collectors and analysts performed the following:

- Conducted comprehensive threat assessments of their Catholic opposition's conspiratorial and anti-Protestant activities
- Analyzed, developed, and updated their understanding of how Catholics developed conspiracies
- Identified and developed profiles on conspiratorial leadership and other individuals they believed would play significant roles in future plots against Elizabeth. The profiles included personal background history, interpersonal and communication skills, leadership styles, character flaws, and psychological biases and exploitable vulnerabilities
- Identified conspiracy planning centers of activity and their most vulnerable points of failure (i.e., traffic flow to and from the French embassy in London)

- Facilitated successful recruitment and penetration of Walsingham's double agents into the Babington conspiracy leadership
- Provided information that enabled Walsingham to use truth reinforcement and disinformation techniques to advance his operational goals and objectives
- Played key roles in controlling conspirators' communication channels and influencing enemy perceptions, decisions, and courses of action

Walsingham's analysts provided him with a critical window into the Babington plotter's leadership decision-making processes, systemic vulnerabilities, and individual psychological inclinations. Using that knowledge, Walsingham skillfully deployed his double agent provocateurs, who successfully manipulated the enemy and turned its manpower and resources against itself. Thus, instead of liberating Mary, the Babington conspirators unwittingly assisted the English intelligencers in sealing her fate at Fotheringhay Castle.

For today's practitioners and students of "the art," a comprehensive examination of the evolution of Cecil and Walsingham's deception plan against a more potent Catholic coalition force provides lessons that are relevant and essential to gaining the advantage against targeted opponents today. It would also behoove those interested in national security issues to heed these historical lessons for future situations requiring similar actions or countermeasures.

## NOTES

1. Baseline personality assessments of Walsingham, Cecil, Queen Elizabeth I and Mary, Queen of Scots, provided insight into their relationships with each other; their decision-making processes; strengths, weaknesses, and skill sets; leadership and management styles; and their psychological biases, vulnerabilities, and behavioral tendencies.

2. A timeline of Cecil and Walsingham's deception activities was developed using publicly released United States military deception planning templates, and WWII and post WWII deception examples (e.g., Operation Fortitude/Bodyguard, XX Committee's double agent program, Mincemeat, Desert Storm). Discussions were also conducted with experts who provided best estimates as to nominal times it takes to transition from the concept development phase to the execution of actual deception activities. The limiting factor of slow communication capabilities was also taken into consideration.

# Appendix B

## *Lingering Questions and Their Implications*

While conducting research for this book, I was struck by the many different explanations concerning some of the events relevant to the Babington Plot's development and evolution. Therefore, I offer my interpretations and answers to the following questions:

- Why isn't there more direct or "smoking gun" evidence to support the argument that Mary, Queen of Scots, was manipulated and eventually entrapped by a Walsingham and Cecil-designed deception operation?
- In the presence of the French Ambassador, Châteauneuf, in April 1586, Elizabeth implied she was aware of everything that was going on in her realm and already knew of the Babington Plot and the origins of Walsingham and Cecil's deception plan. What were the potential unintended consequences of such a public declaration?
- When was Gilbert Gifford, the key double agent provocateur influential in bringing down the conspiracy, recruited by Walsingham? If Gifford was already working for Walsingham, why did the English arrest him at Rye in early December 1585?
- What lessons can be learned from a study of the Stafford "Sham" Plot?

## I. The Missing "Smoking Gun" Evidence

"The Absence of Evidence is Not Always Evidence of Absence." Attributed to Martin Rees, British Cosmologist and Astrophysicist.

Unfortunately, many of Walsingham's papers, including those dealing with sensitive intelligence matters, disappeared after his death in 1590. "A great majority of intelligence reports were burned after they were read."[1] However, several renowned historians have also offered their thoughts on this subject.

Stephen Alford, *The Watchers: A Secret History of the Reign of Elizabeth I*, Page 264: "Just before his death, when he was too sick to carry out his duties, Walsingham handed Burghley (Cecil) his official papers on diplomacy, with special reference to England's relations with Spain. There was also *The Book of Secret Intelligences*." The contents of Walsingham's secure cabinets moved to Burghley's own.

Robert Hutchinson, *Elizabeth's Spymaster,* Page 258: "Burghley's staff must have made a frantic search amongst his papers to discover the identities and locations of his agents . . . Burghley's agents probably also combed through Walsingham's papers and sequestered a huge number of documents to protect the powerful and safeguard the reputation of Elizabeth's government."

Charles Nicholl, *The Reckoning: The Murder of Christopher Marlowe,* Page 221: "Walsingham's death created a vacuum at the heart of the English intelligence service. He succeeded in centralizing the business and getting government money for it, but much of this was due to his magnetic political skills, his compendious involvement in the network he had created. The disappearance of his files in the days following his death remains a mystery."

Alan Haynes, *Walsingham: Elizabethan Spymaster and Statesman,* Page 241: "His home was the safest refuge, and clearly as a house of State secrets, it offered rich pickings for the seekers after maps, position papers, diplomatic correspondence and cipher letters of spies. The finding of such papers at Hatfield suggests that a primary pillager was Robert Cecil, an admiring opportunist who looked to learn much from the man he was being groomed to succeed at some future opportunity. Whoever undertook the raid on the house, it was done with extraordinary alacrity."

Let us not forget there were no incentives whatsoever for the English hierarchy to disclose such potentially sensitive and incendiary information to the realm's subjects. Given Elizabeth's concern about maintaining her positive public image, it was not in her best interest to divulge that Mary was purposely set up to be executed, whether or not aware of William Cecil and Francis Walsingham's behind-the-scenes deception machinations. Likewise, Elizabeth's successor, James I, certainly had no interest in releasing information that would have made him vulnerable to accusations that he only gained the English throne by agreeing to his mother's death.

Of course, from the beginning, Walsingham and Cecil knew they would face severe retribution from the Crown should their activities be exposed either before or after Mary's death. Perhaps for these reasons alone, the documents relevant to the deception operation developed in the early 1580s were never available or permitted to see the light of day.

## II. Elizabeth's Discussion with the French Ambassador

*April 1586*

"You have much secret intelligence with the Queen of Scotland. But believe me, I know everything that is done in my Kingdom. Besides, since I was a prisoner at the time of the Queen my sister, I know what artifice prisoners use to gain over servants and to have secret information."[2] Thus spoke Queen Elizabeth to Ambassador Châteauneuf in April 1586.

Some historians claim this conversation proves Elizabeth knew about the Babington Plot and warned the plotters to cease and desist. However, this warning delivered to Châteauneuf had nothing to do from a deception analysis perspective with the ongoing Babington Plot. Instead, Elizabeth was referring to Castelnau's (the French ambassador at the time) involvement in the earlier Throckmorton Plot. Châteauneuf had just replaced Castelnau, who had been declared *persona non grata*.[3] In effect, Elizabeth was not too subtly putting Châteauneuf on notice that he should not continue on his predecessor's path, or else he would suffer similar consequences.

At the same time, Elizabeth's somewhat bombastic remarks speak volumes about her legendary mood swings, unpredictable behavior, and quixotic personality. It was for these very reasons that her two senior advisors chose not to inform her of their plan to manipulate an unwitting Mary and her group of conspirators into a scenario that would eventually lead to the Scottish Queen's demise.

Regardless, the fact that Elizabeth claimed to have known everything that was going on in her kingdom (a not uncommon trait among all people then and now in power) had absolutely nothing to do with the counter-conspiracy operation already in progress. Nevertheless, Walsingham and Cecil were forced to develop alternative contingency plans to respond to any unexpected actions from her royal braggadocio.

Therefore, beginning in April 1586, they prepared to react quickly should their opposition be tipped off to their ongoing subterfuge. Fortunately for Walsingham and Cecil, it was not until early to mid-summer that their double agent provocateur, Bernard Maude, was compromised by the Catholics. This gave them time to develop deception countermeasures to mitigate the potential consequences of Maude's "blown" cover.

If Elizabeth was, in fact, not aware that the Babington Plot was already in progress in April 1586, then when did she finally learn about it? The answer may be found in the following letter sent by Walsingham to the

Earl of Leicester, Robert Dudley, as he [Dudley] prepared to lead a military force to the Low Countries to support the Huguenots in fighting occupying Catholic forces:

> "My only feare is that her majestye wyll not use the matter with that secreacy that apperteynethe, though yt importyt as ever any thing dyd synthece she cam to this crown. And surely yf the matter be well handeled it wyll breake the necke of all dayngerowse practyces durying her magestyes reigne." Hsuan-Ying Tu, *The Pursuit of God's Glory*, Page 154.

In the communication above, Walsingham was almost certainly alluding to the Babington Plot as it entered a critical stage of communications between Anthony Babington and Queen Mary. Walsingham stated that the English scheme to counter the plot was so sensitive the First Secretary warned Leicester that "none of my fellows here privy thereunto."[4] He also instructed Leicester to burn the letter.

Unfortunately, the first sentence of the letter could be interpreted in two different ways. Was Walsingham saying that Elizabeth already knew about the Babington plot, or was he concerned about her reaction once she became aware of the Catholic conspiracy?

The following is a chronological timeline of events showing when Elizabeth may have first learned of the Babington Plot:

## Timeline

### June

- 25 June—Babington receives a letter from Mary asking for his assistance.
- 29 June—Morgan reports to Mary that Elizabeth exhibits strange behavior. "She [Elizabeth] was going to Chapel . . . when suddenly she was 'overcome by a shock of fear.' The pang was so severe, she could not recover herself, but at once returned to her apartments, 'greatly to the wonder of those present.'"[5]
- Late June—Poley informs Walsingham that Babington seeks a travel license to leave England.

### July

- 3 July—Babington meets with Walsingham to discuss a travel license.
- 4 July—Morgan asks Mary to stop all intelligence with Ballard.[6]
- 6 July—Babington sends a detailed letter describing the conspirators' plan to liberate Mary. This same day Walsingham reads Babington's letter.

- 7 July—Phelippes decodes the letter and sends it to Mary via the "beer keg" network.
- 9 July—Walsingham sends a confidential letter to Leicester informing him of the situation.
- 9–10 July—Walsingham tells Elizabeth that agent Maude's cover has been compromised.
- 13 July—Walsingham tells Babington he is inclined to approve a travel license.
- 16 July—Morgan orders Ballard to stop all activity with Mary.[7]
- 18–19 July—Walsingham tells Elizabeth about Mary's response to Babington's 6 July letter.

## *Factors Bearing on the Question*

- The relationship between Elizabeth and Walsingham was tenuous and strained, especially after 1580. They diametrically differed on how best to deal with Catholic/anti-Protestant issues.
- Cecil acted as a buffer to minimize direct contact between their clashing personalities.
- The Earl of Leicester, Robert Dudley, and Elizabeth had a special relationship. Probably few, if any, secrets were kept between them.
- Elizabeth was politically and psychologically disinclined to support highly controversial activities such as regicide.
- Elizabeth had independently taken actions that nearly compromised sensitive English counter-conspiracy activities (Throckmorton Plot).

## *Conclusion*

With a moderate degree of confidence, I submit Elizabeth became aware of the Babington Plot no earlier than the last week of June 1586 and no later than 10 July 1586. Alternatively, there is no direct evidence she knew that Walsingham and Cecil had developed a deception plan to entrap and implicate Mary Stuart in treasonous acts.

## III. Recruitment of Gifford

### *An Alternative Explanation*

One generally accepted narrative has the recruitment of Gilbert Gifford by Francis Walsingham occurring several days after his arrest by English custom agents at Rye in early December 1585. At the time of his apprehension, he reportedly carried a letter of recommendation from Morgan to Mary, informing her that Gifford would set up a safe letter-carrying system from her new location at Chartley Hall. However, Gifford allegedly escaped from English authorities, told Morgan of his arrest, and assured him that his promise to work for English intelligence to undermine Jesuit activities in Paris was nothing more than a ruse to gain his freedom. To allay Catholic suspicions, he assured Morgan that, in truth, he would continue to work for Morgan and the Catholic cause, regardless of what he had promised Walsingham. Surprisingly, Morgan quickly dismissed his suspicions that Gifford's story was a Walsingham-inspired fabrication and continued to run him as a "trusted" Catholic agent throughout the evolution of the Babington Plot.

> "There are no accidents [coincidences] in intelligence work—only schemes."
> Howard Blum, *The Last Goodnight*, Page 258.

However, upon closer examination of the changing focus, timing, and decisions involving Mary's incarceration at Tutbury Castle and her future relocation to Chartley Hall, Gilbert Gifford may have already been working for English intelligence several months before his arrest by English custom agents in December. This assumption is based on the following observations:

## Focus, Tone, and Intent of Cecil and Walsingham's Activities

*(January–June 1585)*

- *Purposely restricting access to Mary:* In January 1585, the original intent of moving Mary to her much-hated Tutbury Castle had two primary purposes. The first was to significantly make her life more difficult by tightening security to isolate her from the outside world, especially her Catholic supporters. Second, knowing how much Mary detested her incarceration in such a dilapidated, dank, and uncomfortable living space,[8] Cecil and Walsingham hoped that by raising her stress and frustration levels, they could later exploit that to their advantage. Accordingly, Mary was transferred from the accommodating Earl of Shrewsbury and ailing Sir Ralph Sadler to Sir Amyas Paulet, the militant anti-Catholic, to create a more restrictive environment.
- *Applying more pressure:* In March, the same approach to isolate and restrict freedom of movement was applied to Mary's chief intelligencer, Thomas Morgan. Elizabeth requested that Morgan be extradited to England to face accusations that he was guilty of conducting plots to dethrone her. While not fully complying with Elizabeth's demands, the French King arrested Morgan and put him into the Bastille. Like Mary, Morgan's diminished ability to communicate and interface with the

outside world created a growing frustration and sense of helplessness in being unable to advance the best interests of the Catholic cause.

- *Ramping up the pressure:* During the May/June time frame, Cecil instructed Paulet to let Mary and Morgan know that their communications were being read and monitored into and out of Tutbury Castle.[9]
- *Receiving positive feedback:* During the January through September 1585 period, Mary was displeased about her treatment and living conditions at Tutbury and made it known to friends and foes alike.[10] Her constant stream of complaints to Elizabeth fell on deaf ears.
- *Baiting the hook:* Fortuitously, the panacea for all of Morgan's concerns and Mary's dismal situation at Tutbury arrived at the Bastille in the person of Robert Poley. Poley offered a solution to resolve both Morgan and Mary's dilemmas. By mid-summer, with the successful penetration of Morgan's center of gravity in Paris and Poley's acceptance by Mary, Walsingham significantly improved his ability to monitor, control, and react to Catholic activities heretofore denied him.[11]

## Focus, Tone, and Intent of Cecil and Walsingham's Activities

*(July–December 1585)*

- *Mary's communication ability improves:* Once Morgan accepted Poley and Gilbert Gifford as "trusted agents," communications began to consistently reach the Scottish Queen informing her of their efforts to improve her current situation.[12]
- *English Intelligence develops a new communication trap:* In late August/ early September, Walsingham tasked Thomas Phelippes and Sir Amyas Paulet to develop a means to control the information flow to and from Chartley Hall.[13] Moving Mary from Tutbury Castle to a new location became a topic of conversation between Elizabeth's two senior advisors.
- *Purposely decreasing the pressure:* Immediately adjusting to Gifford's defection during the October/November 1585 time frame, the First Secretary convinced Elizabeth that, as a public gesture of goodwill, she should move Mary from her old austere surroundings to the more accommodating Chartley Hall.
- *Mary is relocated to Chartley Hall:* In October, Cecil informed Mary that she and her entourage would be relocated to Chartley Hall. Morgan was also made aware of that planned move. In a personal message to Mary, he informed her that Gilbert Gifford would soon return to England, reconnoiter the area, and identify her supporters who resided near Chartley Hall.[14]

This noticeable shift in emphasis from July to December 1585 occurred despite 1) successful inroads made by isolating and increasing the security around Mary and Morgan, 2) Poley's acceptance as a trusted agent by Mary's chief intelligencer, and 3) the substantial expenditure of English capital, resources, time, and energy used to restrict the ability of Mary and Morgan to communicate with each other. What could explain such a radical reversal in emphasis and focus?

> "Once is Happenstance, Twice is Coincidence . . . Three times is Enemy Action." Ian Fleming, *Goldfinger*, Page 177.

## Happenstance

Cecil and Walsingham's apparent willingness to address Mary's complaints while still in Tutbury Castle and Elizabeth's subsequent approval to move her to the more comfortable and benign Chartley Hall was likely the direct result of Gilbert Gifford's defection to the English intelligence organization in late summer 1585.[15]

## Coincidence

After Gilbert Gifford switched his allegiance, Walsingham dispatched Phelippes and Paulet to Chartley Hall to develop a more user-friendly, flexible, and, most importantly, English intelligence-controlled communication system. Interestingly, Gilbert Gifford's family lived near Chartley Hall, and his "family ties" provided him excellent cover to explain his physical presence in the area once Mary moved to Chartley Hall; in effect, "hiding Gifford in plain sight." Chartley Hall was relatively close to Tutbury (approximately 12–15 miles). It was currently vacant and owned by a staunch Protestant and avid supporter of Elizabeth. Periodic "airing" of Tutbury Castle after more than nine months of Mary's imprisonment provided a plausible explanation for Mary's relocation and that of her entourage.

## Enemy Action

Thanks to Phelippes and Paulet's information gathering in August/early September in the vicinity of Chartley Hall, Walsingham could now more effectively conduct activities specifically designed to expose Mary's role in the plan to murder her cousin Elizabeth.

## Why Chartley Hall?

Ironically, the association of Gilbert Gifford's ancestral ties to the area surrounding Chartley Hall provided both Walsingham and Morgan windfall opportunities that, if successfully exploited, would significantly advance their diametrically opposed goals and objectives. Thus, for Protestants and Catholics alike, control of Gilbert Gifford became the key to the success or failure of their current and future operations against each other.

For Walsingham, Gilbert Gifford offered the means to advance the goal of ridding England of a person claiming his Protestant sovereign's throne. For Morgan, Gilbert Gifford provided the means to destroy a Protestant Queen and return Catholicism to England. As fortune would have it, Gifford's apparent allegiance to Walsingham in late summer 1585 doomed the Babington Plot from the beginning.

## IV. Gilbert Gifford's Arrest at Rye

*Alternative Explanations*

If Gilbert Gifford was already working for Walsingham in late summer 1585 or earlier, why was he arrested by English customs agents in December, especially knowing that such an incident could blow Gifford's double agent cover? If upon receiving word that English custom agents had captured him at Rye, why did Morgan so readily accept Gifford's story about his subsequent escape from their control given the "life and death" struggle between the Protestants and Catholics? Why did Morgan throw caution and suspicion of possible deceit and treachery on the part of Gifford to the winds so quickly?

*Why the Arrest at Rye?*

There are several plausible explanations. The following possibilities deserve further investigation:

- *Serendipity Scenario*: The customs agents at Rye did not know Gilbert Gifford was already working for Walsingham and made their arrest based on evidence found on Gifford. Even in sixteenth-century England, knowledge of running such a sensitive source deep into a mortal enemy's infrastructure would have been tightly protected and placed in an "eyes only" security compartment. Therefore, the arrest was nothing more than a typical bureaucratic foul-up or "the left hand, not knowing what the right hand was doing" situation.
- *Walsingham-inspired Scenario*: Assuming Gifford's earlier recruitment in the fall, the nearly completed English controlled communication

penetration network at Chartley Hall, and the scheduled late December move of Mary from Tutbury urgently required a face-to-face meeting between Walsingham, Gifford, and his new handler, Thomas Phelippes. During that meeting, Gifford would be briefed on the "beer keg" scheme and the significant role he would play in it. Therefore, Gifford's arrest was a Walsingham preplanned event. The Rye custom agents received a description of a suspected spy and were directed to apprehend him on sight. To reinforce the "suspected spy" story, Gifford would ensure that the customs agents would find evidence that directly tied him to the imprisoned Scottish Queen.

- *Gifford-inspired Scenario*: On the other hand, the arrest may have resulted from Gifford's own doing because of the rapidly changing situation inside the Catholic leadership in exile. From his perspective, new turbulence roiling within the Catholic ranks required immediate and extraordinary measures. By setting himself up to be arrested, he was able to alert the First Secretary to the rapidly changing situations, intentions, and decisions that existed inside Morgan's conspiratorial planning cell in Paris. Gifford's arrest and a subsequent face-to-face meeting with Walsingham and his controller, Phelippes, resulted in providing valuable information that would give Walsingham time to anticipate, prepare, and counter Catholic moves before they occurred. In effect, Gifford's almost near-to-real-time intelligence would provide the First Secretary the luxury of designing deception/provocation activities to manipulate, encourage, or control Catholic decisions, behaviors, and events. In the end, these actions would result in the selection of Anthony Babington as the leader of the London-based group of conspirators.

- *Morgan-inspired Scenario*: Morgan, unaware that Gilbert Gifford was already working for Walsingham, and learning that Mary would be moved from Tutbury Castle, devised a scheme that would "dangle" Gifford in front of the First Secretary. In so doing, Morgan offered Walsingham an opportunity to recruit Gifford to work against the Catholic conspirators' cause. Once arrested and "turned" by his Protestant counterpart, Morgan believed he would have his own double agent (Gifford) firmly embedded in the inner sanctum of English intelligence. From Morgan's perspective, possessing such an invaluable, uniquely placed asset would provide the Babington plotters a distinct advantage against Walsingham's counter-conspiracy operations. Unfortunately for Morgan, Walsingham had already co-opted Gifford.

*Why Did Morgan Accept Gilbert Gifford's Cover/
Escape Story?*

Attempting to determine why Morgan responded as he did to Gilbert's story, the following factors must be considered:

*Key Factors Bearing on the Question*

- Walsingham's reputation as a skilled intelligencer, a master manipulator, exploiter of psychological vulnerabilities, and a genius at "turning" captured agents into supporting the English Protestant cause was legend among the English Catholic exile community.
- Morgan was a skilled intelligence practitioner who ran double agent operations against Walsingham's intelligence organization. Like Walsingham, he was well-schooled in the art and tradecraft of espionage and counterespionage.
- Gifford's story that he outwitted Walsingham into believing that he committed himself to the English cause but was only a ruse designed to help him escape from the First Secretary's grasp lacks credibility when considering Walsingham's reputation.
- Morgan was under intense pressure from the English Catholic community in exile to solve a multitude of interrelated problems that demanded immediate attention.

There are several plausible explanations for his seemingly disinterested and incurious reaction:

*The Stress Disabled Argument*: Morgan's dismissal of Gifford's somewhat questionable explanation about his escape from Walsingham may have been due to a psychological paralysis caused by a long period of physical isolation in the Bastille further aggravated by the growing pressure of unrelenting and immobilizing stress. Some of his more intractable problems that demanded his immediate attention included his:

- Losing control of a unified Catholic resistance was vital to the success of any future anti-Protestant initiatives. (Catholic ranks were split into two warring camps—Jesuits and English/Welsh Catholic laymen.)
- Being isolated from day-to-day activities, losing control of actions targeting the Protestant opposition, and a growing inability to participate in making key decisions within the Catholic leadership ranks
- Difficulty communicating with Mary, especially after her move to Tutbury Castle in January 1585

- Inability to stay abreast of the situation surrounding Mary; further aggravated by the recent revelation that she would be relocated to Chartley Hall, a short distance from Tutbury Castle, sometime in December 1585
- Inability to control or positively respond to Dr. William Gifford's last-minute refusal to return to England to lead his (Morgan's) newly developing plot to overthrow Elizabeth from her throne and restore Catholicism to her realm

Given Morgan's extensive and overwhelming list of problems, the added pressure of determining the credibility of Gifford's story may have created a disabling, stressful situation. He, therefore, became psychologically incapable of focusing on and solving this and many other time-sensitive problems. As a result, Morgan could very well have decided it was much easier to believe in Gifford's loyalty and accept him at his word.

*The "Benefit vs. Risk vs. Time" Argument*: Alternatively, Thomas Morgan may have sighed with relief when told that Walsingham, recruiting Gifford, had directed that he (Gifford) periodically return to France to focus his attention on attacking the Jesuit faction that was attempting to gain control of the exiled Catholic movement in France. Fortunately for Morgan, it was a tasking that would disrupt and undermine the very group that was in direct conflict with Morgan's more secular-based group of Catholic conspirators and sympathizers.

Therefore, Gilbert Gifford's feigned promise to provide Walsingham support in disrupting the Jesuit community could be used to his (Morgan's) great advantage. Other factors also came into play with Morgan's decision to throw caution and suspicion to the wind. For example:

- Time was another essential consideration that probably weighed heavily on Morgan's decision to accept Gilbert Gifford's story. Mary's chief intelligencer knew that Mary's relocation to Chartley Hall would soon be a reality, and yet nothing had been done to reconstitute a new communication system for her. Thus, Gilbert Gifford was the ideal person to lay that critical groundwork, similar to what Robert Poley did for Morgan while Mary was imprisoned in Tutbury Castle.
- Gifford could also be used to relieve him of the pressure of advancing, coordinating, and implementing—from London—a "time-sensitive" new plan designed to invade England in mid-to-late summer 1586. This activity had become even more critical when Morgan learned that the person selected to lead the conspiracy from London refused to accept the assignment. Until a replacement was found and vetted, Gifford could be used as "the glue" to keep the other plotters together.

Perhaps Morgan determined that the benefits of accepting Gilbert Gifford's escape story and using him to attain his objectives far outweighed the risk that Gifford had been "doubled" by the hated Protestant opposition. This position gains even more currency when considering a possible course of action that, if successful, would place Catholic "eyes and ears" (Gilbert Gifford) within Walsingham's inner circle.

*The Successful Penetration Argument*: Upon receiving word of Gifford's arrest at Rye and his agent's subsequent story explaining how and why he was set free may have provided Morgan a much-needed boost in morale. The fact that Gifford's story, if closely scrutinized, could reveal glaring flaws in its credibility did not matter to Morgan. The fact that he had penetrated Walsingham's organization took precedence over all other concerns. He was confident that Gifford's commitment to him and the Catholic cause was inviolate. And his loyalty to the plan to free Mary from English imprisonment was unassailable.

Morgan's penetration plan commenced after discovering Mary and her entourage would be moving from Tutbury Castle to a new Staffordshire location. He also found that Gifford's family and fellow Catholic sympathizers lived near Chartley Hall. This advantageous situation made Gifford a valuable commodity for Morgan's future planning purposes. At the time of Gifford's arrest, Morgan was presented with the unique opportunity to develop a way to communicate with Mary "in plain sight" securely. At last, it appeared that providence was indeed smiling upon the forces dedicated to extirpating the heinous, heretical Protestant opposition.

However, unaware that his prized double agent was now working for Walsingham, Morgan assumed that his plan to infiltrate the First Secretary's inner sanctum would help him succeed in defeating Walsingham's counter-conspiracy activities. Instead, it would prove to be just the opposite. The Babington conspirators thought they had a secure means via the Chartley Hall communication network to execute their plan to retake England and dispense with Elizabeth. However, unbeknownst to them, it was because of that same network that they were being influenced to take actions that would lead to the demise of the very person they hoped to save, Mary Stuart.

*The Walsingham Agent Argument*: Morgan had already been recruited by Walsingham before his self-imposed exile to Paris in 1575 and kept Walsingham fully informed of conspiratorial attempts to remove Elizabeth from her throne. Both he and his fellow exile, Charles Paget, were influential members of the Welsh, or more moderate, faction who sought to reconcile their differences with Elizabeth. However, they were opposed by an extreme anti-Protestant Jesuit faction led by Dr. William Allen and Father Robert Persons. The intense rivalry and enmity between these two groups permitted

Walsingham to exploit that factional tension through the *sub rosa* assistance
of both Morgan and Paget.[16]

## V. The Stafford Plot

*(Designed to Deceive)*

Elizabeth's reluctance to try the Scottish Queen for treason and later sign
Mary's death warrant was certainly not unanticipated by her two most senior
advisors. Aware of their Queen's chimerical character and inability to make
difficult decisions, especially if doing so would tarnish her reputation with
her subjects, Cecil and Walsingham had roughly sketched out a rudimentary
contingency course of action in their deception/provocation plan. The overriding purpose of the contingency plan was to force a decision from their
monarch by pressuring her to act in the best interests of her kingdom, people,
and herself.

By late 1586, it became clear that the evidence so assiduously gathered by
Walsingham proving Mary's complicit involvement in supporting Elizabeth's
death was still not enough to force Elizabeth's hand. Therefore, in early
December, it became apparent to both Cecil and Walsingham that even more
pressure had to be put on Elizabeth to bring Mary to justice.[17]

It may have been during his 16–24 December 1586 absence from court
that Walsingham began the final preparations to launch a fake or "sham plot"
and disinformation campaign intended to convince Elizabeth once and for
all that if Mary lived, the threat to Elizabeth and the kingdom would continue unabated.

The operation began on 8 January 1587 with the house arrest of French
ambassador Châteauneuf, who was accused of being involved in a new conspiracy to assassinate Elizabeth.[18] The fictional plot revolved around three
principal characters—William Stafford, the unruly brother of Sir Edward
Stafford, English ambassador to France,[19] Michael Moody, the English ambassador's former Catholic servant, and Léonard de Trappes, the French ambassador's (Châteauneuf) personal secretary. Not surprisingly, William Stafford
and Michael Moody were known to have had past ties to Walsingham. "There
seems little doubt that Stafford was one of Walsingham's agent provocateurs,
and it is perhaps significant that two years earlier, he had acknowledged
some kind of deep obligation to the spymaster . . . Moody for carrying letters
between London and Paris from 1580–1584."[20]

The supposed purpose of the fake conspiracy was to kill Elizabeth by
using gunpowder to blow her up or by poisoning objects that would touch her
skin. Concurrently, Walsingham and Cecil ran a multi-themed disinformation

operation designed to raise the ire of Elizabeth's subjects and increase pressure on Elizabeth to act decisively against her royal cousin.

As the investigation into the alleged Stafford Plot unfolded, the following disinformation themes and rumors were circulated throughout the kingdom and abroad:

1. Elizabeth had been assassinated
2. Philip II of Spain was building up stocks of artillery and military equipment at Lisbon, ready to use against England
3. Spain, under the leadership of the Duke of Parma, had invaded Newcastle
4. Thousands of Spaniards had landed in Wales
5. Scotland had been invaded
6. Certain English noblemen had fled England
7. France, under the leadership of the Duke of Guise, had invaded Sussex and was marching on London
8. London was burning or would soon be burned by the invading forces
9. The Duke of Parma was to mount an operation from the Low Countries to rescue Mary from Fotheringhay
10. Mary, Queen of Scots, had escaped[21]

## Risk of Unintended Consequences

Unfortunately for Walsingham and Cecil, their disinformation campaign proved too successful, and the consequences of that success quickly turned their plan to urge Elizabeth forward into a "double-edged" sword.[22] The Earl of Pembroke, the Mayor, and Alderman of Exeter, Devon, Sir Owen Hopton, Lieutenant of the Tower of London, and even Amyas Paulet were unwitting to the planted rumors and reacted to the misinformation (disinformation). "The rumors had also spread overseas. On 1 February, Walsingham received information from one of his intelligencer's in France that . . . Many Romanists laugh at the report of the Scottish Queen's escape, but the French ambassador never thought her dead till now"[23] Another of Walsingham's agents reported rumors that Paulet himself had murdered Mary.

One would be hard-pressed to deny that Walsingham and Cecil's sham plot and supporting disinformation campaign unleashed in January 1587 did not affect Elizabeth's final surrender to her government and subjects' demands for the Scottish Queen's head. However, determining the degree of the contingency plan's impact in influencing and moving Elizabeth forward in her decision-making process will always remain problematic and a topic of discussion. However, one thing is clear and speaks volumes about the real motive, intent, and objective of the Stafford Plot. Two months after Mary's execution, Elizabeth's government acknowledged that its accusations against

Châteauneuf and France had been based on a terrible misunderstanding. As a result, legal proceedings against the alleged conspirator, William Stafford, were dropped.[24]

## NOTES

1. Hsuan-Ying Tu, in his Doctoral Thesis titled *The Pursuit of God's Glory*, Pages 17–42, provides an extensive and detailed account of why the Walsingham Papers are in such disarray.

2. John Hungerford Pollen, *Mary, Queen of Scots and the Babington Plot.* Edited from the original documents in the Public Records Office, the Yelverton MSS., and elsewhere. (Edinburgh University Press by T. and A. Constable for the Scottish History Society, 1922), Introduction: "The Death Trap," lxiv.

3. Ambassador Châteauneuf replaced the previous ambassador, Castelnau, in September 1585. Francis Edwards, *Plots and Plotters in the Reign of Elizabeth I*, Page 135.

4. Hsuan-Ying Tu, *The Pursuit of God's Glory: Francis Walsingham's Espionage in Elizabethan Politics, 1586–1588* (University of York, Thesis, 2012), 154.

5. Morgan probably received that information from the Spanish Ambassador, Mendoza.

6. *Calendar of the Cecil Papers in Hatfield House: Volume 3, (1583–1589).* (Originally published by the Majesty's Stationary Office, 1889), Cecil Paper #288, 24 June/4 July 1586; Elizabeth Jenkins, *Elizabeth the Great* (G.P. Putnam's Sons, 1958), 269.

7. Pollen, Introduction: "The Catastrophe," cliv–clv.

8. John Cooper, *The Queen's Agent: Sir Francis Walsingham and the Rise of Espionage in Elizabethan England* (Pegasus Books, 2012), 207.

9. Robert Hutchinson, *Elizabeth's Spymaster* (St. Martin Press, 2006), 119.

10. *Letters of Mary, Queen of Scots. Volume II* (Henry Colburn, Publisher, MDCCCXLIV, 1864), 154–155.

11. *Calendar of the Cecil Papers in Hatfield House: Volume 3, (1583–1589).* (Originally published by the Majesty's Stationary Office, 1889) Cecil Paper #170, 10/20 July 1585.

12. Hutchinson, 120–121.

13. Hutchinson, 121.

14. Assuming Gifford was already working for Walsingham, this intercepted message indicates that Gilbert Gifford had been successful in convincing Morgan et al. that he was committed to liberating Mary from English imprisonment.

15. Robert Southwell, a Jesuit priest, in 1591 indicated that the dating of letters between Gifford and Phelippes showed that Gifford had been working for Walsingham well before his arrest at Rye in December 1585. Patrick Martin, *Elizabethan Espionage*, Page 62.

16. L. Hicks, S.J., in his extensively researched study titled *An Elizabethan Problem: Some Aspects of the Careers of Two Exile-Adventurers*, cogently argues that both

Morgan and Paget were recruited by the English and conspired to sabotage Spain's efforts to invade England, assassinate Elizabeth and replace her with Mary. The author bases his conclusions on evidence "partly direct, and partly circumstantial." *Forward,* Page x.

17. Robert Hutchinson writes, that extra pressure would take the form of "a sensational new plot to murder her [Elizabeth] was conveniently discovered that January. It was a baffling affair bearing all the hallmarks of Walsingham's genius for disinformation and timing." *Elizabeth's Spymaster,* Page 176.

18. Charles Nicholl writes, "the purpose of which was to embarrass the French ambassador, and to render him incommunicado during the trial and execution of Mary Stuart, which was deeply deplored in France." *The Reckoning,* Page 164.

19. Selected English ambassador to France in 1583, Sir Edward Stafford was immediately compromised by enormous gambling debts owed, ironically, to Francis, Duke of Alençon, among others. (The Duke must have felt some sense of sweet revenge for the way he was treated by the English during his long courtship with Elizabeth.) Hearing of Stafford's plight, Mendoza, the Spanish ambassador to France, recruited Stafford as a double agent by offering financial assistance in return for information regarding English intentions and military strengths. Walsingham was aware of this situation.

20. Hutchinson, 177.

21. Thomas Wright (editor), *Queen Elizabeth and Her Times: A Series of Original Letters Vol. II* (London: Henry Colburn, Publisher, 1838), 329–331.

22. Robert Hutchinson writes "the misinformation [disinformation] rebounded on the government and came back to harm them . . . it must have frustrated and angered Walsingham and Burghley [Cecil] to continually receive messages reporting back the disturbing output of their own rumor machine." *Elizabeth's Spymaster*, Page 178. Alison Weir states the rumors "[caused] such out breaks of panic throughout the kingdom that many men were going about wearing armor and guards were posted on major roads." *The Life of Elizabeth I*, Page 376.

23. Hutchinson, 179.

24. "The [Stafford] Plot was also designed to isolate the French ambassador from communication with his own king or others in England." Patrick Martin, *Elizabethan Espionage*, Page 64.

# Appendix C
## *Walsingham's Intelligence Organization*

Walsingham's reformed intelligence arm was a significant improvement compared to its past structure. However, it was still a far cry from how contemporary organizational models look today. Nevertheless, extrapolating what scholars have written about Cecil and Walsingham's intelligence services evolution from c. 1573 to c. 1587 and superimposing that information onto a typical modern-day organizational paradigm, Walsingham's intelligence arm may have looked like the following organization chart.[1]

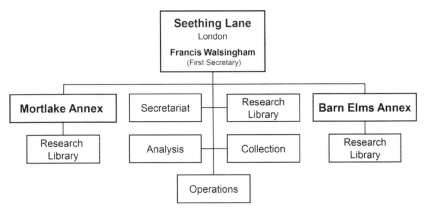

Figure Appendix C.1.
Source: R. Kent Tiernan

## FUNCTIONAL GROUPS

### Operations

This typically proactive directorate has the following responsibilities:

- Special Activities—Planning, implementation, and execution of Deception and Influence activities, penetration, and neutralization of perceived threats. This unit was heavily involved in manipulating the Babington plotters and their "centers of gravity."
- Technical Services—Making and breaking of codes, secret writings, and forgeries.
- Information Support—Developing propaganda themes, rumors, misinformation, disinformation, and psychological operations.
- Domestic Surveillance—Conducting security around and monitoring activities at ports of entry, postal services, and prisons. Identifying recusants supporting Jesuit infiltrators and disseminating seditious materials.[2]

### Collection

This directorate is responsible for providing information that could directly or indirectly impact England's domestic tranquility or national security using two collection methods:

- Open Source (Overt)—Using sources whose type of work permits them access to information without drawing suspicion (e.g., merchants, diplomats, adventurers/explorers, traveling troupes/entertainers, royal servants, etc.). This type of collected information provides contextual background to that collected by covert means.
- Clandestine (Covert)—Using sources (intelligence agents or co-opted individuals) specifically assigned to penetrate and collect a target's (e.g., France, Spain, Papacy, etc.) most sensitive secrets that could threaten England's domestic and national security.

### Analysis

This directorate is responsible for assessing the credibility and value of the collected information by people with specialized knowledge or skill. If that information proves relevant to a particular area of concern or interest, it is forwarded to subject matter experts for further analysis in one of the following categories:

- Scientific intelligence
- Economic intelligence
- Geographic intelligence
- Political/Military intelligence
- Biographic intelligence
- Psycho/Social intelligence
- Forecasting/Predictive intelligence

## Secretariat

This directorate is responsible for providing Walsingham and his key members administrative, operational, courier service, Privy Council liaison, and fiduciary support. "Some in the Secretariat were also assigned to do a great deal of preliminary reading and sifting [vetting/analysis], which would weed out the inconsequential requiring no more response than a line of acknowledgment, praise, or rebuke, and that not always very prompt."[3] Note: Hsuan-Ying Tu asserts that by 1581, Walsingham's Secretariat was six times the size of the Lord Treasurer's [Cecil's] pre-1573 administrative support structure. *The Pursuit of God's Glory: Francis Walsingham's Espionage in Elizabethan Politics, 1568–1588*, Page 77.

## Mortlake and Barn Elms Annexes

While Walsingham primarily conducted his intelligence activities from Seething Lane near the Tower of London, he also provided support activities to his intelligencers from the Mortlake residence of Elizabeth's astrologer, John Dee, and Walsingham's Barn Elms home outside of London.

Both annexes, approximately ten miles distance from Seething Lane, were locations probably used for research, generation of baseline threat assessments, production of support materials, strategic brainstorming sessions, sensitive operational planning, and archival storage. They could have also acted as "safe houses."

## NOTES

1. Many of the people associated with the organization had numerous responsibilities and supported multiple directorates. For example, Robert Beale was involved in Operations, Secretariat, and Analysis activities, while Charles Sledd likely supported the Collection, Analysis, and Operations areas of responsibilities.

2. Today, a number of these focal points are considered to have counter-intelligence responsibilities. Separation of intelligence and counter-intelligence functions in

England did not occur until the early 20th century. MI5 was created in 1909 to focus on internal/domestic security threats and reports directly to the Home Secretary. MI6 was founded the same year to deal with external/foreign national security threats and reports directly to the Foreign Secretary.

3. Alan Haynes, *The Elizabethan Secret Services* (Sutton Publishing, 1992), 15.

# Appendix D

## *Countering the Catholic Threat*

Agents and Helpers[1]

**A**

*Solomon Aldred*
(Operations Directorate/Double Agent)
(Secretariat Directorate/Operations Support)
A field agent at the seminary in Rome and one of Francis Walsingham's (FW) key collectors and provocateurs in France. He was sent to Paris to convince William Gifford to return to England and work for FW. In that capacity, he carried a letter from FW with a travel license for Gifford and delivered them to Stafford, the English ambassador in Paris. Recruited in 1583.[2]

*William Ashby*
(Secretariat Directorate/Courier Services)
Ashby began his career in the Foreign Service as a letter carrier for FW. Between 1576 and 1588, he was frequently employed as a confidential messenger traveling to and from English representatives in Brussels, Frankfurt, Augsburg, and other towns.[3]

*Anthony Atkinson*
(Operations Directorate/Domestic Surveillance Activities)
He was a postal searcher at the port of Hull.[4]

**B**

*Richard Baines*
(Operations Directorate/Domestic Surveillance Activities)

Attended seminary at Rheims in 1578 and was ordained a Jesuit priest. He probably began working for FW c. 1580. Baines collected and agitated against Catholics, sent information to the Privy Council, and was discovered to be a spy by William Allen—leader of the Jesuit anti-Protestant faction in France. He subsequently was imprisoned by Catholics on May 29, 1582, but eventually convinced his captors he was innocent. He repented but continued working for FW.[5]

*Peter Bales*
(Operations Directorate/Technical Services)
He may have tutored Thomas Phelippes in the clandestine arts. A master of microscopic penmanship, he was also a deviser of ciphers employed by FW.[6]

*Christopher Barker*
(Secretariat Directorate/Finance)
He signed for Walsingham's annuities in 1577.[7]

*Robert Beale*
(Operations Directorate/Special Activities/Plans and Programs, and Technical Services)
(Secretariat Directorate/Chief of Staff/Operations Support)
Clerk of the Council; part of the intelligence service management; case officer, confidential messenger, and private secretary to FW. Active in sifting out intelligence from reams of malicious rumor. Beale advised FW to "Be not too credulous," "Hear all reports, but trust not all," "Weigh them with time and deliberation and be not too liberal of trifles. Observe them that deal on both hands, lest you be deceived." Brother-in-law of FW, he worked with FW's ciphers, knowing most if not all of them. Beale decoded incoming letters and occasionally fell to working on an intercepted item. In FW's absence, he many times acted as his stand-in. He worked for FW as his secretary in the Paris embassy from 1571–1573. Beale was worried about government continuity and particularly keen that paperwork be maintained and passed on intact to the next generation of Crown servants. He was closely connected with Seething Lane and was very familiar with the FW agent network located in forty-six places. Beale was considered a brilliant archivist.[8]

*Nicholas Berden alias Thomas Rogers*
(Collection Directorate/Clandestine)
(Operations Directorate/Special Activities and Domestic Surveillance Activities)
Berden was one of the most prolific spies employed during the 1580s. He was a field agent in France, a prison informer, and a Jesuit spotter. He

probably began working for FW c. 1582–1583. He provided a rich harvest of intelligence from deep within the Catholic underground. He reported on safe houses, priests, and books stowed away on French coasters bound for Newcastle; and the networks that supported seminary priests and Jesuits in England. He also discovered a new significant postal connection. Finding himself in possession of key enemy codes, Berden stumbled across a treasure trove of secret ciphers. In April 1586, he returned from Paris with information about a Morgan spy who had penetrated the royal household and kept company with Jesuits living secretly and illegally in London. Upon his recall to London, FW used the "flipped" Morgan spy to vet a list of priests and recusants already imprisoned in London before the Babington conspirators' arrests in midsummer 1586. He retired in 1587 when Catholics began to suspect him of being FW's agent.[9]

*William Bland*
(Secretariat Directorate/Administration)
Worked in Custom affairs.[10]

*Thomas Bodley*
(Collection Directorate/Open Source)
Worked out of the Netherlands.[11]

*Robert Bowes*
(Collection Directorate/Open Source)
Hard-working ambassador to Scotland who built an active intelligence cluster, using as many sources as possible. The letters written by Bowes were dense with intelligence matters.[12]


# C

*Maliverny Catlin*
(Analysis Directorate/Biographic Intelligence)
(Operations Directorate/Domestic Surveillance/Prisons)
Catlin served as a soldier in the Low Countries. FW used him to get a sense of Catholic resistance, strength, and support in England's North counties. Maliverny Catlin was one of FW's most prolific collectors, along with Nicholas Berden and Thomas Phelippes. Based on information from local contacts, Catlin wrote a long paper that revealed the names and descriptions of Catholic men and women in England.[13]

*Lisle Cave*
(Secretariat Directorate/Administration)
In mid-1571, he served Walsingham in Paris. He later was a filing clerk for Mylles, "Ciprian," and Thomas Lake. Cave also edited the French language letter book of 1571–1589.[14]

*"Charles"*
(Secretariat Directorate/Administration)
Performed secretarial duties in the 1580s.[15]

*Richard Cholmeley*
(Operations Directorate/Domestic Surveillance Activities)
He was employed by the Privy Council "for the apprehension of papists and other dangerous men."[16]

*"Ciprian"*
(Secretariat Directorate/Administration)
Performed secretarial duties in the 1580s.[17]

*John Cottesforde*
(Secretariat Directorate/Finance)
Signed for Walsingham's annuities in 1575.[18]

*Company of Queen's Men*
(Collection Directorate/Open Source)
A traveling front group of playwrights and actors gathering information as they traveled throughout England and the continent.[19]

*Claude de Courcelles (Nicholas LeClerc)*
(Collection Directorate/Clandestine)
French embassy official who Henry Fagot recruited in 1583. He was employed as a secretary to Castelnau, the French ambassador in London.[20]

# D

*John Dee*
(Analysis Directorate/Scientific Intelligence, Economic Intelligence, Geographic Intelligence, Research Library, and Prediction Analysis)
(Operations Directorate/Technical Services)
Magician, Astrologer, Mathematician, and Occultist. He owned a substantial library of over 2000 books at Mortlake. In 1551, he was introduced to William Cecil, who became an avid collector of maps—an essential

element in serving the State's needs. A consultant and strong advocate of seeking the north-east passage to Asia. Mortlake was a storehouse for all sorts of equipment relating to exploration and discovery. Frequent visitors were FW, Hakluyt, and Frobisher. In public and private, FW was a part of an intense literary culture. Dee's library was used by the First Secretary to support and enhance England's secret service needs. He was also interested in secret writing—ciphers and codes. Dee and FW first met in 1577. A year later, FW briefed him before a trip to Germany on some sort of government mission. During his travels, Dee found an extremely rare manuscript of the *Steganographia* that referred to the art of writing secret messages and communicating them long distances by occult means.[21]

*"Digbye"*
(Secretariat Directorate/Courier Services)
A confidential letter-carrier to and from England.[22]

*Roger Draunsfelde*
(Secretariat Directorate/Finance)
Signed for Walsingham's annuities in 1578.[23]

## E

*Thomas Edmondes*
(Secretariat Directorate/Administration)
Joined the Secretariat in the mid-1580s and acted as Elizabeth's Latin secretary.[24]

*George Eliot*
(Operations Directorate/Domestic Surveillance Activities)
Executed warrants issued by Elizabeth and her Privy Council. In the 1580s, Eliot was busy hunting for priests and putting Catholic recusants in prison. Called "Judas" because of the key role he played in capturing the popular and influential Catholic priest Edmund Campion.[25]

## F

*Nicholas Faunt*
(Secretariat Directorate/Acting Chief/Courier Services/Operations Support)
FW's secretary from c. 1580, "very honest and discrete" and much employed in France. Attended Cambridge; his college was the same as Christopher Marlowe's: Corpus Christi. Faunt was a possible talent-spotter (recruiter) and

carried dispatches to English agents abroad. During Walsingham's absences in the 1580s, he was acting chief of the Secretariat.[26]

*William Fowler*
(Operations Directorate/Special Activities)
Fowler began working for FW c. 1583. He was a poet, scholar, and spy. Fowler studied in France and had even lent money to Mary, but his imprisonment in England undermined his Catholic loyalties, and he likely agreed to work for FW as a means of gaining his freedom.[27]

# G

*Gilbert Gifford*
(Operations Directorate/Special Activities)
Gifford proved to be a double, or possibly, triple agent extraordinaire. Considered an unruly aspirant initially to the Catholic priesthood, the Catholic exile community considered him a loyal defender of Mary Stuart's claim to the English throne. In early autumn 1585, Gifford was selected by the English Catholic exile community to carry secret messages to Mary while she was incarcerated at Chartley Hall. However, unbeknownst to her loyalist supporters, Gifford was already working for Walsingham. Given the code name "Number 4," he played an essential role in ensuring that Walsingham had access to all of Mary's secret communications to and from Chartley Hall. By the end of May 1586, Gifford returned to support the exiled anti-Jesuit, Welsh faction in Paris. He assisted in writing a short book attacking the more strident Jesuit faction's approach to returning the Catholic faith to Protest England.[28] (Author Alan Haynes claims Walsingham recruited Gifford as early as c. 1580. Other historians claim he was recruited in December 1585 as a result of his arrest at Rye. This Author asserts Gifford was "turned" during the late summer to early fall of 1585. See Appendix B.)

*Arthur Gregory*
(Operations Directorate/Technical Services)
Gregory's specialty was "the art of forcing the seal of a letter (flaps and seals); he was another regular in FW's back-room entourage. "Ingenious," as he was said to be, he had perfected "the art of forcing the seal of a letter, yet so invisibly that it still appeareth virgin to the exactest beholder."[29]

# H

*"Harcort"*
(Secretariat Directorate/Courier Services)

A letter carrier to and from England stationed in Paris.[30]

*Richard Hakluyt*
(Analysis Directorate/Economic Intelligence and Geographic Intelligence)
(Collection Directorate/Open Source)
His principal preoccupation was stocking up information about overseas trade. Starting in 1580, he collected material and interviewed mariners about the unexplored regions of the world. Using his chaplaincy as cover, he gathered a mass of information on French and Spanish interests in North America. He had a close relationship with FW and John Dee.[31]

*Anthony Hall*
(Operations Directorate/Domestic Surveillance Activities/Safe House)
Robert Poley used his lodgings as a safe house in his dealings with the Babington conspirators. Hall ran various errands for the government; he was considered a "minor" secret policeman.[32]

*William Harborne*
(Collection Directorate/Open Source)
Agent in Constantinople working under commercial cover.[33]

*Sir Thomas Heneage*
(Secretariat Directorate/Privy Council Liaison)
Treasurer of the Queen's Chamber, he disbursed funds to agents for courier work and continental missions. Liaison between Privy Council and the espionage world, he was in daily contact with FW's couriers and informers.[34]

*William Herle*
(Collection Directorate/Clandestine)
Herle began his intelligence work in the early 1570s as a prison informant for William Cecil. He later provided services to both Cecil and FW. Herle became the intelligence "cut-out" between the mole, Henry Fagot, in the French embassy in London and FW and Cecil. "He knew of a great international plot that involved the Duke of Guise, the Throckmorton brothers . . . earlier he had told Secretary Walsingham of Throckmorton's secret meetings with the French ambassador in London . . . a partye very busy and an enemye to the present State"[35]

*Christopher Hoddesdon*
(Collection Directorate/Open Source)
Agent/merchant reported on trading activities in Eastern Europe.[36]

*"Horcle"*
(Secretariat Directorate/Administration)
He performed secretarial duties in the 1580s.[37]


# I

*Paul Ive/Ivy*
(Analysis Directorate/Political/Military Intelligence)
Soldier, military engineer, spy; he had a checkered career in the Netherlands/
Low Countries. Wrote a manual on "garrison fortifications" and dedicated
it to FW.[38]


# J

*Thomas Jeffries*
(Collection Directorate/Open Source)
A merchant working out of Calais.[39]

*David Jenkins*
(Operations Directorate/Domestic Surveillance Activities)
Executed warrants issued from Elizabeth and her Privy Council. In the 1580s,
he was busy hunting for priests and putting Catholic recusants in prison.[40]


# L

*Thomas Lake*
(Secretariat Directorate/Operations Support/Finance)
(Operations Directorate/Domestic Surveillance Activities)
Lake began work in the Secretariat in the mid-1580s and was initially
involved in customs affairs. Lake earned the nickname of "Swiftsure" for his
speed and accuracy in the Secretariat business, and he also assisted in decod-
ing letters. He compiled Walsingham's table book of 1588.[41]


# M

*Jacobo Manucci*
(Collection Directorate/Clandestine)
(Secretariat Directorate/Courier Services)
From London, he controlled part of the English network of agents in Europe
and conducted sensitive missions for FW. He also carried letters to and from
England.[42]

*Christopher Marlowe*
(Operations Directorate/Domestic Surveillance Activities and Special Activities)
Collector of intelligence, watcher, pamphleteer, a source of recruitment, socially mobile, intelligent, well-traveled, spoke many languages. Marlowe was considered an insider in the English literary world. His life as a playwright was intertwined with that of Thomas Walsingham who was his case officer.[43]

*Bernard Maude*
(Operations Directorate/Special Activities)
Maude was Ballard's fixer and constant companion whom Ballard trusted with travel arrangements, especially forged travel licenses. Present at the Plough Inn during the first meeting with Babington and his coterie of plotters. While in prison, FW offered him freedom if he agreed to work for him in March 1586.[44]

*Michael Moody*
(Operations Directorate/ Domestic Surveillance Activities and Special Activities)
Moody was the key FW agent behind the Stafford Plot. Prison informer and projector; Robert Poley was his handler (case officer). He was assigned to work in the Low Countries.[45]

*Thomas Middleton*
(Secretariat Directorate/Finance)
Joined the Secretariat in the mid-1580s. He was involved in customs affairs.[46]

*Anthony Munday*
(Operations Directorate/ Domestic Surveillance Activities/Special Activities)
He was an agitator and disrupter at English Catholic seminaries in Rome and Paris. Informer, watcher, and anti-Catholic propagandist and pamphleteer. Munday was a prolific poet, romancer, balladeer, and dramatist who published his works for over forty years. A reluctant scholar and skilled writer with a gift for telling exciting tales. He knew his audience and could both enthrall and horrify them. In 1578, after two years of apprenticeship, Munday skipped his indenture and left for Europe. The following February, under the alias of "Antonius Auleus," he enrolled at the English College in Rome. Among those studying or employed at the Rome seminary in 1579 were Gilbert Gifford, Salomon Aldred, and Charles Sledd. With Sledd, his diary of Catholic activities on the continent became the basis for FW's biographical intelligence capabilities. Munday provided FW the means to spread anti-Catholic rhetoric

and propaganda throughout England. In 1582, Munday had become a regular agent for ferreting out popish plots while running down priests. By 1584 he was one of the messengers of the Queen's chambers. Munday was frequently employed from that time forward as a pursuivant (informer).[47]

*Francis Mylles*
(Operations Directorate/Special Activities)
(Secretariat Directorate/Chief of Staff/Finance/Operations Support)
Began working for FW c. 1584. Responsible for matters of "intelligence ciphers and secret advertisements." Senior intelligence secretary during the Babington Plot. Mylles disbursed covert payments (black funding), conducted surveillance of Babington conspirators, ran the surveillance team in London, and personally arrested Ballard at Poley's lodgings. Following Ballard's arrest, Mylles wrote it "was handled so circumspectly" that neither FW nor his agents "need be known in the matter." Mylles screened letters delivered to FW from businessmen for gossip and information. He was primarily responsible for matters concerning the capture and examination of Jesuits and seminary priests.[48]

# N

*Dr. Hector Nunez*
(Collection Directorate/Clandestine)
Nunez was one of FW's most thorough agents and an organizer for Iberian espionage. Nunez provided FW and Cecil with up-to-date information about Spanish activities in the Low Countries and Iberia and later reported on his countrymen and fellow exiles. One of many correspondents receiving letters from abroad on FW's behalf.[49]

# O

*Thomas Oldesworth*
(Secretariat Directorate/Finance)
Signed for Walsingham's annuities from 1580–1581.[50]

*Pierre d'Or alias Chasteau-Martin*
(Collection Directorate/Open Source)
Acted on behalf of English merchants trading out of Bayonne. He provided reports on Spanish activities.[51]

# P

*Sir Horatio Pallavicino*
(Collection Directorate/Clandestine)
Pallavicino was a highly skilled man with excellent contacts in foreign courts and embassies who provided FW with secret intelligence. His business connections made him extremely useful, especially in foreign exchange dealings. However, he also became a target of the opposition's disinformation campaign against Walsingham.[52]

*Ralph Pendlebury*
(Secretariat Directorate/Finance)
Signed for Walsingham's annuities in 1575.[53]

*Edmund Palmer*
(Collection Directorate/Open Source)
Acted on behalf of English merchants in St.-Jean-de-Luz.[54]

*Thomas Phelippes*
(Operations Directorate/Special Activities and Technical Services)
(Secretariat Directorate/Finance/Operations Support)
He was FW's chief assistant in running the secret service, handling agents, and disbursing the blood money (black funding). He was also highly skilled in codebreaking; no one was more closely involved in grassroots intelligence-gathering and code-breaking than Phelippes. He controlled numerous FW agents, notably Gilbert Gifford. Phelippes was known to work closely with FW, his secretary, Francis Mylles, and other watchers and informants such as Nicholas Berden, Maliverny Catlin, and Arthur Gregory.[55]

*Robert Poley*
(Operations Directorate/Domestic Surveillance Activities and Special Activities)
He began working for FW c. 1584–c. 1585 as a prison informer. His reward for undertaking such an unattractive assignment was the trip abroad to carry messages between Blount and Morgan. Poley had a reputation for providing extravagant hospitality to Catholic priests in his Bishopgate house, which Cecil had provided. Poley inveigled his way into the circle and confidence of Anthony Babington.[56]

*Peter Proby*
(Secretariat Directorate/Finance)
Signed for Walsingham's annuities from 1587 to 1588.[57]

# R

*Stephen de Rorque*
(Collection Directorate/Open Source)
Acted on behalf of English merchants in Lisbon.[58]

*John de Rosse*
(Secretariat Directorate/Unknown)
He served Walsingham in France.[59]

# S

*Henry Sanderson*
(Operations Directorate/ Domestic Surveillance Activities)
A postal searcher (Newcastle).[60]

*Captain Tomasso di Vicenzo Sassetti*
(Collection Directorate/Clandestine)
Italian, diplomatic courier, decipherer, and intelligencer, from 1570–1585.
Sassetti made frequent trips to Paris. FW recruited Sassetti to represent him
in an intelligence network that would ultimately stretch from Constantinople
to Canada and Virginia's new found lands. He supported various English
ambassadors, informants, and spies for many years.[61]

*Nicholas Skeres*
(Operations Directorate/Special Activities)
(Secretariat Directorate/Courier Services)
A government "plant" in the Babington Plot. Skeres associated with Thomas
Walsingham, cousin of Francis, as a confidential courier. He worked in
France until 1584.[62]

*Charles Sledd*
(Analysis Directorate/Biographic Intelligence)
(Collection Directorate/Clandestine)
(Operations Directorate/Domestic Surveillance Activities)
Worked as a "serving man" at the English college in Rome. On his arrival in
Paris and return to England, Sledd developed an immensely detailed logbook
about English Catholics on the continent. He found a niche as an informer for
FW and provided a deluge of information on English Catholics abroad. His
lengthy descriptions and specific details must have been valuable to watchers
and port searchers alike. For example, Humphrey Ely wore a short brown
beard and was in his late thirties. Henry Orton, a lawyer, was about thirty

years old and an excellent French speaker. Robert Johnson, a priest, was perhaps forty. He was slim, with an untrimmed flaxen yellow beard, a face full of wrinkles, and two teeth were missing from the right side of his upper jaw. He spoke Italian fluently. Sledd was initially vetted by Francis Mylles and probably began working for FW in 1580. Sledd's surviving document is an extraordinary compilation of facts. He names nearly 300 English and Welsh Catholics abroad and pensions they received from the Pope, as well as physical descriptions of the priests he knew. He also wrote details of meetings, dinners, conversations, and events in Rome and his journey through Italy and France in his diary. His documents significantly enhanced Walsingham's anti-Catholic infiltration and domestic surveillance activities. Sledd's narrative was a secret document read only at the highest levels of Elizabeth's government. Later it was used as evidence in one of the most important treason trials (Mary Stuart) of Elizabeth's reign.[63]

*John Somers*
(Operations Directorate/Technical Services
(Secretariat Directorate/Chief of Staff/Operations Support)
Somers was primarily responsible for revealing the material in the coded letters sent to Mary. He and Phelippes undertook the breaking of particularly tricky letters from Europe. He acted as a principal secretary when FW was ill in 1577.[64]

*Anthony Standen alias Pompeo Pellegrini alias B.C.*
(Collection Directorate/Clandestine)
Information collector on the Iberian Peninsula. Standen ran a group of sub-agents who gathered information on the status of Spanish military operations. A first-class spy with unrivaled access to the Spanish camp, he assumed a new identity as Pompeo Pellegrini. He recruited an agent of his own who sent letters to him from Lisbon by way of the diplomatic bag at Madrid. In 1588, Standen reported to FW directly from Spain.[65]

*William Stubbs*
(Secretariat Directorate/Finance)
Signed for Walsingham's annuities.[66]

# T

*Lawrence Tomson*
(Operations Directorate/Technical Services)
(Secretariat Directorate/Chief of Staff/Operations Support)

Employed by Walsingham from at least 1577, Tomson dealt with incoming correspondence from the Paris embassy, semi-official correspondents in the Low Countries, and numerous special envoys abroad. In the mid-1570s, he undertook deciphering when his employer was especially busy. He was sent to the northern Italian city of Bologna in 1580 to meet a papal agent with information to sell.[67] *Note*: This may be an indication of the early stages of the Throckmorton Plot.

*Alexander de la Torre alias Batzon*
(Collection Directorate/Open Source)
He worked in Antwerp and Rome on behalf of English merchants.[68]

*Anthony Tyrell*
(Collection Directorate/Domestic Surveillance Activities)
(Operations Directorate/Special Activities)
Prison informer and double agent Tyrell escaped from Gatehouse prison with John Savage. In September 1584, he accompanied Savage in Rome, seeking papal approval for Savage to kill Elizabeth.[69]

# W

*William Waad*
(Secretariat Directorate/Operations Support/Administration/Courier Services)
Clerk of the Council; part of intelligence service management; case officer, confidential messenger, and private secretary to FW. Involved in covert work in 1585, Waad was sent to Paris with extradition papers for Thomas Morgan.[70]

*Thomas Walsingham*
(Operations Directorate/Special Activities)
(Secretariat Directorate/Operations Support/Courier Services)
A second cousin to Sir FW, Thomas was involved in intelligence matters at age seventeen, "bringing letters in post for Her Majesty's affairs" from the English ambassador (Sir Henry Cobham) in France. Acquainted with Thomas Phelippes, he returned to England c. 1584 and was promoted to a case officer position. By the mid-to-late 1580's he also may have become Christopher Marlowe's handler. Thomas likely became the intelligence liaison with the English literary community.[71]

*Ralph Warcop*
(Secretariat Directorate/Administration)

Warcop began serving Walsingham in 1570 and worked with Robert Beale. After his return from Paris in 1573, Warcop pursued an academic career at New College, Oxford.[72]

*Thomas Watson*
(Collection Directorate/Open Source)
(Secretariat Directorate/Courier Services)
One of a group of writers/poets/spies tasked with infiltrating suspected literary groups. Watson was related to Robert Poley through his sister's marriage to Poley. He became a letter carrier for FW because FW trusted him with important matters. Watson also worked for Thomas Walsingham and carried confidential letters for both Sir Francis and Thomas.[73]

*"Weekes"*
(Secretariat Directorate/Administration)
Performed secretarial duties in the 1580s.[74]

*"Wilkes"*
(Secretariat Directorate/Administration)
Performed secretarial duties in the 1580s.[75]

*Walter Williams*
(Operations Directorate/Domestic Surveillance Activities)
(Secretariat Directorate/Courier Services/Operations Support)
He was a multi-lingual messenger who worked for FW for fifteen years. Williams often communicated using the Welsh language to confuse foreign agents. He was, at times, also employed as a prison informer. In 1582, he was assigned to a surveillance operation at home. Inserted into Rye Prison in August 1582 to investigate Catholic sedition, he reported how traitors were conveying intelligence via secret writing hidden by using orange juice. By August 1583, he acted as FW's contact with Laurent Feron, a mole inside the French embassy. Eventually, FW put Williams in charge of housekeeping duties at Seething Lane.[76]

*John Wolley*
(Secretariat Directorate/Administration)
Joined the Secretariat c. 1577 and concurrently served as Elizabeth's Latin secretary.[77]

*Jan Wychegerde*
(Collection Directorate/Open Source)
A grain and sundries merchant/agent, originally from Germany.[78]

# Y

*Richard Young*
(Operations Directorate/Domestic Surveillance Activities)
A tracker of priests in Westminster and Middlesex.[79]


## NOTES

1. I wish to thank Mr. Robert Hutchinson, who in his book *Elizabeth's Spymaster: Francis Walsingham and the Secret War that Saved England (2006)*, produced and consolidated a list of Walsingham's spies. Using Mr. Hutchinson's list as a baseline, I have added new names and biographical information from the writings of Stephen Alford, Stephen Budiansky, John Cooper, Alan Haynes, Charles Nicholl, and a doctoral thesis titled *The Pursuit of God's Glory* submitted to the University of York (2012) by Hsuan-Ying Tu.

2. Charles Nicholl, *The Reckoning: The Murder of Christopher Marlowe* (Harcourt, Brace and Company, 1992), 109; Alan Haynes, *Walsingham: Elizabethan Spymaster & Statesman* (Sutton Publishing, 2004), 148–149.

3. Haynes, *The Elizabethan Secret Services*, 52–53.

4. Haynes, *Walsingham: Elizabethan Spymaster & Statesman*, 98.

5. Nicholl, 91, 123–124, 126–127; Cooper, 180.

6. Haynes, *Elizabethan Secret Services*, 15.

7. Hsuan-Ying Tu, *The Pursuit of God's Glory: Francis Walsingham's Espionage in Elizabethan Politics, 1586–1588* (University of York, Thesis, 2012*)*, 78.

8. Nicholl, 108, 112; Haynes, *Walsingham: Elizabethan Spymaster & Statesman*, 21, 56–57, 107; Haynes, *Elizabethan Secret Services*, 28; Cooper, 42–43, 168, 175; Alford, 19, 263–264, 313; Tu, 71, 77–79.

9. Nicholl, 110; Haynes, *Walsingham: Spymaster & Statesman*, 160, 169, 178; Cooper, 183–184, 203; Alford, 200–201; Haynes, *Elizabethan Secret Services*, 47–48.

10. Tu, 78.

11. Nicholl, 106.

12. Haynes, *Elizabethan Secret Services*, 35.

13. Nicholl, 136; Haynes, *Walsingham: Elizabethan Spymaster & Statesman*, 91; Cooper, 180–181; Alford, 200.

14. Tu, 77, 80–81.

15. Tu, 78.

16. Nicholl, 110, 270–271.

17. Tu, 78, 80.

18. Tu, 78.

19. Cooper, 180.

20. Cooper, 157; *Haynes, Elizabethan Secret Services*, 32.

21. Nicholl, 36, 194; Haynes, *Walsingham: Spymaster & Statesman*, 34–35, 77–78; Cooper, 202; Haynes, *Elizabethan Secret Services,* 22.

22. Tu, 77.

23. Tu, 78.

24. Tu, 78–79.

25. Alford, 102–103; Haynes, *Elizabethan Secret Services*, 42–43.

26. Nicholl, 119; Cooper, 168; Tu, 75, 77–78.

27. Haynes, *Elizabethan Secret Services*, 34.

28. Nicholl, 131–132; Haynes, *Elizabethan Secret Services*, 63, 77.

29. Nicholl, 108; Alford, 217; Haynes, *Elizabethan Secret Services*, 14; Stephen Budiansky, *Her Majesty's Spymaster* (A Plume Book, 2005), 146.

30. Tu, 77.

31. Haynes, *Walsingham: Spymaster & Statesman*, 99; Cooper, 270–271, 277–278.

32. Nicholl, 137.

33. Haynes, *Elizabethan Secret Services*, 28.

34. Nicholl, 109, 222.

35. Alford, 162–163; Tu, 176.

36. Haynes, *Elizabethan Secret Services*, 29.

37. Hsuan-Ying, 78.

38. Nicholl, 119–120; Cooper, 302.

39. Nicholl, 106.

40. Alford, 102–103.

41. Tu, 78, 81.

42. Budiansky, 95; Haynes, *Elizabethan Secret Services,* 27; Tu, 71, 77.

43. Cooper, 179–180.

44. Nicholl, 148–149; Haynes, *Walsingham: Spymaster & Statesman*, 153; Haynes, *Elizabethan Secret Services,* 53–54, 70; Haynes, *Elizabethan Secret Services*, 154.

45. Nicholl, 252–253; Haynes, *Walsingham: Spymaster & Statesman*, 184.

46. Tu, 78.

47. Nicholl, 173–176; Haynes, *Walsingham: Spymaster & Statesman*, 190; Alford, 87–88; Haynes, *Elizabethan Secret Services*, 43–44.

48. Nicholl, 109, 161; Haynes, *Walsingham: Spymaster & Statesman*, 66, 172; Alford, 217; Haynes, *Elizabethan Secret Services*, 28; Tu, 71, 76–77, 79–82, 84.

49. Haynes, *Walsingham: Spymaster & Statesman*, 117.

50. Tu, 78.

51. Alford, 264.

52. Haynes, *Walsingham: Spymaster & Statesman*, 192; Alford, 252; Haynes, *Elizabethan Secret Services*, 49.

53. Tu, 78.

54. Alford, 264.

55. Nicholl, 105–106, 108, 223; Haynes, *Elizabethan Secret Services*, 14–15; Alford, "Spies, Cyphers and Sleights of Hand: Uncovering the Conspiracy to Kill Queen Elizabeth I." An article in *Command Posts—A Focus on Military History, Policy and Fiction*, February 11, 2013; Tu, 76, 78, 80–81, 90.

56. Nicholl, 134–135; Haynes, *Elizabethan Secret Services*, 75–76.

57. Tu, 78.

58. Alford, 264.

59. Tu, 77.

60. Haynes, *Walsingham: Spymaster & Statesman*, 98.

61. Haynes, *Walsingham: Spymaster & Statesman*, 91–92; Cooper, 2, 62; Haynes, *Elizabethan Secret Services,* 27.

62. Nicholl, 28,116–118.

63. Nicholl, 125; Haynes, *Walsingham: Spymaster & Statesman*, 47–48; Alford, 69–70, 76, 83–84, 103; Haynes, *Elizabethan Secret Services*, 44.

64. Budiansky, 145; Haynes, *Elizabethan Secret Services*, 28, 32.

65. Haynes, *Walsingham: Spymaster & Statesman*, 201–202; Cooper, 297; Alford, 253; Haynes, *Elizabethan Secret Services*, 101.

66. Tu, 78.

67. Haynes, *Elizabethan Secret Services*, 28; Tu, 78.

68. Alford, 264.

69. Cooper, 186–187; Haynes, *Elizabethan Secret Services*, 28, 69.

70. Nicholl, 40, 108, 141; Haynes, *Walsingham: Spymaster & Statesman*, 189; Alford, 295, 310.

71. Nicholl, 116–117.

72. Tu, 79.

73. Nicholl, 182–183, 200–201.

74. Tu, 78.

75. Tu, 78.

76. Haynes, *Walsingham: Spymaster & Statesman*, 21; Cooper, 168–169, 181, 201; Tu, 77–78.

77. Tu, 79.

78. Haynes, *Elizabethan Secret Services*, 102.

79. Alford, 210.

# Appendix E

## *Facts, Fiction, and Inferences[1]*

Fact: Something that has happened or is true.

Fiction: An imaginary statement/story. Literary narratives with imaginary characters/events.

Inference: A conclusion based on reasoning from something known or assumed.

Throughout this book, facts and inferences are used to explain the evolution of Walsingham and Cecil's Indirect Preemption strategy and the supporting deception planning process. The sequence of facts and inferences is described below in ascending order, from Mary's escape to England in 1568 to the arrest of Mary for treason in August 1586.

### Chapters 1–3 (1568–1572)

*[Facts]*

- A large percentage of English subjects are Catholic. However, the loyalty of those subjects is problematic; England is geographically isolated and surrounded by Catholic-controlled countries with larger populations and superior military forces.
- Mary Stuart, a legitimate Catholic claimant to the English throne, arrives in England seeking sanctuary.
- Following Mary's request for protection, a series of Catholic-inspired activities attacked the legitimacy of Elizabeth's reign and Protestant rule in England.
- Elizabeth is disinclined to use war as a legitimate tool of statecraft.

*[Inferences]*

- Elizabeth's government and Protestant subjects perceive a growing threat to England's domestic tranquility and Protestant control.
- A motive is created to seek new, counter-Catholic courses of action to mitigate the perceived threat.

## Chapters 4–7 (1573–1580)

*[Facts]*

- Sir Francis Walsingham replaces Sir William Cecil as First Secretary. Walsingham is a strident, aggressive anti-Catholic.
- Walsingham and Cecil are exceptional, learned leaders and highly effective statesmen, administrators, and managers of people.
- Walsingham and Cecil are frustrated with Elizabeth's approach to statecraft.
- The writings of Niccolò Machiavelli and Sir Thomas More offer innovative approaches that reject the idea of direct military confrontation against an opposing force.
- Significant changes in England's diplomatic, military, and domestic courses of action take place. The most dramatic change focuses on improving England's intelligence collection and analysis capabilities.

*[Inferences]*

- Walsingham, Cecil, and Elizabeth are familiar with the writings of Machiavelli and More.
- Elizabeth's two top advisors seek more effective ways to counter the perceived Catholic threat that will not only support Elizabeth's priorities but more effectively counter the growing advances of Catholic resistance.
- They choose to employ deception as the best course of action to counter perceived Catholic advances against England.
- The significant advances in intelligence capabilities provide Walsingham and Cecil the means to plan and develop a successful deception operation.
- Walsingham and Cecil begin the deception planning process by determining Catholic vulnerabilities and resources available to Walsingham to support a large-scale deception operation.

**Chapters 8–10 (1580–1585)**

*[Facts]*

- Two Catholic plots against Elizabeth, an incidence of potential violence directed against her, and an assassination of a prominent Protestant leader (William of Orange) increased tensions to a breaking point between Catholics and Protestants in England.
- Queen Elizabeth significantly increases funding for her Intelligence Service.
- Walsingham's agents successfully infiltrate the French embassy in London and English-exile Catholic conspiracy group in Paris.
- Walsingham and Cecil openly justify their past actions (Mary's reincarceration at Tutbury Castle, promulgating the Act of Association, imprisoning Mary's chief intelligencer in the Bastille, and weakening Mary's influence by isolating her from her son, James VI) as necessary countermeasures to prevent future attempts on Queen Elizabeth's life.
- At the direction of Walsingham, two of his agents developed a communication intercept system designed to control message traffic between Paris, the French embassy in London, and Mary's new location of incarceration—Chartley Hall.
- Mary and her entourage are moved from Tutbury Castle to Chartley Hall on 24 December 1585. Mary and her Catholic supporters are unaware that Walsingham controls what they believe to be secure communication between the Scottish Queen and her supporters.
- The exiled Englishman, William Gifford, selected to lead to a new Catholic conspiracy from London, rejects the offer leaving the position unfilled.

*[Inferences]*

- The anti-Protestant events provide Walsingham and Cecil with the opportunity to develop their counter-Catholic deception plan further.
- Walsingham and Cecil use the Catholic-inspired and supported events against English Protestants and Queen Elizabeth to cover/hide their ongoing deception-related planning and implementation events from public scrutiny. In truth, England's countermeasures to Catholic anti-Protestant activities are pre-meditated actions designed to support Walsingham's deception objectives (entrapping Mary in traitorous acts).
- Before Mary's relocation to Chartley Hall, Walsingham's deception planners are refining deception events and themes, or storylines, that will be used to influence key Catholic conspirators and their decisions.

## Chapters 11–12 (January–May 1586)

*[Facts]*

- Walsingham strategically places his double agents in the English Catholic exile, conspiracy "center of gravity."
- A person to lead the conspiracy from London is still in limbo.
- The English communication intercept system at Chartley Hall is fully operational and controlled by Walsingham.
- The Catholic conspirators are in a "fact-finding" mode to determine the extent of French, Spanish, papal, and in-country English noble support for their plan.
- Thomas Morgan, John Ballard, and Mary Stuart choose Anthony Babington as the London focal point for the conspiracy.
- By the end of May, Walsingham has evidence that Mary is committed in principle to the conspiracy and the invasion plan.

*[Inferences]*

- Walsingham's double agents' access to key conspirators provides an excellent opportunity to influence conspirator decisions about who should act as *de facto/de jure* conspiracy focal point in London.
- By the end of May, Babington and many of his supporters begin to doubt the conspiracy's invasion plans.

## Chapter 12 (June–July 1586)

*[Facts]*

- From this point hence, Walsingham's counter Catholic conspiracy now focuses on three specific individuals—Babington, Ballard, and Queen Mary.
- Babington requests three meetings with Walsingham to discuss providing services to Elizabeth if he is approved to travel to the continent.
- Walsingham agents Robert Poley and Gilbert Gifford convince an unwitting Babington to provide invasion plan details to Mary. Another agent Thomas Philippes reads the message and informs Walsingham before sending it on to Mary at Chartley Hall.
- By the end of July, with Mary's response to Babington's letter and her later request to Spanish Ambassador Mendoza for King Philip II's support of the plan to invade England and remove Elizabeth, Walsingham now possesses the "smoking gun" evidence required to charge the Scottish Queen with treason.

*[Inferences]*

- Walsingham's success conducting such a highly complex counter-conspiracy operation against the Babington plotters resulted from a deliberate, well-thought-out, coordinated, and precisely orchestrated deception plan.

## NOTE

1. "Analysis, good or bad, is about producing judgments, forecasts, and insights. A judgment is a conclusion or inference based on analysis of incomplete and uncertain information . . . Analytic judgments are typically expressed without accompanying statements of probability or confidence . . . When customers of intelligence receive analysis that offers a fresh, new perspective, or when it causes them to think about a hard problem in a new way—even if it does not present any new information—they appreciate the insight that analysis has brought them. Analytic insights are less about facts than they are about contextualizing them." James B. Bruce and Roger Z. George. Chapter 1 "Intelligence Analysis, What Is It and What Does It Take?" Pages 1, 5. *Analyzing Intelligence: National Security Practitioners' Perspectives.*

# Appendix F

## *Chronology of Catholic and Protestant Events*

**The 1560s**

- The early 1560s: Spain suppresses Protestants in Low Countries (Catholic Event)
- The early 1560s: England provides financial support to Scottish Protestants (Protestant Event)
- 1568: Mary seeks asylum in England (Catholic Event)
- 1569: English nobles in northern England revolt (Catholic Event)
- 1569/1570: Elizabeth brutally "puts down" the Northern Rebellion (Protestant Event)

**The 1570s**

- The 1570s: Increasing reports of Spain preparing to invade England (Catholic Event)
- 1570: Pope excommunicates Elizabeth (Catholic Event)
- 1571–1572: Ridolfi Plot supported by Pope, Spain, and France (Catholic Event)
- 1572: Ridolfi Plot defeated (Protestant Event)
- 1572: St. Bartholomew Day Massacre (Catholic Event)
- 1573: English intelligencer, Robert Beale, produces a dire assessment of the Catholic threat (Protestant Event)
- 1573: Cecil becomes Lord Treasurer, Walsingham becomes First Secretary (Protestant Event)

- 1573: Indirect Preemption strategy, Intelligence reorganization begins (Protestant Event)
- 1574–1575: First wave of infiltration: Earliest Catholic students from Douai, France, return to England (Catholic Event)
- 1579: Desmond uprising in Ireland (Catholic Event)

## The 1580s

- 1580: Second Wave of infiltration led by Robert Persons and Edmund Campion (Catholic Event)
- 1580: Pope excommunicates William of Orange (Catholic Event)
- 1580: Deception planning begins—Concept Development (Deception Planning Event)
- Late 1582–1584: Throckmorton Plot active (Catholic Event)
- 1582–1584: Deception plan transitions to the Implementation phase (Deception Planning Event)
- 1583: Somerville incident focused on assassinating Elizabeth uncovered (Catholic Event)
- 1584: William of Orange is assassinated (Catholic Event)
- 1584–1585: Domestic surveillance and military preparedness activities in England significantly increase (Protestant Event)
- 1584–1585: Parry Plot to assassinate Elizabeth uncovered (Catholic Event)
- 1585: England provides financial and manpower support to the Protestant rebellion in the Low Countries (Protestant Event)
- 1585: Spain declares war on England (Catholic Event)
- 1585: New Catholic plot begins to develop in Paris (Catholic Event)
- 1585: Deception plan transitions from Implementation to Execution—identification/penetration of the (Babington) plot (Deception Planning Event)
- 1586: Babington Plot becomes active (Catholic Event)
- 1586: Deception plan transitions from Identification/Penetration to provocation/influence activities against plotters (Deception Planning Event)
- 1587: Mary, Queen of Scots, executed at Fotheringhay Castle (8 February 1587) (Protestant Event)

# Appendix G

## *Chronology of Significant Deception Plan Execution Events*

### 1585 to January 1586

*1585*

- January—Mary is moved to Tutbury Castle for security reasons. (This is a planned execution event.)
- January—Mary signs the Bond of Association, condemning anyone who threatens Elizabeth's life.[1] Mary's surprise acceptance of this planned execution event essentially legitimizes and legalizes the death penalty for royal monarchs. (This fortuitous, unplanned event advances Walsingham and Cecil's primary objective.)
- January/February—Morgan and Paget believe their ability to communicate with Mary securely has been severely impacted by her move to Tutbury.[2] (This information confirms to Walsingham that the planned execution event is causing the desired reaction—stress, angst, and frustration.)
- February—Paget and Morgan tell Mary that they are trying to reconstitute a secure means of communicating with her.[3] (This information provides valuable feedback that Morgan is searching for a solution to the communication problem.)
- February/March—Mary/James VI split is irreconcilable, and Scotland allies itself with England. (This is the desired objective of a planned execution event.)
- March—Thomas Morgan is placed in the Bastille, awaiting extradition to England. (This is a planned execution event.)

- May thru September—Mary voices her discontentment to Elizabeth and many others over her imprisonment at the "hated" Tutbury Castle. Mary asks that she be moved to a more comfortable and accommodating location, given her rank and royal stature.[4] (This information provides valuable feedback that the planned execution event of moving Mary to Tutbury Castle in January has produced the desired target reaction—stress, angst, frustration.)
- May/June—Cecil instructs Paulet to tell Mary her communication network at Tutbury is not secure and that French Ambassador Castelnau's letters are being monitored.[5] (This is a planned execution event designed to increase target frustrations. Thus, increasing the likelihood that Morgan and Mary will be more susceptible to accepting new solutions to their perceived communication problem.)
- June—Robert Poley gains access to Morgan. (This is a planned execution event.)
- July—Morgan tells Mary that he has been contacted by Robert Poley, who can be trusted to help reconstitute a secure communication link with her supporters. Morgan informs Mary that Poley will be returning to England to assist in the effort. He also informs Mary that he has passed this information to James Seaton, her ambassador in Paris, and Charles Paget. Also, Morgan asks Seaton to forward the information to the Spanish ambassador in Paris, Bernardino de Mendoza.[6] (This information provides valuable feedback that the planned execution event has produced the desired target reaction—Poley is accepted as a trusted agent.)
- July—Morgan/Paget mention Robert Poley as a possible ally. In addition, they recommend that Mary contact Anthony Babington as he might be of excellent service in furthering her intelligence-related capabilities.[7] (This information highlights and identifies a potentially high-value target for Walsingham's deception plan.)
- August/September—Gilbert Gifford becomes a Walsingham agent.
- September—Walsingham tells Paulet to examine Chartley Hall as a possible new place of confinement for Mary.[8]
- September—Walsingham instructs Phelippes and Paulet to develop a communication network at Chartley Hall that Walsingham will control.[9]
- September—French ambassador, Châteauneuf, replaces Castelnau in London.[10] (Both are likely aware Mary will be moved from Tutbury Castle to a healthier and more commodious place.)
- October—Morgan informs Mary that Gilbert Gifford is returning to England to reconstitute her communication network. Gifford has also been instructed to surveil the area of her imprisonment and identify her loyal supporters. Morgan vouches for Gifford's loyalty. His uncle, living

near Chartley Hall, is to renew an old friendship with Mary's jailor, Paulet, "to gain his confidence and some advantage to her."[11] (Gifford's successful penetration of Morgan's center of gravity is a planned execution event.)

- October/November—Cecil informs Mary she will be moved to Chartley Hall. (This is a planned execution event.)
- December—Gilbert Gifford is arrested by English customs officials at the Rye.
- December—Morgan sends Mary a cipher code to be used at Chartley Hall. Walsingham and Phelippes already possess the means to read all message traffic going to and from Chartley Hall.[12]
- 24 December—Mary and her entourage relocate to Chartley Hall. (This is a planned execution event.)

*1586*

- January—Gifford begins delivering letters from the French embassy in London to Chartley Hall.[13]
- January—Mary approves of her new, secure communications network at Chartley Hall.[14] Receipt of this information not only supports Walsingham's deception/provocation objectives but also continues to validate the effectiveness of his feedback loop.

## NOTES

1. Antonia Fraser, *Mary Queen of Scots* (Delacorte Press, 1969), 473; Anne Somerset, *Elizabeth I* (Anchor Books, 1991), 410.
2. *Calendar of the Cecil Papers in Hatfield House: Volume 3, (1583–1589),* (originally published by the Majesty's Stationary Office, 1889), Cecil Papers #139, 31 January/10 February 1584, and #140, 4/14 February 1585.
3. Cecil Papers #139, 31 January/10 February 1584, and #140, 4/14 February 1585.
4. *Letters of Mary Queen of Scots* (now first published from the originals), Volume II (Henry Colburn publisher, 1844), 153–155.
5. Robert Hutchinson, *Elizabeth's Spymaster* (St. Martin's Press, 2006), 119.
6. Cecil Paper #170, 10/20 July 1585.
7. Cecil Papers #170, 10/20 July 1585; #172, 16/26 July 1585; #173, 17/27 July 1585; Alan Haynes, *Elizabethan Spymaster & Statesman* (Sutton Publishing, 2004), 158.
8. Hutchinson, 120.
9. Hutchinson, 121.
10. Hutchinson, 120.
11. Cecil Paper #202, 5/15 October 1585.

12. John Hungerford Pollen, *Mary, Queen of Scots and the Babington Plot*. Edited from the original documents in the Public Record Office (T. and A. Constable for the Scottish History Society, 1922), Introduction: "The Death Trap," lviii.

13. Conyers Read, *Lord Burghley and Queen Elizabeth* (Alfred A. Knopf, 1960), 343.

14. Hutchinson, 121–122.

# Appendix H

## *Walsingham's Deception Capabilities Flow Chart*[1]

### NOTE

1. The original generic flow chart depicting foreign adversary deception planning and execution dynamics was designed by Mr. John Wilhelm, a member of the author's staff (2006–2014).

# Walsingham's Deception Capabilities Flow Chart

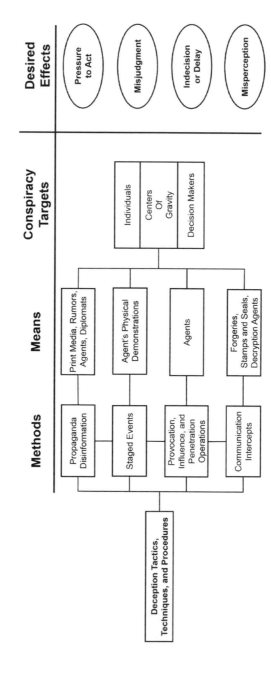

**Figure Appendix H.1.**
Source: R. Kent Tiernan

# Appendix I

## *Walsingham's Role in Defeating the Babington Plot*

### LITERATURE REVIEW

John Hungerford Pollen (1922) concludes, "He [Walsingham] encouraged, assisted, and 'recompensed the pains' of his informers, and by doing he clearly made himself . . . responsible for the treachery and lies, and wickedness of their multiplied and prolonged plotting against the life of his victim [Mary]."[1]

Stefan Zweig (1935) writes that "Walsingham . . . began one of the most incredible though documentarily attested acts of perfidy known to history . . . the 'frame-up' by which Walsingham made Mary Stuart privy to a plot of his own manufacture, the so-called Babington Plot, which was, in reality, a Walsingham conspiracy."[2]

Antonia Fraser (1969), weighing in about English intelligence chicanery, observed that "Walsingham, through his many devious agents, set about enmeshing Mary in two separate conspiracies against Elizabeth, which together made up the complicated and, in part, bogus machinations which are known as the Babington Plot . . . "[3]

Rosalind K. Marshall (1991) stated, "Sir Francis Walsingham, therefore, initiated a series of elaborate conspiracies designed to ensnare Mary. The Babington Plot of 1587 was not the first but was the most successful."[4]

Charles Nicholl (1992) submits that Jesuit Robert Southwell claimed: "there was not a shadow of a doubt that the [English] government was responsible for the entire plot . . . the matter of Babington was wholly of their plotting and forging, and his accomplices were drawn blindfold to be workers of their own overthrow."[5]

Alan Haynes (1992) notes, " . . . the Babington Plot was a dramatic coup for Walsingham . . . Babington and his friends had been prodded into something much more significant with a compelling blend of effort and ingenuity."[6]

Robert Hutchinson (2006) writes, "Never far from the forefront of his [Walsingham] mind was the brutal suppression of Protestantism by Mary . . . [It] can have left no room for any doubts or scruples to prevent him from deploying all the dark instruments of the Tudor state to destroy any threat he perceived as emanating from the repressed Catholic majority or from England's enemies overseas. To him, bribery, treachery, blackmail, coercion, internment, torture, and state-sponsored murder were merely handy tools . . . to stamp out the contagion of Popish treason and conspiracy.[7]

G.J. Meyer (2010) believes "none of the most notorious and supposedly dangerous plots against Elizabeth had the slimmest chance of success and Walsingham himself probably actively encouraged at least one of them to entrap gullible young true believers. He may even have concocted that last of the conspiracies (the so-called Babington Plot)."[8]

A.N. Wilson (2011) contends that "the Babington Plot was a real one, but what none of the conspirators realized was that Walsingham had known about it from the beginning and that the consummate spy-master had decided to use it as a way for finally entrapping the Scottish queen."[9]

Stephen Alford (2012) asserts that "Sir Francis Walsingham and Thomas Phelippes led Mary, Queen of Scots, to the headman's block. By secret means they uncovered her correspondence with Anthony Babington and his fellow conspirators, unearthing with great patience the evidence they needed to prove Mary's complicity in a plot to murder Elizabeth . . . they dabbled [in] a little forgery. Even at the time, the word entrapment was used by their enemies to describe the way Mary had been caught and held fast."[10] Adding to Alford's characterization of Walsingham's counter-conspiracy activities, John Cooper (2012) affirms that "The most striking allegation against Walsingham, from the pen of a modern Jesuit, is that he fabricated the Babington Plot in a Machiavellian scheme to obliterate Catholicism from the map of England."[11]

Hsuan-Ying Tu (2012) opines that "Elizabethan plots did arise from Catholic ambition—though the plotters did not realize that how far they could go was decided not by their own efforts, but by the English government, more precisely by the spymaster, Walsingham. Instead of nipping them in the bud, Walsingham's espionage adopted a wait-and-see strategy, allowing plots to develop until he could obtain enough fatal evidence to put Mary on trial."[12]

# NOTES

1. John Hungerford Pollen, *Mary Queen of Scots and the Babington Plot.* Edited from the original documents in the Public Record Office, the Yelverton MSS., and elsewhere (Edinburgh University Press by T and A. Constable Ltd. for the Scottish History Society, 1922), Introduction: "Walsingham's Political Morality," xxxiii.

2. Stefan Zweig, *Mary Queen of Scotland and the Isles* (Lancer Books, 1935), 310.

3. Antonia Fraser, *Mary Queen of Scots* (Delacorte Press, 1969), 480.

4. Rosalind K. Marshall, *Elizabeth I* (HMSO Publications, 1991), 121.

5. Charles Nicholl, *The Reckoning: The Murder of Christopher Marlowe* (University of Chicago Press, 1992), 162.

6. Alan Haynes, *The Elizabethan Secret Services* (Sutton Publishing, 1992), 92.

7. Robert Hutchinson, Elizabeth's Spymaster (Thomas Dunne Books, St. Martin's Press, 2006), 262–263.

8. G.J. Meyer, *The Tudors: The Complete Story of England's Most Notorious Dynasty* (Delacorte Press, 2010), 515–516.

9. A.N. Wilson, *The Elizabethans* (Farrar, Straus, and Giroux, 2011), 232.

10. Stephen Alford, *The Watchers: A Secret History of the Reign of Elizabeth I* (Bloomsbury Press, 2012), 243.

11. John Cooper, *The Queen's Agent: Sir Francis Walsingham and the Rise of Espionage in Elizabethan England* (Pegasus Books, 2012), 131.

12. Hsuan-Ying Tu, *The Pursuit of God's Glory: Francis Walsingham's Espionage in Elizabethan Politics, 1568–1588*, Ph.D. Thesis, University of York, September 2012, 173.

# Bibliography

Alford, Stephen. "Spies, Cyphers and Sleights of Hand: Uncovering the Conspiracy to Kill Queen Elizabeth I." An article in *Command Posts—A Focus on Military History, Policy, and Fiction*, February 11, 2013.

———. *The Watchers: A Secret History of the Reign of Elizabeth I.* Bloomsbury Press, New York, 2012.

*Analyzing Intelligence: National Security Practitioners' Perspectives.* Edited by George, Roger Z. George, and James B. Bruce, Georgetown University Press, 2014.

*Army Field Manual 90–2, Chapter 4, Deception Planning Considerations*, Department of Army, Washington D. C., 1988. Note: Found on the Internet.

Blum, Howard. *The Last Goodnight: A World War II Story of Espionage, Adventure and Betrayal.* Harper Perennial Press, New York, 2017.

Bowyer, J. Barton. *Cheating: Deception in War, Magic, Games, Sports, Sex, Religion, Business, Con Games, Politics, Espionage, Art, and Science.* St. Martin's Press, New York, 1982.

Budiansky, Stephen. *Her Majesty's Spymaster: Elizabeth I, Sir Francis Walsingham, and the Birth of Modern Espionage.* Penguin Group, New York, 2005.

Burleigh, Nina. *Unholy Business: A True Tale of Faith, Greed, and Forgery in the Holy Land.* Harper Collins/Smithsonian Books, New York, 2008.

*Calendar of the Cecil Papers in Hatfield House, Volume 3, (1583–1589)*, originally published by Her Majesty's Stationary Office, London, 1889. Note: Digitized by British History Online.

*Calendar of State Papers (Domestic Series) on the Reign of Elizabeth (1581–1590), Volume CXLVII.* Edited by Robert Lemon, preserved in Her Majesty's Public Records Office, Printed by G. Eyre and W. Spottiswoode, her Majesty's printers, London, 1865. Note: Google digitized.

Campbell, James Stuart. *The Alchemical Patronage of Sir William Cecil, Lord Burghley* (Thesis submitted to the Victoria University of Wellington in fulfillment of the requirements for the degree of Master of Arts in History), 2009.

Community Assessment, *Foreign Threats to 2020 U.S. Federal Elections*, Office of Director National Intelligence, March 10 2021.

Conant, Jennet. *The Irregulars: Roald Dahl and the British Spy Ring in Wartime Washington.* Simon and Schuster Paperbacks, New York, 2008.

Cooper, John. *The Queen's Agent: Sir Francis Walsingham and the Rise of Espionage in Elizabethan England.* Pegasus Books, New York/London, 2012.

Duffy, Eamon. *Fires of Faith: Catholic England under Mary Tudor,* Yale University Press, New Haven and London, 2009.

————. *Reformation Divided: Catholics, Protestants and the Conversion of England,* Bloomsbury, London, Oxford and New York, 2017.

Durant, Will. *The Reformation,* Simon and Schuster, New York, 1957.

Durant, Will, and Ariel. *The Age of Reason Begins: The Story of Civilization, Vol. VII.* Simon and Schuster, New York, 1961.

Dziak, John J. *Chekisty: A History of the KGB.* Lexington Books/D.C. Heath and Company, Lexington, Massachusetts, and Toronto, 1988.

Edwards, Francis. *Plots and Plotters in the Reign of Elizabeth I.* Four Courts Press Ltd., Dublin, Ireland, 2002.

Fleming, Ian. *Goldfinger.* Ian Fleming Publication Ltd., 1959 Thomas and Mercer edition, October 2012, Las Vegas, NV.

Fraser, Antonia. *Mary Queen of Scots.* Delacorte Press, New York, 1969.

Grant, Natalie. *Disinformation: Soviet Political Warfare, 1917–1992,* Leopolis Press, Washington, D. C., 2020.

Harkness, Deborah E. *The Jewel House,* Yale University Press, New Haven and London, 2007.

Hayden, Michael V. *Playing to the Edge.* Penguin Press, New York, 2016.

Haynes, Alan. *The Elizabethan Secret Services.* Sutton Publishing, England, 2000.

————. *Walsingham: Elizabethan Spymaster & Statesman.* Sutton Publishing, England, 2004.

Hicks, L, S.J. *An Elizabethan Problem: Some Aspects of the Careers of Two Exile Adventurers.* Fordham University Press, New York, 1964.

Hutchinson, Robert. *Elizabeth's Spymaster: Francis Walsingham and the Secret War That Saved England.* Thomas Dunne Books/St. Martin's Press, New York, 2006.

Jenkins, Elizabeth. *Elizabeth the Great: A Biography.* Capricorn Books/G. P. Putnam's Sons, New York, 1958.

Joint Publication 3–13.4 (Formerly JP 3–38), *Military Deception,* Director for Operations, United States Joint Forces Command, Joint Warfighting Center, Suffolk, Virginia, July 13, 2006.

Kersten, Jason. *The Art of Making Money: The Story of a Master Counterfeiter.* Gotham Books, New York, 2009.

*Letters of Mary, Queen of Scots.* Edited by Agnes Strickland, Vol. I and II, Henry Colburn Publisher, London, MDCCCXLIV (1864).

*Letters and Papers relating to Patrick Master of Gray, afterwards Seventh Lord Gray.* Presented to the Bannatyne Club by Lord Gray, Edinburgh Printing Company, 1835. Note: Google digitized.

Luke, Mary M. *Gloriana: The Years of Elizabeth I.* Coward, McCann & Geoghegan, Inc., New York, 1973.

Machiavelli, Niccolò. *The Prince and Other Writings.* Translation, Introduction, and Notes by Wayne A. Rebhorn, Barnes and Noble Classics, New York, 2003.

Mahl, Thomas E. *Desperate Deception: British Covert Operation in the United States, 1939–44.* Brassey's, Dulles, Virginia, 1998.

Marshall, Peter. *Heretics and Believers: A History of the English Reformation,* Yale University Press, New Haven and London, 2017.

Marshall, Rosalind K. *Elizabeth I.* HMSO, London, 1991.

Martin, Patrick. *Elizabethan Espionage: Plotters and Spies in the Struggle Between Catholicism and the Crown.* McFarland & Company, Inc. Jefferson, North Carolina, 2016.

Meyer, G. J. *The Tudors: The Complete Story of England's Most Notorious Dynasty.* Delacorte Press, New York, 2010.

Microsoft Encarta College Dictionary, St. Martin's Press, New York, 2001.

More, Thomas. *Utopia.* Introduction and notes by Wayne A. Rebhorn. Translated by Ralph Robinson, Barnes and Noble Classics, New York, 2005.

Nicholl, Charles. *The Reckoning: The Murder of Christopher Marlowe.* Harcourt, Brace, and Company, Chicago, 1992.

Norwich, John Julius. *Absolute Monarchs: A History of the Papacy.* Random House, New York, 2011.

Plowden, Alison. *The Elizabethan Secret Service.* St. Martin's Press, London/New York, 1991.

Pollen, John Hungerford. *Mary Queen of Scots and the Babington Plot.* Edited from the original documents in the Public Record Office, the Yelverton MSS., and elsewhere, 1858–1925. Edinburgh printed by T. and A. Constable for the Scottish History Society, 1922. Note: Google digitized.

*Queen Elizabeth and Her Times, a series of original letters, Volume II,* Selected from the inedited private correspondence of Lord Treasurer Burghley, the Earl of Leicester, the Secretaries Walsingham, and Smith, Sir Christopher Hatton and most distinguished persons of the period. Edited by Thomas Wright in two volumes, Henry Colburn, publisher, London, 1838. Note: Google digitized.

Read, Conyers. *Lord Burghley and Queen Elizabeth.* Alfred A. Knopf, New York, 1960.

Ridley, Jasper. *A Brief History of the Tudor Age: 100 Years of Splendor and Squalor.* Robinson, Great Britain, 2018.

Rowse, A. L. *The England of Elizabeth.* PAPERMAC/Macmillan Publishers, London, 1981.

Scott, Maxwell. *The Tragedy of Fotheringhay.* Founded on the Journal of D. Bourgoing, Physician to Mary Queen of Scots, and on Unpublished MS. Documents, Sands and Co., London, 1912.

Scott, Sir Walter. *Marmion: A Tale of Flodden Field*, Printed by J. Ballantyne & Company, Edinburgh, 1806.

Sherman, William H. *John Dee: The Politics of Reading and Writing in the English Renaissance.* The University of Massachusetts Press, 1995.

Smith, Alan G. *The Babington Plot.* Macmillan and Co Ltd., London, 1936.

StGeorge, Michael. *Survival of a Fitting Quotation.* Anonymous Press, New York, 2005.

Somerset, Anne. *Elizabeth I*, Anchor Books, A Division of Random House, Inc. New York, 1991.

*The Trust.* Senior editor, Pamela K. Simpkins, text edited and republished by the Security and Intelligence Foundation, Reprint Series, July 1989.

Tu, Hsuan-Ying. *The Pursuit of God's Glory: Francis Walsingham's Espionage in Elizabethan Politics, 1568–1588*, Ph.D. Thesis, University of York/History, September 2012.

*Two Missionaries Under Elizabeth: A Confessor and an Apostate (Father William Weston).* Edited by John Morris (Priest/Society of Jesus), London, Burns and Oates, 1891. Note: Google digitized.

Unger, Miles J. *Machiavelli: A Biography.* Simon & Schuster, New York, 2011.

Weir, Allison. *The Life of Elizabeth I.* Ballantine Books, New York, 1998.

Whaley, Barton. *Covert German Rearmament 1919–1939: Deception and Misperception.* University Publications of America Inc., Frederick, Maryland, 1985.

———. *Practice to Deceive.* National Institute Press, Annapolis, Maryland, 2015.

———. *Sun Tzu: The Principles of War:* 37th translation with commentary and annotations. Lybrary.com eBooks, Sommerville, Massachusetts, 2012.

Williams, Neville. *The Life and Times of Elizabeth I.* Doubleday and Company, New York, 1972.

Wilson, A. N. *The Elizabethans.* Farrar, Straus and Giroux, New York, 2011.

Wooley, Benjamin. *The Queen's Conjurer.* Henry Holt and Company, New York, 2001.

Zweig, Stefan. *Mary Queen of Scotland and the Isles.* Translated by Eden and Cedar Paul, A Lancer Book/The Viking Press, New York, 1935.

# Index

# About the Author

**R. Kent Tiernan** received a Bachelor of Arts degree in History from Stanford University (1967) and a Master of Arts degree in Western European Area Studies from the University of Notre Dame (1971), followed by twenty years of service in the United States Air Force. Before his military retirement in 1987, Kent served as an intelligence officer at various locations worldwide. In addition, he was an assistant professor of history at the United States Air Force Academy. He also commanded the Air Force Intelligence Service Special Studies Division focused on foreign denial and deception tactics, techniques, and procedures.

From 1987 to May 2000, Kent was a defense contractor providing planning, analysis, and training support to the Joint Staff, Defense Intelligence Agency, National Security Agency, and the United States Army and Air Force. In May 2000, he joined the Central Intelligence Agency's National Intelligence Council, Foreign Denial and Deception Committee (FDDC) staff.

In June 2008, Kent was promoted to the Senior National Intelligence Service, where he held the FDDC[1] vice chairman and staff director positions until his retirement in July 2014.

Kent, his wife, Carole Sue, their beloved parrots and greyhounds now live in Southern Arizona—all enjoying their "golden years."

## PUBLISHED AND REVIEWED ARTICLES

*Walsingham's Entrapment of Mary Stuart: The Modern Perspective of a Deception Analyst/Planner*, American Intelligence Journal, Vol.34, No.1, 2017.

*Hiding in Plain Sight*, Defense Intelligence Journal, 2006, Reprinted in the American Intelligence Journal, Vol.32, No.2, 2015.

Reviewed *The Anti-Appeasers: Conservative Opposition to Appeasement in the 1930s* by Neville Thompson. The review is in *The Review of Politics*, Vol.35. No.1, January 1973.

## NOTE

1. The FDDC, an important component of the National Intelligence Council (NIC), provided vital work advising the Director of National Intelligence on foreign denial and deception (D&D) activities. The FDDC actively led research, collection, analysis, and training initiatives to counter foreign D&D efforts to stem the flow of information on intelligence community sources and methods to foreign entities. The FDDC was also the interagency hub for the collaboration and integration of the counter-foreign denial and deception mission across the intelligence community.